Cognitive Behavioral Training
A How to Guide for Successful Behavior

Mark Le Messurier

CORWIN PRESS
A SAGE Publications Company
Thousand Oaks, CA 91320

For information:

Corwin Press
A SAGE Company
2455 Teller Road
Thousand Oaks, California 91320
www.corwinpress.com

SAGE Ltd.
1 Oliver's Yard
55 City Road
London EC1Y 1SP
United Kingdom

SAGE India Pvt. Ltd.
B 1/I 1 Mohan Cooperative Industrial Area
Mathura Road, New Delhi 110 044
India

SAGE Asia-Pacific Pte. Ltd.
33 Pekin Street #02-01
Far East Square
Singapore 048763

Printed in the United States of America.

ISBN 1890455032

This book is printed on acid-free paper.

07 08 09 10 11 9 8 7 6 5 4 3 2 1

Contents

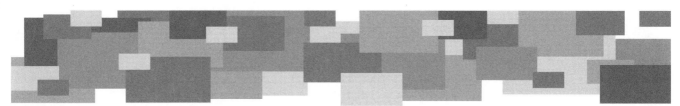

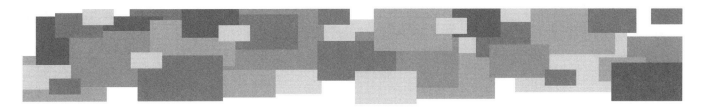

About the author

Mark Le Messurier is a teacher and mentor to children, adolescents and their families. He works in private practice providing educational advice, counseling, literacy and numeracy remediation programs, independent assessments, and social skills training. His background spans twenty years in the classroom which includes special education, adult education, child-centered education and community education projects. He is a recipient of the prestigious National Excellence in Teaching Award.

His expertise is developing cognitive behavioral training (CBT) programs to reinforce the success of students diagnosed with ADD/ADHD, LD, personality syndromes, processing deficits and behavioral difficulties. CBT strengthens self-awareness, self-regulation, goal-setting, motivation, confidence and relationships, the very elements proving elusive in the everyday life of many students. The CBT strategies contained within this book are derived from Mark's work. They are tried and proven techniques and continue to be used with remarkable success.

Mark regularly presents at workshops and conferences for public and independent schools, parents and interested groups. These relate to optimism, cognitive behavioral training, ADHD, Asperger Syndrome, Dyslexia and teaching children with challenging behaviors. He recently co-authored a book and video entitled STOP & THINK Friendship. This is a social skills program for primary-aged students and young adolescents.

Recently, Mark has completed a training and development film about Dyslexia, designed for teachers, parents and students. *Reflections on Dyslexia* is available for sale to individuals, schools, and colleges on the Peytral Publications website (www.peytral.com).

Mark can be contacted as follows: Email: <lemess@ozemail.com.au>

Intellectual property

Establishing the intellectual property with absolute clarity is difficult for some cognitive behavioral training strategies. Many of these ideas have been born from generations of modifications, adjustments and change. Through necessity they are fluid and dynamic. It is common to see the wing of one idea evolve into a new concept, depending on the need presenting itself at the time. This is the way it is with CBT. Wherever possible, the obvious and traceable sources have been acknowledged. If, by chance, an original source has been omitted, I apologize. The overriding motivation has been to add to the easily accessible repertoire of 'thinking strategies' that benefit the young people entrusted to our care: our children and students.

Dedication

As happens with many things in my life, I leapt into this project not realizing its enormity. Instrumental in achieving a satisfying end was Sharon, my wife, who graciously gave me the opportunity to be an absent partner on weekends and very early weekday mornings for two years to write. My dear friend Frank, for his early encouragement. My daughters, Kim and Noni, who both generated the original graphics, offered insight and remained my harshest critics. My colleagues and clients at Fullarton House, whose steady, gentle interest buoyed my motivation and perseverance. And of course, my meticulous editors, Catherine, Jenny and Jane, who spent hours poring over the manuscript considering anything from typing mistakes, referencing issues and grammatical considerations, to whether strings of sentences actually said what I wanted them to say. Finally, my editor Margaret at Hawker Brownlow Education: nothing was too much trouble, and you believed in the value of this work right from the start. Each of you has my heartfelt thanks. It is due to our combined effort that this book exists.

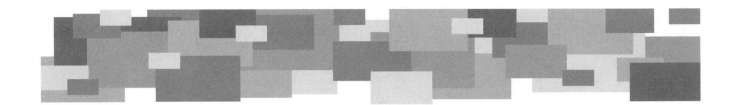

Introduction

What is cognitive behavioral training?

Cognitive behavioral training (CBT) is at the heart of good management. It is a safe, win-win system to get children to do what we need them to do, even though it may not be what they naturally choose to do. As the name implies, the approach links behavior to thinking. It supports all individuals in the move from habitually doing and reacting in the same old ways to thinking about what they are doing and incorporating new behaviors. For some, performance at home or at school may be delayed by impulsive, anxious, lazy, thoughtless or resistant behaviors. CBT sustains the adoption of new habits, new routines and new ways of thinking. It immerses students in practices that encourage goal-setting, emotional resilience, perseverance and motivation: practices that develop 'can do' attitudes. This mind-set is the stuff from which successful lives are made. For a number of children and teenagers, the link between choice and outcome must be taught explicitly, and may prove to be the greatest gift we can hand to them.

Who is this book for?

This book is for educators, counselors, health professionals and parents. It is for those who already embrace, or wish to explore, the notion that our children always do better when placed in situations that stretch their self-awareness, self-regulation and independence. The foundations of this success-based pathway are the strategies embodied in cognitive behavioral training. Cognitive behavioral training encourages improvement, as students are explicitly taught to acquire new skills and learn new ways to think their way around naturalistic difficulties. It addresses problems concerning organization and planning, remembering, perseverance, self-awareness, task completion, motivation and confidence encountered by children and adolescents with or without clinical diagnoses such as Attention Deficit Hyperactivity Disorder, Auditory Processing Disorder, Cerebral Palsy and so on.

How to use this book

This book is designed acknowledging that it is always the practical, easy-to-use ideas which become our most effective tools. The ideas and engaging exercises offer a reliable way to change the wavering behaviors and transient skills displayed by many students. These proactive approaches, enriched by case studies, illustrate how to implement attitudinal and behavioral changes, without needing to waste time reinventing the wheel.

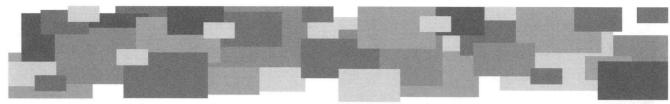

As case studies often fire our enthusiasm for making a difference for a student we may be working alongside, I have included case studies throughout the book. For easy recognition, case studies are identified by this icon:

Small versions of the worksheets are embedded in the text to help connect the reader with the ways in which these visual ideas can be used. For photocopiable sizes, black-line masters are located at the end of each chapter.

Why develop this book?

In recent years my work has taken me into many classrooms to visit teachers and students. The truth is, I'm astonished by the ingenuity of my talented colleagues. They grapple with so much, ranging from meeting the exacting daily classroom and system challenges - organizing curriculum, presenting lessons, responding to the concerns of parents, providing extracurricular activities - to individually mentoring students to ensure their dignity remains intact. I'm also indebted to the children and families I've worked alongside. While I may have played a part in steering them towards a solution to their difficulties, they are also responsible for many of the ideas contained within. Consequently, this book is an amalgamation of effective cognitive behavioral practices engaged by clever educators and parents. It is not intended to be an exhaustive problem-solver, but rather a sensible start for parents, educators and health professionals to align their thinking, language and approach to create opportunities for all children. Managing these niggling, sometimes debilitating, problems more effectively requires strategic, teamed input.

The book is presented to sustain the children who 'do it tough': for those who forget, fail to get around to tasks, think they can't, lose interest or display reactive, unpredictable behaviors. These strategies, presented in a win-win spirit, are geared to ease natural difficulties and promote opportunities for practice and skill-strengthening. Used well, the result will be children and young adolescents who interact and operate more effectively at home and within the classroom.

A note for parents

There appears to be a widely held belief that good intervention results in cure, or something very similar. So, when interventions do not translate to cure or rapid change, the assumption is that the intervention is flawed. In this sense, the 'cure it now' model has the potential to heighten anxiety, defeat optimism and allow negative management cycles to perpetuate. It is more effective to come to grips with the truth; that is, progress is slower for children with difficulties and developmental delay. It is the simple, practical things we do that will make the greatest difference to children's development and happiness.

Without this awareness, parents are far more likely to jump on board the professional merry-go-round. First, a diagnosis is sought for their child. This sensible beginning sharpens understandings about the difficulty and the available interventions, and can provide refinement of management techniques. Then, seemingly innocuous visits to a plethora of counselors, occupational therapists, sound therapists, speech pathologists, educational tutors, physiotherapists, chiropractors, naturopaths, dietitians, acupuncturists and others intensifies the quest to unlock the cure. In these situations it is usually the child who loses out. Being carted from one professional to another for years

is emotionally demoralizing. After all, if we treat children as ill, disordered and dysfunctional, it's easy to guess who will lose. Of course there is a place for skilled, well-targeted intervention, but too much intervention, too intensively, for too long delivers a message to children that something is seriously wrong. It reinforces to children that someone else must take responsibility for their difficulties.

The ideal model focuses on the emotional stability of children. Adopting thoughtful interventions - friendship-building, academic remediation, negotiating clear expectations, curriculum adjustments and appreciating the unique attributes of children - is most effective. The alternative is clinging to the belief that someone else will fix the problem.

Take a moment. Reflect on what you see and think when you look at your child. Do you carry too many magnifying glasses? Do you look too intensely, too critically, and feel entangled in your own emotion? Do you see too many problems which overshadow your child's strengths, interests, resources and potential? Sometimes, when a parent has long been immersed in a child's difficulties, their poise, priorities and sense of humor become casualties. Make a resolution to see your child more favorably, to prioritize what should be tackled and inspire your child to participate in their life.

A note for educators

Education in United States is now fixed on inclusivity. Teachers have become increasingly responsive to incorporating children with diverse abilities into their classrooms. Contemporary teachers realize that the effective management of students, especially those with delayed self-regulatory and learning capacities, depends on the knowledge, artfulness and persistence of themselves. Progressive practitioners now find themselves in a position of re-examining their teaching approach, re-evaluating what they deliver and how they execute it.

With the *Individuals with Disabilities Education Act* (IDEA), *Americans with Disabilities Act* (ADA), and *Section 504 of the Rehabilitation Act* educators can now focus on providing the services their students need. Rather than seeing the problem as being solely with the student, educators now have to be thinking about what they can do to assist when the child's self-regulatory and learning systems have not developed naturally. This requires a strengthening of the 'islands of competence' in children and appreciation of the praise deficit these children so commonly suffer - focusing on what children can do, rather than criticizing them for what they can't do (Giorcelli 2000).

More than ever, there is a responsibility on every school, college, university and teacher to manage students with learning differences far more vigorously. As new education standards are implemented, education providers will be expected to welcome, guide and accommodate the needs of students with differences and ensure they are included, as opposed to simply presenting curriculum material and hoping the rest might follow. This further strengthening of inclusive education, by law, is the new order.

To everyone

This book aims to reignite creative cognitive behavioral interventions, which encourage the acceleration of awareness and skills in individuals. These interventions are at the heart of good management and are concerned

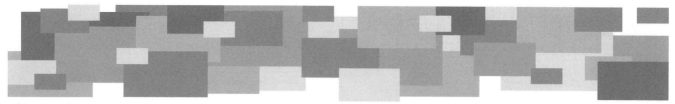

with energizing everyone to work towards successful outcomes. Cognitive behavioral training assumes that the vast majority of children and young adolescents are healthy. They may experience developmental delay, attention, social, learning or behavioral problems, but they are all capable of learning and changing.

Over the past several decades, it seems we have become overly focused on 'medicalizing' various behavioral conditions. Attention Deficit Hyperactivity Disorder presents a prime example of the struggle to rationalize the gap between an individual's behavior and what is happening in the brain. In other words, what lies behind how these individuals behave? We have witnessed a proliferation of new authorities, new understandings, new theories, new medications and new literature: an enormous industry has blossomed around ADHD. Very recently, highly sophisticated brain imaging has permitted us to see precisely what is happening in the brain. This continues to intrigue, educate, confuse and mesmerize. New methodologies and understandings may allow more accurate diagnosis and legitimize the diagnosis by providing physical evidence.

Yet a fixation with 'medicalizing' can detract from the wonderful possibilities of change. A medical overemphasis runs the risk of convincing some that these neurological problems are so fixed, so ingrained that little hope for change to behavior exists outside the medical domain. The fact is that the influences within a child's environment are fantastic: how they are loved, taught, parented, accepted and guided. Some children just take longer to meet the demands of school and day-to-day expectations.

With the benefit of hindsight, we know these difficulties tend to right themselves with maturity and well-targeted intervention. However, until this occurs these children can attract their unfair share of criticism and failure. They hear too many negative messages too often, and, in some cases, begin to believe this is what they must be. They develop reputations. Surely if we treat children as though they are will fully noncompliant, disobedient and naughty, this is what they are likely to become.

After years of this, even the most agreeable of children accept their role: the clown, the victim, the runaway, the disrupter, the aggressor or the outcast. By the time some begin secondary school they think and act in negative ways, and efforts to help are met with belligerence. When children are hounded by a constant barrage of criticism it is impossible for them to remain in a position which invites transition and change. They are forced to react aggressively or despairingly, or to give up, uttering, 'I don't care!'. When students reach this position it is very difficult to influence them to change.

If we wish to guide, change and redirect the attitudes of our children we must start by examining and changing our own attitudes and practices. We need to examine what we are doing and appreciate that our children will change and modify their habits, routines and attitudes according to the levels of management we choose to put in place. With this in mind, the design of this book has as much to do with redesigning the thinking of adults as it has with redesigning the thinking of children. Improving our management will make the greatest difference for our children.

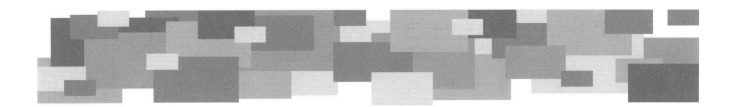

The North Wind and the Sun

A dispute arose between the North Wind and the Sun, each claiming that he was stronger than the other. At last they agreed to try their powers on a traveler to see which could soonest strip him of his cloak. The North Wind had the first try; and, gathering up all the force for the attack, he came whirling furiously down upon the man, and caught up his cloak as though he would wrest it from him by one single effort: but the harder he blew, the more closely the man wrapped it around himself. Then came the turn of the Sun. At first he beamed gently upon the traveler, who soon unclasped his cloak and walked on with it hanging loosely about his shoulders: then he shone forth in his full strength, and the man, before he had got many steps, was glad to throw his cloak right off and complete his journey more lightly clad.

(Aesop)

Cognitive Behavioral Training

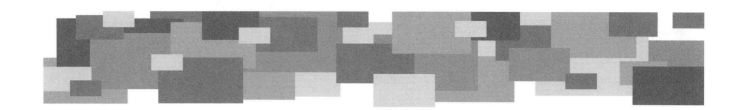

Chapter 1
Cognitive behavioral training

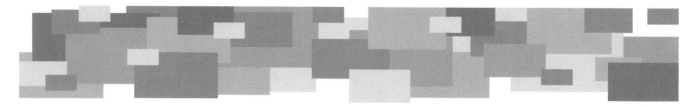

Cognitive behavioral training explained

What is it?

Cognitive behavioral training (CBT) has existed for as long as we have parented and educated children. Consciously, and more often unconsciously, we have relied on it to ensure their success. Yet amazingly, this code of practice often abandons us, or is poorly applied, in situations when it can lend most benefit.

Behavior is driven by the way one thinks. For some children and young adolescents the quickest way to feel as though a problem has been solved is to discount it, ignore it, blame someone, lash out or refuse. Over time, habitual reaction, fuelled by emotion rather than thought, sees these individuals stuck in a difficult position. Their response often spills over into the domains of family, friendships and school. CBT presents a framework that allows individuals to gradually modify their behavior. It helps them move from reactive thought processes to logical thought processes (Kernberg, Weiner & Bardenestin 2000). The result, reinforced through thoughtful day-to-day management, is the production of more independent, socially acceptable and successful behaviors. Westwood, in *Common Sense Methods for Children with Special Needs*, appeals to educators and parents to design approaches which encourage students to think about their thinking in a variety of learning situations.

> Teaching a student how to learn and how to regulate and monitor his or her own performance in the classroom, how to become a more self-regulated learner, must be a major focus in any intervention program.
>
> (1999, pp. 40-41)

The ability to understand and control one's thinking places the individual in a position to understand what they are doing, why they are doing it and what they really want. Without this, they are learners without direction and without the ability to review their progress, accomplishments and future directions (O'Malley et al. 1985; Sinclair & Ellis 1992). Students, struggling to acquire metacognitive thinking, require instructions that are tailored to their needs, practice in how to think and frequent opportunities to evaluate their performance. They are far more dependent on hearing the right questions to stimulate their internal awareness. They require specific practice prior to commencing, during tasks and at the completion of tasks. Critical reflective questions that invite thought might be:

- *How do you want this to work out?*
- *Where will you start?*
- *What will you do next?*
- *What do you need to make this work?*
- *Who can help you?*
- *What do you want them to do?*
- *What helped in the past?*
- *How will you know if it is working out?*
- *What will make this successful for you?*

On the other hand, once the task or event is complete, reflective questions might include:

- *Was it successful?*
- *Why?*
- *What were the things that really made the difference?*

or

- *Why didn't it work out?*
- *What other reasons might there be?*
- *Is there one thing you could have done to make a difference?*
- *What would you do next time that you did not do this time?*

Asking the right questions in the right way guides students to prepare, pace themselves and reflect on their performance. The aim is to externalize the very thing they find difficult to do.

When is it best to begin?

Think of CBT as drown-proofing children by stimulating their thinking. It's never too early. The earlier a system is established and reinforced, the greater the benefits that are achieved. Even quite young children demonstrate a modest metacognitive capacity, or the ability to think about themselves (Flavell 1970). By the time they reach middle primary there is usually a significant development in their formal reasoning and self-awareness. Consequently, encouraging them to reflect critically on how they think and what they do has strategic value around this time.

Middle primary is a significant transitional period as the links between thinking about their behavior and likely outcomes are naturally accentuated. As these links are strengthened, the tendency to exclusively blame others begins to diminish. Scope emerges to guide children to understand their natural thinking style. This period provides an exciting time for children to learn more about themselves. It opens precious moments for them to self-evaluate, to wrestle with social and behavioral issues and to work on simple strategies to overcome them.

> It is considered that metacognition helps a learner to recognize that he or she is either doing well, or is having difficulty learning or understanding something.
>
> (Westwood 1999, p.41)

How can it help?

Cognitive behavioral training delivers a design for students to think and a platform for educators to teach thinking. It alerts individuals to the link between their actions and the likely consequences. Motivation is more often driven by children wanting to please and do well for their teacher, parents, friends or themselves. 'In general, cognitive behavioral training has been among the most effective psychotherapy approaches for many disorders of childhood and adolescence including depression, obsessive compulsive disorder and post traumatic stress disorder.' (Hendren 1999, p. 162)

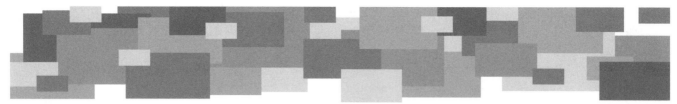

Cognitive behavioral training is a profound modifier of behavior. Guiding children to be more aware of what they are doing and why they are doing it systematically reshapes their approach to thinking. It stretches their self-awareness and optimizes outcomes.

Who benefits?

Many students fall into a category where their difficulties are not acute enough to attract a formal diagnosis. As a result, this sizeable, moderately at-risk group frequently drifts along year in, year out without being led to engage in simple, success-based cognitive behavioral interventions. This leaves them in a position where their difficulties are able to worsen and become habitual.

Their poor internal management causes them to perform as if they are out of balance, unsynchronized, constantly falling short of what is required. To varying degrees, they exhibit forgetfulness, impulsiveness, disorganization, day dreaminess, distractibility and/or avoidance, and may be attention-demanding or restless. Sometimes their behaviors are global, sometimes situational, sometimes transitory and sometimes entrenched. Their reduced capacity to pay attention, to remember what has just been explained, to follow directions, to keep track of belongings or to prioritize what needs to be said, written or done next muddles their ability to perform socially or academically. Invisible memory and concentration, as well as egocentric and impulsive forces make these students look as though they are selfish, thoughtless and unmotivated. They have more than their share of careless moments, and they display a consistent spill of frustration.

Other children display clusters of behaviors that are well understood and therefore attract a clinical diagnosis. See Appendix 1 (page 323) for a discussion of common clinical diagnoses and their implications. Whether or not an individual attracts formal identification, what these students have in common are habits that do not work for them. Cognitive behavioral training is able to provide benefit to every individual.

The value of diagnosis

Motivating children to do what we determine is best is usually a challenge. Naturally, it's doubly hard for students with diagnosed working memory weaknesses, inflexibility, reduced concentration, impulsivity, learning difficulties and maturational delays. Diagnosis is often referred to as a therapeutic act (Barkley 1990). This because it attracts our attention, taking us closer to understanding an individual's unique functioning. It allows us to acknowledge the gap between what the child is able to give and what is expected. Diagnosis helps to make sense of the problem, to depersonalize it and redirect interest to remediation, accommodation and promoting success (Hannell 2002).

Individuals diagnosed with these difficulties, disorders or disabilities, and those possessing similar characteristics, will remain dependent on our intelligent management and success-rich attitudes for some time. They will remain dependent on consistent structures, clear expectations, well-established routines, appropriate incentives and matter-of-fact consequences, as opposed to being exposed to emotionally charged win-lose situations. Without effective cognitive-behavioral strategies in place these students will miss out. They rely on us to be balanced, motivated and inspired.

This places the management responsibility squarely with us, the adults.

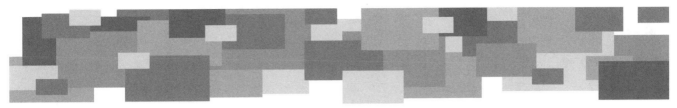

Constructing success pathways

We have long known that successful individuals, with or without difficulties, rarely become successful by accident. Successful individuals know there is an unmistakable pathway to tread in order to be successful, and they know how to put themselves on the path. They demonstrate characteristics that are success-worthy; their thinking, words and actions are more likely to be based in optimism. They have traits which are likely to include:

- the capacity to determine goals, to prioritize, to organize and to start

- passion, zest, even mild obsessiveness to help maintain motivation

- common sense; the ability to look widely, 'read the play' and anticipate

- the ability to take calculated risks and determine possible outcomes

- self-belief, and perhaps a degree of perfectionism to drive persistence

- the ability to ask the right questions at the right time, and know how to listen

- emotional resilience permitting the acceptance of failure and, in turn, allowing improved future performance.

What leads young individuals to success?

A twenty-year study, designed to identify factors that lead some students with learning disabilities to success and others to failure, concluded there are a set of personal attributes, attitudes and behaviors which are predictive of success (Raskind et al. 1999). Similarly, earlier comprehensive studies addressed what shapes individuals with learning disabilities into successes (Gerber, Ginsberg & Reiff 1992; Reiff, Gerber & Ginsberg 1997). Their focus was to understand the process of acquiring success, and one of their most powerful conclusions concerned the creation of 'can-do' attitudes. Previous and current research point to self-awareness, emotional stability, goal-setting, proactivity, organizational skills, perseverance, motivation, and healthy support networks as strong predictors of future success (Gottesman 1979; Hoffman et al. 1987; Johnson & Blalock 1987; Kavale 1988).

> Specifically the attributes of self awareness, perseverance, proactivity, emotional stability, goal setting, and support systems were more powerful predictors of success than numerous other variables such as IQ, academic achievement, life stresses, age, gender, socioeconomic status and ethnicity, and many other background variables.
>
> (Raskind et al. 1999, p. 46)

Transferring research to practice

Our challenge as educators must be to take the next step; to transfer these research findings into effective school and classroom practices. Structuring pathways, programs and processes to 'teach' and sustain successful ways is especially important for students with difficulties. This emphasis on teaching 'success pathways' needs to carry as much weight as the effort to improve academic skills (Raskind et al. 1999). Many students rely on being explicitly taught and being kept in touch with the attributes of success. They rely on precise guidance to remain successful.

ADD therapist and mentor Jane Massengill believes that students who make it from difficult, even apparently hopeless, situations, have often had just one significant adult take an interest in them (Amen 2002b, p. 334). When a classroom teacher chooses to take the role of mentor, especially if the student's problems are largely classroom or school based, it indisputably makes a significant difference. As soon as a student realizes their teacher is engaged and on-side, changes in their thinking, optimism, effort, cooperation and appreciations usually unfold. Old barriers melt. The scope for new energies and new beginnings emerge. They see someone is on their side, providing encouragement and advice within the context of a meaningful relationship. Increasingly, there is a realization that mentoring is a powerful treatment for individuals with ADHD, ADD, Asperger Syndrome and learning difficulties.

Mentoring aside, teachers can still influence significant change by managing within the cognitive behavioral framework and nurturing the success attributes of:

- self-awareness
- goal-setting
- emotional stability
- proactivity
- organizational skills
- perseverance and motivation.

In this way students gain the advantage of being engaged and guided in proactive, success-based systems. Many students willingly accept, depend on and flourish through the development of artificial structures and scaffolding systems (Thomas & Pashley 1982). The key is constructing and maintaining strategies which add value at the student's point of performance. It is in their public performance - that is, how they function in the classroom and school environments - that the outcome really matters. Our children's access to the attributes of success is entirely contingent on the success attitudes of the adults around them.

Chapter 2
Promoting self-awareness

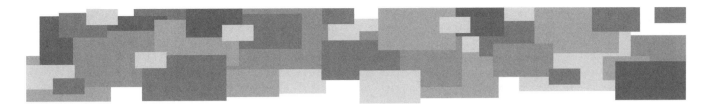

Developing relationships

No one strategy to influence change and benefit for students works in all situations. The approach needs to be designed to discover what works best for each student. This, of course, highlights the emphasis on relationships (Kohn 1996). As obvious as it sounds, relationship is a prerequisite when attempting to develop self-awareness in students and support change. Without quality relationships, cognitive behavioral strategies hold little more than a collection of short-term props and fixes resulting in flimsy temporary control. Without recognizing relationships we miss the vastness of potential gains. Relationships are fundamental.

Ironically, some are convinced that the 'control mentality' is the best way to change or suppress unwanted student behaviors. An example of this attitude was highlighted when a teacher recently discussed his teaching methodology with me. He stated, 'I'm the boss. It's my classroom, and your kids will learn that fast.' Instead of engaging with students and proactively managing behavior, this style of teaching relies on power and control. The words 'you should', 'you will' and 'I want' are used and overused as adults who use this method react to what they don't like. They subscribe to an irrational belief that has long been termed as demandingness (Ellis 1985). That is, to assert their control, they use their authority to demand students change to what they consider are more desirable ways without contemplating the value in building relationships and strengthening the students' self-awareness. They ignore the repertoire of natural, warm human behaviors, and the extraordinary benefits they bring: a smile, a wink, a nudge, a dare, a joke, a thumbs-up, a kind or reassuring comment. These teachers tend not to respond to students who are doing well because they expect them to do well, but react dramatically to poor behavior, often reinforcing it. Demandingness discounts the impact of friendly human interactions and overlooks the results of empirical research that consistently confirms the effectiveness of teacher praise on student behavior (Maag & Katsiyannis 1999).

Changing the behavior of students has as much to do with changing the values of teachers as it does with the students themselves. Teacher values and attitudes can be altered. All teachers can profit from being shown how to improve the classroom climate, how to build relationships with students and how to plan positive approaches to promote appropriate student behaviors. The alternative is running the risk of haphazardly reacting to inappropriate student behavior and relying on tell-offs, demerits, detentions, exclusions and suspensions as a management mainstay (Maag 2001).

Case study

Good chemistry can be built

Sometimes good chemistry is spontaneous, but good chemistry can also be deliberately built. Not long after the year had started, Dom, a fourth grade teacher, was at his wit's end with Robert's challenging behaviors. He had been aware of Robert's reputation, but wasn't prepared for the reality. Robert wriggled and squirmed in his chair, was often out of his seat wandering the room, and incessantly called out. His greatest joy was acting as class clown and receiving a laugh from others. While there were many endearing qualities about Robert, he was downright disruptive. Intuitively Dom knew the quality of his relationship with Robert would likely tip the balance. He organized, in consultation with Robert's parents and his principal, to take Robert on an outing with his wife and himself one weekend. Robert helped to select a new barbecue, spent twenty minutes playing a computer game while Dom's wife bought software. The three of them concluded the outing by having a milkshake together. Three weeks later, Robert accompanied Dom and Jo to a movie. Much later in the following

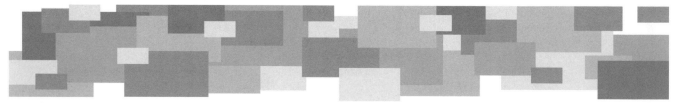

term I recall asking Robert why his behavior was so different at school now. His response: 'Well now I know Mr. Larconis, I like him. I can't do what I used to do.'

Dom achieved this change in attitude and behavior in two easy outings. If you get the relationship balanced, then it's startling just how effective CBT techniques are.

Home visits offer WHAM! value

What a remarkable impact just one home visit can have on the relationship between a teacher and their student. A brief home visit offers an explosion of information: information about the student, family relationships, attitudes, interests, difficulties, barriers to learning, motivating forces and ambitions, just to mention a few. What a privilege to be able to see, touch, listen and smell the fabric of a student's life. Yet, most students see it as a privilege to have their teacher visit, especially when the visit is aimed at connecting with the student: sitting on the living room floor together looking at their collection, checking out the bedroom, or seeing some of their favorite belongings. Home visits can be successfully orchestrated by parents discreetly prearranging the student to have something to show, share and talk about.

How much do you really know about your student?

Find time to talk. Let the conversation wander so even the seemingly inconsequential matters are discussed. Free flowing discussion often reveals insightful glimpses. Dig a little deeper, past the bravado and past the superficiality of behavior. Do they play a sport? Where? What are their hobbies or interests? Do they collect cards or stamps, or play computer games? Do they have favorite places they enjoy visiting? Are there special skills or abilities they have that can be brought to the classroom? What annoys them? What worries them? What inspires them? If they had a magic wand, what would they want to change about themselves, school, home or their life? Do you know? Together, develop 'A Book about You'. Here's a practical way to glimpse their world, to understand the way they see it and how it impacts on them.

Find out what kids worry about

Many children worry or enter phases where worrying and anxiety features more prevalently in their lives. For a few these can escalate into debilitating and restrictive behaviors, and at this level of intensity, professional, even medical, intervention may be required. Most children worry, but are able to keep their worries in check. Occasionally there are times when worry seems to get the better of them. In such circumstances strategies to reduce the problem are called for (Hallowell 1997).

Wilson's worry tin

I worked with Wilson for two years. When I first met him he was a tall, robust-looking ten-year-old who spent a lot of time worrying. Worry, for the moment, had got the better of Wilson. His worry made him feel nervous and cautious, and doubt his capabilities. He had begun to skirt around some day-to-day challenges because he thought he might fail or look silly. Yet, Wilson was well liked and highly regarded by his peers. Academically he was bright and showed gifts within numeracy and logic problem-solving domains. Outwardly, he was the kind of boy who appeared to have it all. At night his worries became so powerful that he found it difficult to fall asleep. To help Wilson take control of his worries he and his mother bought a strong tin, beautifully decorated, with a slot on the top. It could be locked with a small, strong padlock. This became his Worry Tin.

Wilson agreed that whenever the worries started to eat at him, he would write each on a small piece of paper and insert it into his locked tin. We had fun sharing some of our worries. Wilson especially enjoyed hearing my worries, and watching me model writing them on small pieces of paper and inserting them in the tin. During our conversations I learned Wilson was convinced that most people are untouched by worry. He viewed his worry problem as unique. We set up the cue that once the worry was written, folded up and put away; it was dealt with for the day and didn't need any further thought. Wilson was enthusiastic about the trial, as he wanted to make a difference for himself. When I saw him a week later I asked how his Worry Tin was going. 'I think it's almost full,' he replied. His mother caught my eye and mouthed the words 'There aren't any worries anymore. I haven't heard of any'. This was an impressive result, and was assisted by his parents' sensible handling. It would have been easy for them to rush in, counsel, question, delve deeply and try to explain his worries away. Although well intentioned, this approach may have strengthened his worries and not helped Wilson at all.

Over the next six weeks Wilson continued to add his worries to the tin, although fewer worries were added in the last four weeks than he'd manage to write in the first night! Sessions continued, and discussion about worry and sadness dissipated, giving way to Wilson happily exploring his gifted areas.

Several months later, I asked Wilson whether he would be prepared to bring in his Worry Tin so we could look at them. He was tentative about this, but agreed. Next session we unlocked the Worry Tin and unfolded each of the old worries. As we finished reading them Wilson said, 'They seem pathetic!'.

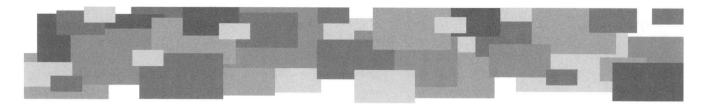

Worry tree and worry scale

Draw or copy a worry tree and display it on a pin-up board. Have students spend time discussing their worries. Ask them to write each worry on a leaf and attach the leaves to the board around the worry tree (Garth 1994). Bringing worries out into the open is the first step. Talking about worries, and listening to the worries of others, lets students see that worrying is normal, even though keeping worries under control can be tricky sometimes. Teach students that when

 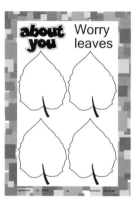 

they have a worry to deal with they can start at the worry scale. This gives them an idea whether they can deal with the worry independently or need the help of someone else.

What happens when I worry?

It's useful to discuss the common physiological responses human beings have when they worry, are stressed, scared or anxious. The Resourceful Adolescent Program (RAP), an experiential resilience-building program designed to promote positive coping abilities for young adolescents, has been developed by Ian Shochet and colleagues at Griffith University (Shochet et al. 1997). RAP provides calming techniques, and approaches on how to restructure thinking to resolve problems. One of their student handouts examines typical stress indicators. It is a practical catalyst to identify stress reactions and spark discussion about how students deal with them.

Write to students

All students enjoy receiving letters and emails. Writing friendly, uplifting letters to students is another means to dissipate their worries, bolster their persistence and enrich relationships. Using the computer, letters can be made to look inspirational as well as letting students know how well they are managing and where remaining challenges lie. It is an easy way to present a visual map reminding them of their goals, their progress, and the next few remaining steps to achieve the next goal. Letters also deliver a message without the student having to listen. This is refreshing! Some students hear well-intentioned criticism and advice all too often. In this way there are no voices, just silent print congratulating and reflecting on achievements.

Getting the balance right

Balance is the way individuals choose to divide their time between the different areas of life. It is a strong indicator of emotional well-being. To help students see this and move towards a better-balanced life, create a pie diagram, or balance wheel. Each segment reflects their satisfaction about an area in their life; the number ten represents the greatest degree of satisfaction and the number one indicates frustration or despair.

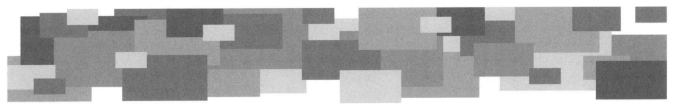

Consider breaking the balance wheel into six categories, and ask students to rate their feelings of satisfaction about school, their relationship with their class or home group teacher, friendships, mother and father relationships, recreational interests and brother and sister relationships. To prepare the balance wheel, take the data to the computer and have a spreadsheet automatically calculate and print the pie graph. This way it is quick, accurate and colorful. It is possible to do the results for an entire class in less than a half an hour! This visual tool helps individuals to recognize areas in their lives that need greater attention. It helps to set the stage to determine goals (Amen 2002b).

Example:

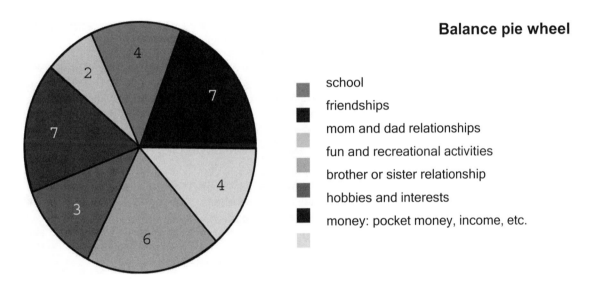

Balance pie wheel

- school
- friendships
- mom and dad relationships
- fun and recreational activities
- brother or sister relationship
- hobbies and interests
- money: pocket money, income, etc.

Do you see a difficulty?

Students whose performance is difficult to manage at school or at home usually are aware of the problems. In their own way they know that their poor concentration, hyperactivity, loudness, bossiness, shyness, over- or under-reaction or learning difficulty bring negative comments and reactions from others.

Cognitive Behavioral Training

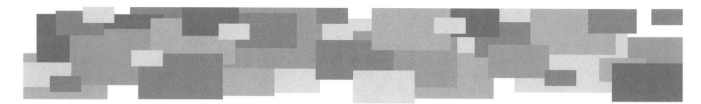

Graph your personality

Finding the right balance is difficult for many - children, adolescents and adults alike. This exercise guides students to appreciate their natural style. It leads them towards discovering their strengths and remaining challenges. As they gain glimpses of themselves the scope for new awareness is created, and thoughts turn to accepting ideas and systems to recognize difficulties.

Graphing Kathryn's package

Case study

Kathryn, an intelligent, vivacious and highly reactive fourteen-year-old described her personality as 'living with the dragon inside me!'. She knew that her volatile personality traits meant she lived with uncertainty. This was part and parcel of her package. She had to be on guard, as it seemed so easy for her not to follow through on assignments, to forget school and home commitments, to be reactive to suggestions from others, and to just drift along arguing and making excuses for poor performance. Kathryn used this graphing technique to identify her challenging and developed areas. She chatted freely about her thoughts as she colored the squares.

The thermometer graph

For younger children, coloring in the thermometers is an easy way to help them reflect. It enables a visual profile to be built which mirrors the intensity of feelings concerning their strengths and difficulties. Each of these domains play a crucial role in how children function and see themselves. This simple approach, linked to conversation, offers valuable insights in a small parcel of time.

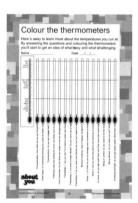

The 'tough stuff' inventory

Determining the 'tough stuff' alerts students to their challenges. These are the habits or behaviors that need to be thought about. Plant optimistic seeds suggesting that one of these challenges may become a future goal. Lead the students to understand that thinking about what they do will always give them an edge.

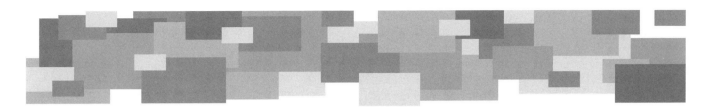

The 'tough stuff' questionnaire

Not having some of the tough stuff under control does not have to be a problem forever, providing we engage students to recognize, and be mildly accepting of, the need to make changes. Explain that they are beginning to find out the sorts of things that are easy, and others that are more challenging. Ask, *How did you rate? Do you think there is room for improvement? What would you start with? Maybe you need a thinking trick to help you along! Do it once, do it a few times, start feeling good about it, and it can become a brand new habit!*

Which window do you look through?

Using the idea of looking through different windows helps students appreciate how they naturally view the world. Each window provides a different view. Large picture windows allow those standing behind them to see the world in its entirety, to see what might happen, what is happening right now, what really caused it and what the likely consequences will be. But some people look awkwardly through much smaller windows that do not allow them to see as much of the world. This can be a problem! Rather than being proactive about life, their blurred view of the world pushes their behavior to be constantly reactive. Ask students: *What does your window look like? How small, big, clear or blurred is your window? Can you see well enough? What sort of view do you get?* Ask them to choose their window or draw themselves standing in front of theirs.

Yourself as others see you

Once students have completed these exercises, encourage them to take the next step and learn how 'significant others' see them. Asking a safe, significant person (mother, father, teacher, principal, grandmother, grandfather, special educator, tutor, aunt, uncle, Scout leader, friend etc.) to choose the sort of window they think the student sees the world through helps the student to appreciate how others see them. Feedback from others by reusing the questionnaires allows students to compare the viewpoints of others with their own responses.

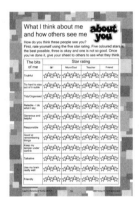 

Exchanging this information permits the student to better interpret their world. Defining problems, seeing who they affect and seeing why a problem occurs opens pathways to make changes. Clever management guides students toward new strategies providing them with the freedom to move to different windows when needed. It may take a while to discard old habits and develop new routines, but knowing which window they instinctively look through awakens understandings concerning cause and effect.

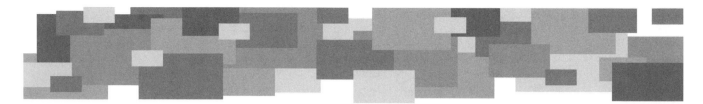

Nonverbals are a powerful language

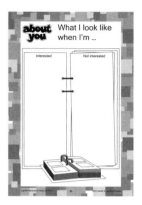

Explicitly teach body language so children and young adolescents are aware of their look and what it says to others. The judgements others make hinges on whether they pick up positive or negative nonverbal gestures. The way we sit, stand, lean, use eye contact and facial expressions, in particular, and the tone of voice send persuasive messages. Knowing simple facts (e.g. that maintaining eye contact suggests confidence and interest, or that sitting up and leaning slightly forward while listening is seen as being interested), works in one's favor when communicating. Conversely, mumbling and looking toward the floor expresses uncertainty, and folding arms gives the impression of low confidence, defensiveness, even disinterest.

Enjoy role-playing body and facial expressions seen in others when things do not go right. Play with facial expressions together. Make disgruntled faces, draw them and attach expressions often used to describe them. Ask students to draw faces aligned to common expressions. Start with *A face like a torn sock* or *The cat's bum face,* and note next to each the overriding feeling being conveyed.

Mime feelings by using facial expressions and body language. Uncontrolled, these faces give away too many of our feelings and can set individuals up as victims. Why not video or take a series of photographs of posed facial expressions? Then, discuss what the student is probably feeling, and how others might respond to somebody with that kind of expression. It is a huge asset for students to know how others are likely to perceive them, even before they speak.

Appreciating the total package

Lead students to see themselves beyond a diagnostic label. By all means explore how it affects them, but also help them see their talents and interests. Recognizing the link between what the student has as strengths, and what they need to make more of, has a direct influence on tenacity and motivation.

Discuss strengths versus challenges. Make displays to highlight this dynamic connection. Collate class responses and display lists so students develop a sense that many people work to overcome similar difficulties.

Explain, for example, that the organization of the brain which produces the Dyslexic difficulty is also thought to account for unique artistic, personal, musical, dramatic and athletic abilities, and mechanical gifts. Yet, sadly many of our 'out of balance' children fall from the success pathway because they lose sight of their natural abilities. They give up, failing to see this dynamic connection. With our insight and our perseverance, a healthy balance can be restored, helping students to hold a healthier perception. Learning more about oneself provides a reason to make changes. It reassures them that their difficulties

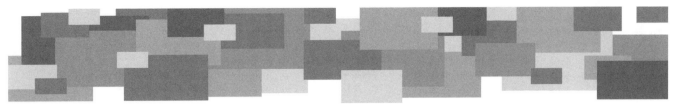

are not total. By compartmentalizing problems, individuals are less likely to become overly defined by their difficulties, and more likely to see their difficulty as only one aspect of themselves.

Dispelling mythology

Discover, and in some cases rediscover, the facts regarding a student's clinical diagnosis. Visit quality websites together to learn straightforward explanations. Read biographies, view documentaries and videos which dispel the popularized fallacies. The exercise below presents an opportunity for educators and students to compare popular myths and misunderstandings with the facts. Next, begin to prioritize real things that can be done! The goal is to deliver optimism and sensible solutions.

Successful people with difficulties

Investigate a few of the amazing individuals from the past and present diagnosed with Dyslexia, Attention Deficit Hyperactivity Disorder or Asperger Syndrome. Assist students to discover their rich, wonderful lives, and the contributions these individuals made. Many of their autobiographies and biographies are inspirational (Smith 2004). Examine the problems they faced, how they got around them and why they became successful. Reinforce that most say they would never trade away their difficulty, as without it they would not be complete.

Outstanding individuals believed to have Dyslexia:

- Winston Churchill, former prime minister of England
- Whoopi Goldberg, leading actress
- Agatha Christie, prolific author
- Thomas Edison, scientist and inventor
- Tom Cruise, actor
- George W. Bush, President of the United States
- Cher, leading actress and entertainer
- Vanessa Amorosi, singer and song writer
- Edward Hallowell, MD, author and psychiatrist
- Henry Winkler, actor, producer and director
- Charles 'Pete' Conrad Junior, astronaut
- Jamie Oliver, chef and television personality
- Jodie Kidd, international model
- Richard Branson, businessman and CEO of Virgin Atlantic Airways

Cognitive Behavioral Training

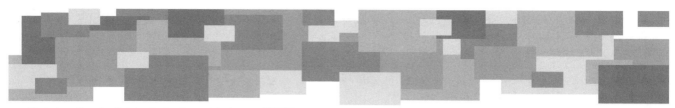

Outstanding individuals believed to have ADHD

- Thomas Edison, scientist and inventor

- Alexander Graham Bell, inventor

- Ludwig van Beethoven, composer

- Leonardo da Vinci, artist, writer and inventor

- Walt Disney, famous producer of animated cartoons and movies

- Albert Einstein, mathematician and scientist (rumored also to have characteristics of Asperger Syndrome and Dyslexia)

- Ben Polis, Australian author who has written about his ADHD

- Benjamin Franklin, statesman

- Robin Williams, comedian and actor

- Woody Harrelson, actor

Outstanding individuals believed to have Asperger Syndrome

- Andy Warhol, artist (also rumored to have ADHD)

- Henry Cavendish, scientist (discovered the element hydrogen)

- Temple Grandin, inventor of machinery to handle livestock

- Ludwig Wittgenstein

- Thomas Jefferson, former American president

- Glenn Gould, pianist

While this list provides a good starting point, it is wise to keep in mind that obtaining a definitive diagnosis for each of these individuals is difficult. Some of course are deceased, and it is simply assumption based on their behavioral characteristics that makes identification likely. Further to this, never underestimate the reassurance provided to students when given the opportunity to explore closer to home. Discovering that their father, uncle or grandmother made their way successfully in the word, despite being identified with or having obvious traits of ADHD, Asperger Syndrome or Dyslexia, is powerfully stabilizing and energizing.

Recognize and unite students with difficulties

This can be as simple as making the adaptive education or learning center welcoming for students. Make it the place to be. Offer hot chocolate in winter, cool drinks in summer and the opportunity for casual conversations where students can debrief and offload their worries. Embracing and inclusive attitudes create an environment where students with learning difficulties want to be.

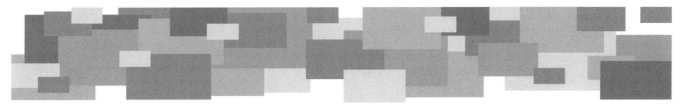

Provide scope (ultimately a student choice) to form a club, an association or an advisory group to have input into school policy, adjustments and modifications.

Arrange meetings with inspirational adults

Bring adults who experience the same difficulties into the classroom or make arrangements to introduce them to a student on an individual basis. Ask these adults to speak about their experiences, struggles and achievements. Is there a secret to their success? How did they find their success pathway? To illustrate the magnitude of this sort of experience, one of my young teenagers with cerebral palsy attended a seminar presented by Catriona Webb, an Australian athlete with the same condition. When I saw her again I asked the student how she found the evening. Her reply was, 'It made me feel so good about me. I understand it now. I know the power of learning to love my disability. She made me understand that it's no good struggling against it. I may as well use it. It was the first time for ages I've gone to bed feeling happy about me.' Through listening to significant others students can identify pivotal points that shaped potential difficulties into success. They learn first-hand what made the difference, and how this thinking and attitude can work for them.

Use the difficulty

Michael Caine, in an interview with Michael Parkinson (Parkinson 2003), was quizzed about his axiom, 'use the difficulty'. Caine recounted a situation as a young actor when his entrance onto the set was foiled by a chair. He was later berated by the director and told 'always use the difficulty'. Rather than complaining about the chair, he could have used it to dramatically intensify his entrance. 'Use the difficulty' is an excellent phrase to promote discussion with the students. Reflect on others who have a similar difficulty and how they have used it to excel.

Is your brain working for you?

Stir students to think about what they are doing, why they do it and whether it fits into what they really want for themselves. Often, individuals locked into one way of reacting seem to be unaware about the impact their behavior has on others. They need to know there is a reason they behave like this. They do it because the emotional or reactive part of their thinking is convinced it gets them what they want. It might be showing off, going against others, calling out in class, opting out, looking angry or sulky, being violent, answering back or storming off when they can't have their way. The behavior may have become habitual, and because they have received so many negative messages it is difficult for them to see how to make changes.

Explain that some people have better connections to the frontal part of their brain where their problem-solving can get easily tangled with their emotions. This results in behaviors triggered by emotions, which force the thinking, logical process to desert them. Others are 'wired' differently. They have stronger connections to the logical part of the brain, and are able to use their thinking tools more easily. Obtain a model of a brain. Let students hold it. Use colored slides or overhead projection sheets of brain images to identify the working parts of the brain. Alternatively, display and discuss John Joseph's 'learning brain poster' (http://www.focuseducation.com.au). Locate where doing math takes place; find the center for emotion. This is worth knowing more about because the brain is the boss of our behavior. It steers us in every direction. As students learn how their brains work, the realization dawns that they can

Cognitive Behavioral Training

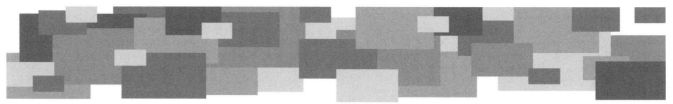

do it differently. It is possible to 'rewire' and make new, improved brain circuitry. With practice, they can learn to compensate for their innate 'wiring'.

> Your brain is like a muscle. The more you use it, the more you can use it. Every time you learn something new, your brain makes a new connection. Learning enhances blood flow and activity in the brain. If you go for long periods without learning something new, you start to lose some of the connections in the brain and you begin to struggle more with memory and learning. New learning actually causes increased brain density and weight. Strive to learn something new every day even if it just for a short period of time.
>
> (Amen 2002a, p. 4)

Ask students to divide the brain into the automatic and manual parts. The automatic parts take care of our heart beating, blinking, breathing and body temperature, all without us needing to think. The manual part of our brain thinks. This is the part that determines our behavior, thoughts and words. Make two lists detailing the automatic (uncontrollable) and manual (controllable) characteristics. This is a step closer to seeing that we have the capacity to control our thinking and actions.

Encourage students to collect magazine pictures, or prompt them to write comments typical of messages delivered from the thinking and reactive parts of the brain. With a few essential brain understandings in place, ask students whether their current behavior, especially when they're under stress, comes from the thinking or reactive part of their mind. Ask if it is likely to get them what they really want in the future. Is it a behavior they can see working successfully for themselves as a teenager or an adult?

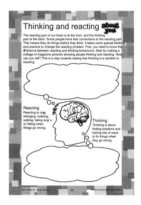

Behavior and time of day

There are patterns which link an individual's moods, behavior and learning, and their alertness. For most, alertness rises throughout the morning until midday, then gradually falls throughout the afternoon. Knowing that short-term memory peaks early in the day and long-term memory operates best from midafternoon to late afternoon explains why formal learning is scheduled before midday.

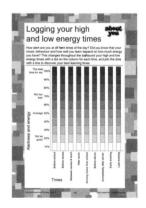

There is value in leading students to appreciate their high-energy and low-energy times. Each of us knows what happens to our energy levels, or degree of alertness, throughout the day and how this influences what we feel like tackling. It is the same for students, and more so for the out-of-balance, reactive or asynchronous students (Armstrong 1997). Help students keep a daily log of their energy levels, behavior and learning. This will begin to highlight their peak time for focused attention. It also alerts teachers and parents to times that are likely to be most productive, least productive and potentially challenging. It is important to know this, especially when tackling homework. Some students are able to commence their homework the moment they arrive home, but for others this

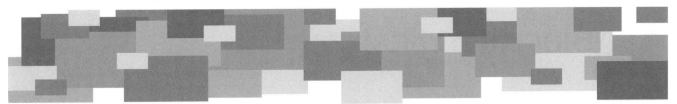

is genuinely difficult. They need to regroup their resources, and are likely to regain a peak energy time later in the afternoon or evening.

Play 'What if I ... ?'

What if I did this? What will happen? What else might happen? What if I chose to do something different? Then, what's likely to happen? How would I feel about it?

'What ifs', through structured activities, conversations or day-to-day dealings, must become the focus. Focusing on this approach consistently reinforces the link between feelings, choices and outcomes. Gradually, this leads young and older students to see that choice always exists. Everyone has choice, and to realize ambition and success, everyone needs to discover the interplay of feelings, choice and consequence.

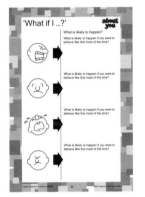
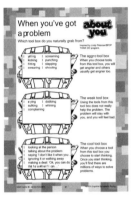

This is real life, and for many individuals it must be taught explicitly and may prove to be a life-altering gift. Start developing this gift now by beginning to play 'What if I ... ?'.

The recipe for success

Use 'recipe for success' as a discussion point with students. Discuss the most important qualities to determine success. Prioritize them from most important to least important. Discuss which are hardest to put into action and why this might be so. The recipe for success delivers a succinct framework for individuals to walk the 'success pathway'.

Blackline masters

- A book about you
  - ★ Things I like
  - ★ Things I don't like
  - ★ Worries
  - ★ I wish …
  - ★ Teachers
  - ★ I try
- My feelings and me
- Are Wilson's worries yours?
- Checklist of typical troubles
- Worry tree
- Worry leaves
- Worry scale
- My stress indicators
- Subject hotspots
- Classroom hotspots
- Family hotspots
- Patterns of independence
- The independence quiz
- Find the problem bulges
- Kathryn's graph
- Color the thermometers
- The 'tough stuff' inventory
- How close are you to having the 'tough stuff' under control?
- Which window do you look through?
- What I think about me and how others see me
- Is what they get what they expect?
- What I look like when I'm ...
- Things I have done
- Things I can do
- Maintaining a balance
- Exploring the differences between mythology and fact
- Thinking and reacting
- Logging your high and low energy times
- When you've got a problem
- 'What if I ... ?'
- On loan to you: The recipe for success

A book

Name _____

Birthday ___/___/___

A drawing or a photo of me

Cut out words and pictures from magazines that describe the sort of person you are.
Paste them around a drawing or photo of yourself.

Star sign ....

The people in my family are ....

....

My best friends are ....

....

My pets ....

....

....

Things I like

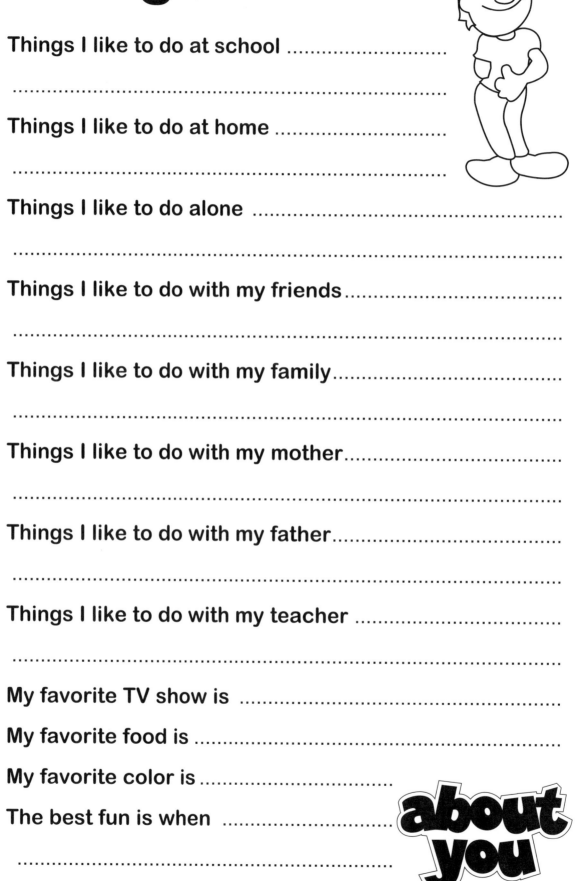

Things I like to do at school ....

....

Things I like to do at home ....

....

Things I like to do alone ....

....

Things I like to do with my friends.................................

....

Things I like to do with my family..................................

....

Things I like to do with my mother.................................

....

Things I like to do with my father.................................

....

Things I like to do with my teacher ....

....

My favorite TV show is ....

My favorite food is ....

My favorite color is ....

The best fun is when ....

....

about you

Things I don't like

Things I don't like to do at school ....

....

Things I don't like to do at home ....

....

The worst time for me is when ....

....

Great thoughts

My favorite daydream ....

....

....

....

The happiest times for me are when ....

....

Soon ...

Things I would like to do but can't do now

....

....

....

about you

Worries

List things which worry you ....

....

....

I'm afraid that ....

....

....

What helps when you're worried? ....

....

....

I get the most scared when ....

....

....

I would be really upset if ....

....

Changes

List things about yourself you can change ....

....

List things you can't change about yourself ....

....

....

I wish ...

I wish other students at school ....

....

I love Mom, but I wish ....

....

I love Dad, but I wish ....

....

I really wish that.......................................

....

I wish teachers would ....

....

If I had three wishes, I would wish ....

....

....

Mom and Dad

It would please Mom if I ....

....

....

It would please Dad if I ....

....

....

Teachers

The trouble with my teachers ....

....

....

....

....

....

I know

I know other people think that I ....

....

....

I know I make people angry when I ....

....

....

I know if I ever did anything really wrong ....

....

....

I know things would be better for me if ....

....

....

I Try

I really try my best when ....

....

....

I don't feel like trying hard when ....

....

....

Oops!

My three worst faults are ....

....

....

But my three best points are ....

....

....

People don't realize that I ....

....

....

I get really angry when ....

....

I feel really pleased when ....

....

My feelings and me

What makes me feel …	Worried or sad	Happy and smiling
At home		
At school		
With friends		

Are Wilson's worries yours?

Big kids kicking and punching me.

People telling me to do stuff I can't do.

Looking stupid.

Having no-one to play with.

Kids teasing me about my laugh.

Getting teased because I kiss Dad goodbye in the car at school.

People planning to gang up on me.

People saying that I think I'm the best. I'm not the best, but I want to be good.

My teacher doesn't understand how I feel.

People teasing me for having long legs.

Feeling like a wimp.

Everybody bossing me around and not knowing what to do.

Feeling dumb.

What if Mom or Dad dies?

People thinking I'm a dumb.

Kids pushing me into the wood chips at school.

Getting teased about the way I speak.

My teacher picking on me in class.

Not being able to do everything.

Being kept in class later than usual and everyone has gone.

Kids in choir teasing me about my singing when their singing is even worse.

People saying I love Marina. I like her.

People saying I've got a fat face.

If someone's going to hijack a plane and crash it.

Not going out late with my friends any more.

Checklist of typical troubles

Check the box if any of these look like your kind of troubles.

* I don't listen. I don't remember.

* If I can't do it the first time, then I won't do it.

* Monday is my worst school day. Everyone talks about what they've done with their family. It makes me think, 'Where's my dad?'.

* I feel dumb with my schoolwork.

* Home is bad. We fight, especially in the mornings.

* I say dumb things and think afterwards, 'How dumb was that?'.

* School is boring.

* I get beat up.

* Mom and Dad split up. I miss Dad.

* Dad/Mom is angry a lot!

* Times tables. I can't learn them.

* I act funny in class.

* I want to do better with my

* I fight with other kids too much.

* I have to stop hitting.

* I go crazy when I get criticized.

* I can't do homework

* I don't have friends.

* I put people down before they do it to me.

* I forget.

* I just lose it with Mom.

* There's no-one home when I get home. I can't make myself start my homework.

* I get teased. I hate it.

* I can't concentrate.

* I daydream. I count the flowers on the bush outside my window most afternoons rather than do my homework.

Worry tree

about you

about you

Worry leaves

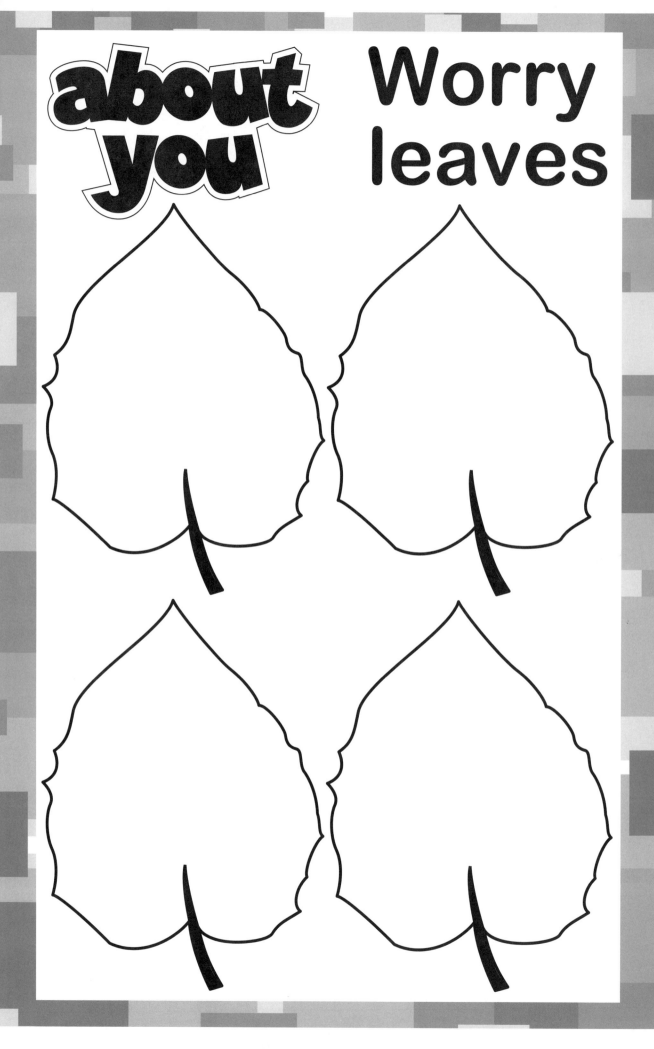

Worry scale

Talking about your worries and listening to the worries of others lets you see that worrying is normal, even though keeping worries under control can be tricky. When you have a worry, begin dealing with it using the Worry scale. It helps you know if it is a worry you can deal with, or a worry needing the help of someone else.

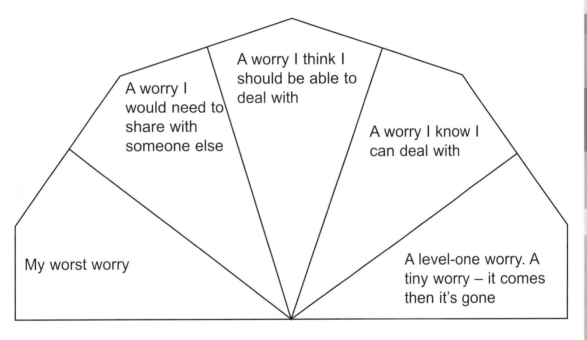

Some worry questions

What is your worst worry?

What is a small worry you dealt with by yourself?

Name a worry you just had to share with someone else.

Describe a worry you dealt with alone that turned out all right.

What are the worries that cause you most trouble?

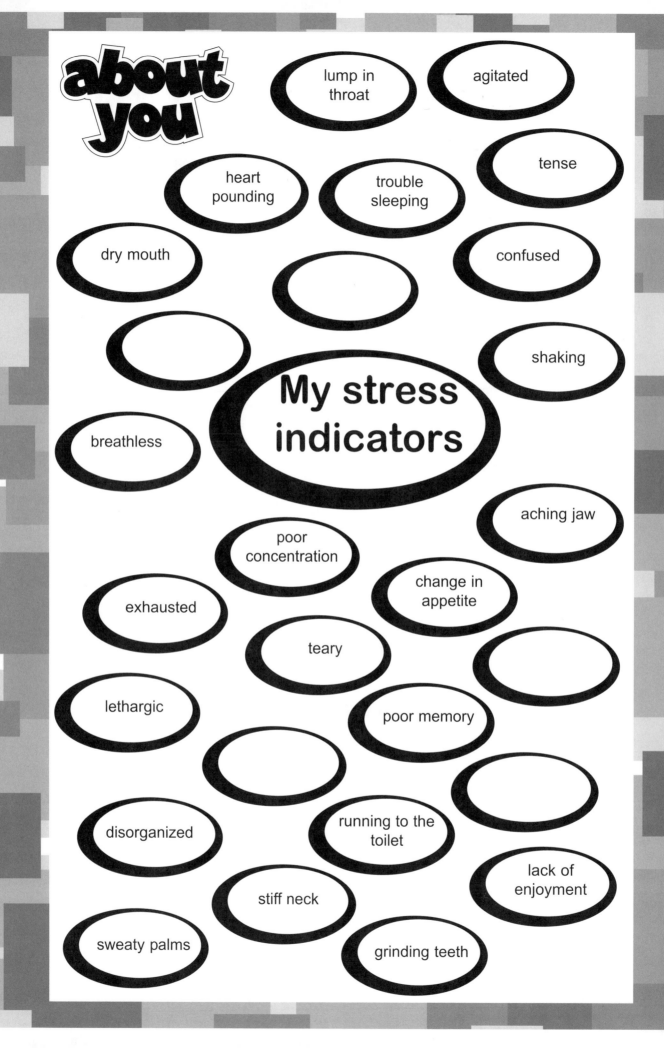

Subject hotspots

★☆☆☆☆ I don't like it
★★☆☆☆ It's ok
★★★☆☆ It's good
★★★★☆ It's good and I like doing it
★★★★★ It's a brilliant subject and I'm brilliant at it

about you

How do I rate my subjects?

Spelling ☆☆☆☆☆

Story-writing ☆☆☆☆☆

Reading ☆☆☆☆☆

Math ☆☆☆☆☆

Multiplication tables ☆☆☆☆☆

Foreign languages
(Italian, French, Spanish, etc.) ☆☆☆☆☆

Science ☆☆☆☆☆

P.E. ☆☆☆☆☆

Music ☆☆☆☆☆

Computing ☆☆☆☆☆

Classroom hotspots

These are the things most students have trouble with at school. Look at each and rate it according to the trouble it causes you.

1 Talking out in class.

| No problem at all | Sometimes | Mostly | Almost always | Always |

2 Not staying in my chair.

| No problem at all | Sometimes | Mostly | Almost always | Always |

3 Distracting others during lessons.

| No problem at all | Sometimes | Mostly | Almost always | Always |

4 Finding it difficult to start and finish my work.

| No problem at all | Sometimes | Mostly | Almost always | Always |

5 Forgetting instructions and not knowing what to do.

| No problem at all | Sometimes | Mostly | Almost always | Always |

6 Learning problems.

| No problem at all | Sometimes | Mostly | Almost always | Always |

7 Troubles with friends.

| No problem at all | Sometimes | Mostly | Almost always | Always |

8 Not completing my homework.

| No problem at all | Sometimes | Mostly | Almost always | Always |

 # Family hotspots

These are the things most kids have trouble with at home. Look at each and rate it according to the sort of trouble it causes you.

1 Getting out of bed independently in the morning.

| No problem at all | Sometimes | Mostly | Almost always | Always |

2 Getting ready for school on time in the morning.

| No problem at all | Sometimes | Mostly | Almost always | Always |

3 Getting homework done independently.

| No problem at all | Sometimes | Mostly | Almost always | Always |

4 Keeping my bedroom organized.

| No problem at all | Sometimes | Mostly | Almost always | Always |

5 Remembering daily chores.

| No problem at all | Sometimes | Mostly | Almost always | Always |

6 Keeping to my bedtime or going to bed and staying in bed.

| No problem at all | Sometimes | Mostly | Almost always | Always |

7 Remembering to get my lunch box out of my schoolbag.

| No problem at all | Sometimes | Mostly | Almost always | Always |

8 Too much television, phone or computer games.

| No problem at all | Sometimes | Mostly | Almost always | Always |

Patterns of independence

It's a good idea to think about the things you do. The patterns of what you do give an idea of your independence – where you are in the journey of growing up. Build an inventory to check out your independent skills. Compare with friends if you like.

	I do this	I don't do this much	I never do this
read short novels			
read long novels			
use the washing machine by myself			
hang out clothes on the clothesline			
iron my clothes sometimes			
prepare a simple meal for myself or others (e.g. sandwich, a boiled egg or cereal)			
send an email independently			
make or buy and mail a birthday card			
stay focused for an entire lesson and get the work done well			
boot up the computer or shut it down			
complete written work on the computer, save it and print it			
clean my bedroom without help			
help out around the house with vacuuming, dusting, cleaning, sweeping, car washing etc			
do something pleasant and unexpected for my parents, brother or sister (e.g. smiling, helping, making a cup of coffee, bringing them breakfast in bed, bringing them some flowers)			
perform (e.g. sing, do a speech or perform a play in front of the class)			
attend an activity outside school that makes me feel good			
take out the garbage, feed the cat, clean up the doggy doo, sweep leaves etc.			
ride a bike			
play a sport with enjoyment			
do homework without being nagged or helped every night			
look after the neighbor's pets when they go away			
look after younger children			
go to the local shops on errands to help out my parents			

The independence quiz

Name _____

Date _____

Here's a quiz to help you rate how independent you are. Gaining independence is all about being able to think things through yourself, being your own boss, taking control and not having to rely too much on other people.

	YES! (3 points)	Sometimes (2 points)	I don't do this much (1 point)
When I'm not sure what to do, I try to work it out before asking my teacher.			
I do my homework without Mom or Dad having to sit with me and help me along.			
I can always get started on my homework without Mom and Dad telling me to.			
If I have a problem at school I try to work it out myself without making a big deal about it.			
Kids know I'm organized and borrow things from me.			
I'm sensitive. I notice the feelings of others and help them.			
I'm one of the first to finish my work fairly well.			
I'm chosen by the teacher to do responsible tasks.			
I ask the same amount of attention from the teacher as most others in class.			

Independence questions
What was your score?

Above 24: That's a lot of points. There are strong signs of independence here!

16 to 23: Not bad. There are some areas that could do with improving.

9 to 15: There's work to be done. What's best to start with?

Find the problem bulges

Finding the right balance is tricky. Here's a way to learn more about your balance. By answering the questions and coloring the squares you'll start to see what's easy and what's challenging for you.

Name _____ **Date** _____/_____/_____

Question										
Procrastination: how often do you put things off?										
Great ideas: how annoying is it knowing you could do better work, but not doing it?										
Overreactions: do you get angry too fast?										
Following rules and waiting for turns: are these hard to do?										
Can't remember: do you think you forget or are disorganized more than others?										
Friendships 1: are you shy? Is it hard to make new friends?										
Friendships 2: is it hard to keep friends? Do you have more fights than you'd like?										
Friendships 3: do you wear your friends out, but can't seem to										
Teasing & bullying: does it happen very much?										
Study 1: is it hard for you to manage your homework at home?										
Study 2: do you worry about how you are managing your learning at school?										
At home: do you fight with Mom and Dad more than most kids?										
Being in control: is it hard if you're not in charge? Do you need to be the boss?										
Being different: do you think you are? Why?										
Emotional strength: do you get easily upset, and upset more than										

0%	50%	100%
Never	Average – just like most people	A lot

Kathryn's graph

about you

Find the problem bulges

Finding the right balance is tricky. Here's a way to learn more about your balance. By answering the questions and coloring the squares you'll start to see what's easy and what's challenging for you.

Question	0–10%	10–20%	20–30%	30–40%	40–50%	50–60%	60–70%	70–80%	80–90%	90–100%
Procrastination: how often do you put things off?	■	■	■	■	■	■	■	■		
Great ideas: how annoying is it knowing you could do better work, but not doing it?	■	■	■	■	■	■	■			
Overreactions: do you get angry too fast?	■	■	■	■	■	■				
Following rules and waiting for turns: are these hard to do?	■	■	■	■	■	■				
Can't remember: do you think you forget or are disorganized more than others?	■	■	■	■	■	■				
Friendships 1: are you shy? Is it hard to make new friends?	■	■	■	■	■	■	■	■	■	■
Friendships 2: is it hard to keep friends? Do you have more fights than you'd like?	■	■	■	■	■					
Friendships 3: do you wear your friends out, but can't seem to	■	■	■	■	■	■	■			
Teasing & bullying: does it happen very much?	■	■	■	■	■					
Study 1: is it hard for you to manage your homework at home?	■	■	■	■	■					
Study 2: do you worry about how you are managing your learning at school?	■	■	■	■	■	■	■	■		
At home: do you fight with Mom and Dad more than most kids?	■	■	■	■	■	■				
Being in control: is it hard if you're not in charge? Do you need to be the boss?	■	■	■	■	■					
Being different: do you think you are? Why?	■	■	■	■	■	■				
Emotional strength: do you get easily upset, and upset more than	■	■	■	■	■	■				

0% — Never
50% — About average – just like most people
100% — Almost always

Color the thermometers

Here's a way to learn more about the temperatures you run at. By answering the questions and coloring the thermometers you'll start to get an idea of what's easy and what's challenging.

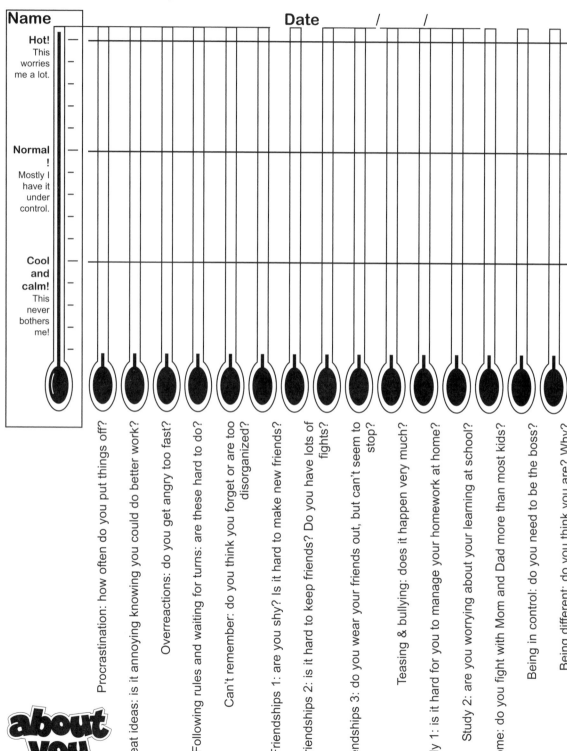

Name

Date / /

Hot!
This worries me a lot.

Normal!
Mostly I have it under control.

Cool and calm!
This never bothers me!

- Procrastination: how often do you put things off?
- Great ideas: is it annoying knowing you could do better work?
- Overreactions: do you get angry too fast?
- Following rules and waiting for turns: are these hard to do?
- Can't remember: do you think you forget or are too disorganized?
- Friendships 1: are you shy? Is it hard to make new friends?
- Friendships 2: is it hard to keep friends? Do you have lots of fights?
- Friendships 3: do you wear your friends out, but can't seem to stop?
- Teasing & bullying: does it happen very much?
- Study 1: is it hard for you to manage your homework at home?
- Study 2: are you worrying about your learning at school?
- At home: do you fight with Mom and Dad more than most kids?
- Being in control: do you need to be the boss?
- Being different: do you think you are? Why?

The 'tough stuff' inventory

What's tough for you?

Go through the checklist. Check the things that you do.

These are your warning signs:

* fidgeting and wriggling
* being bossy with your friends
* having trouble remembering homework and chores around home
* can make friends, but can't keep them
* drawing neat little pictures on your page, or scribbling in your book without thinking
* having more fights than most kids
* 'drifting off' and looking out the window – 'a real daydreamer'
* keep on thinking about things you want to do later
* trying to be funny and getting people to laugh at you
* being impatient when playing games and waiting for your turn
* not being very good at following the teacher's instructions
* starting things without finishing what you've been doing first
* talking too much
* not listening to others
* wandering around the room almost without knowing it
* saying dumb things because you don't think first or don't really listen
* have one or two friends, but they get you into trouble
* being nagged by your teacher more than most.

Why not turn one of your warning signs into a goal? Make one small change, then another. Soon, new helpful habits will grow.

Knowing what you are doing makes life better. It helps you to:

• listen • remember • keep friends • have more fun • feel happier
• know what's happening around you • control your feelings • learn
• understand other people's feelings.

How close are you to having the 'tough stuff' under control?

about you

Here are the good signs. This is a list of the things students do when the 'tough stuff' is under control. Score yourself and see how you rate!

Rate yourself:
3. means you do this all the time
2. means you can do it sometimes with effort
1. means you never really do it.

	getting off to a quick start with your written work
	not letting others distract you from what you're asked to do
	not yelling out right away when something goes wrong
	finding different ways to solve problems
	holding back your temper when things go wrong
	finishing your written work on time
	waiting patiently for turns
	listening carefully so you remember stuff
	doing your homework without Mom or Dad nagging you and checking up
	remembering to get assignments in on time
	having that feeling that you're on top of things and feel cool
	getting ready for school easily and on time
	sitting still for fairly long times (like when the teacher reads to the class)
	keeping friends
	TOTAL SCORE

Total your score and fill in the box. How did you rate? Where do you want to start?

WOW! There's lots of things we can start with.	Are you ready to work on one or two things?	There's some room for 'fine-tuning'	You're doing really well!
14 to 20	21 to 27	28 to 35	36 to 42

Now we're beginning to find out the things that are easy, and others that are more challenging. Next you need a thinking trick or idea to help! Do it once, then do it a few times and it will become a helpful habit.

Which window do you look through?

Each window gives a different view of the world. People who look at the world through large windows see lots of the world. They see what might happen, what is happening, what caused it and what the consequences will be. Others who look through smaller windows cannot see as much of the world.

Which is the view you get?
Color in the window you think you look through.

What I think about me and how others see me

about you

How do you think these people see you? First, rate yourself using the five star rating. Five colored stars is the best possible, three is okay and one is not so good. Once you've done it, give your sheet to others to see what they think.

The bits of me	Star rating			
	Self	Mom/Dad	Teacher	Friend
Truthful	☆☆☆☆☆	☆☆☆☆☆	☆☆☆☆☆	☆☆☆☆☆
Try hard to stay out of trouble	☆☆☆☆☆	☆☆☆☆☆	☆☆☆☆☆	☆☆☆☆☆
Tidy/Organized	☆☆☆☆☆	☆☆☆☆☆	☆☆☆☆☆	☆☆☆☆☆
Reliable – I do what I say	☆☆☆☆☆	☆☆☆☆☆	☆☆☆☆☆	☆☆☆☆☆
Generous and helpful	☆☆☆☆☆	☆☆☆☆☆	☆☆☆☆☆	☆☆☆☆☆
Responsible	☆☆☆☆☆	☆☆☆☆☆	☆☆☆☆☆	☆☆☆☆☆
Good at remembering things	☆☆☆☆☆	☆☆☆☆☆	☆☆☆☆☆	☆☆☆☆☆
Keep my temper under control	☆☆☆☆☆	☆☆☆☆☆	☆☆☆☆☆	☆☆☆☆☆
Talkative	☆☆☆☆☆	☆☆☆☆☆	☆☆☆☆☆	☆☆☆☆☆
Use my brain really well	☆☆☆☆☆	☆☆☆☆☆	☆☆☆☆☆	☆☆☆☆☆
Friendly	☆☆☆☆☆	☆☆☆☆☆	☆☆☆☆☆	☆☆☆☆☆

Is what they get what they expect?

Looking through the windows of expectations

My parents expect …	My friends expect …
What they get is …	What they get is …
My teacher expects …	My school expects …
What they get is …	What they get is …

What I look like when I'm ...

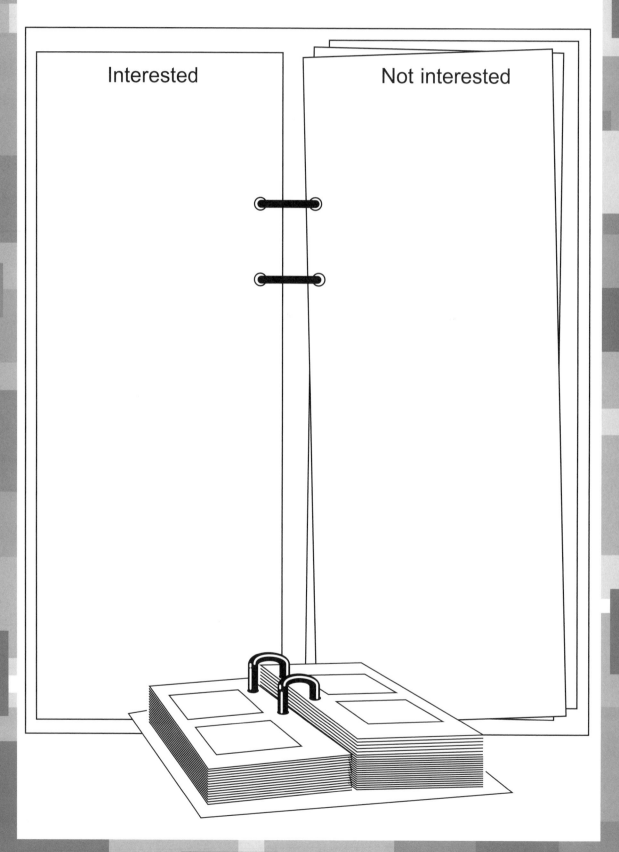

Interested

Not interested

Things I have done

Name _____

Things I like doing

1. _____

_____

2. _____

_____

3. _____

_____

Things I've done well at

1. _____

_____

2. _____

_____

3. _____

_____

Things I can do

Name: _____

Things about me that I'm proud of

1. _____

2. _____

3. _____

4. _____

5. _____

Things I've achieved that I'm proud of

1. _____

2. _____

3. _____

4. _____

5. _____

Maintaining a balance

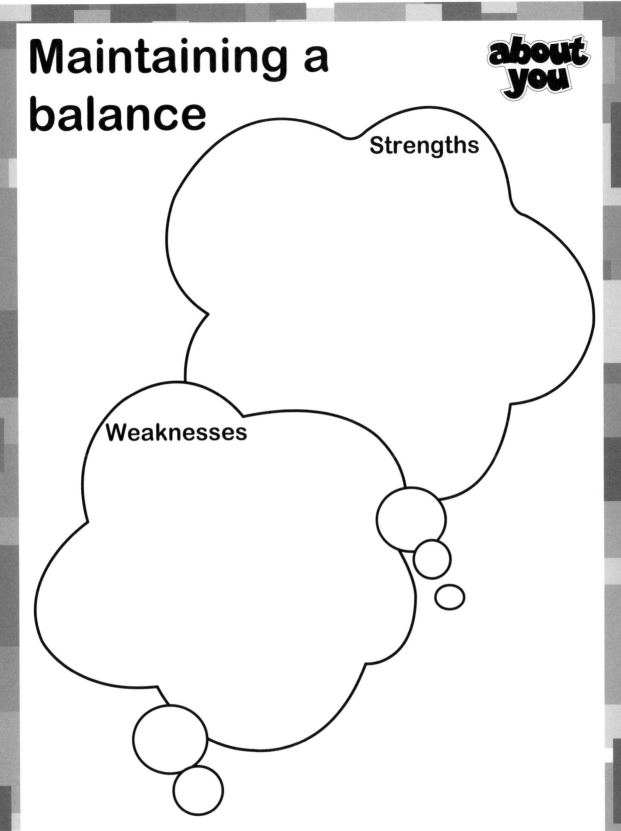

Strengths

Weaknesses

Look at your total package

Everyone has talents and weaknesses. It's normal. What are yours? It's important to know your problem areas so you can work on them, but don't ever forget or give up on your natural abilities!

Exploring the differences between myth and fact

Difficulties	Myth The weird, crazy and strange things people think	Facts The truth
ADD	☒ _____ ☒ _____	☑ _____ ☑ _____
ADHD	☒ _____ ☒ _____	☑ _____ ☑ _____
Dyslexia	☒ _____ ☒ _____	☑ _____ ☑ _____
Auditory Processing Difficulties	☒ _____ ☒ _____	☑ _____ ☑ _____
Asperger Syndrome	☒ _____ ☒ _____	☑ _____ ☑ _____
	☒ _____ ☒ _____	☑ _____ ☑ _____

Thinking and reacting

The reacting part of our brain is at the front, and the thinking part at the back. Some people have fast connections to the reacting part. This means they do things before they think. It takes some special thinking and practice to change the reacting problem. First, you need to know the difference between reacting and thinking behaviors. Start by making a collage of magazine pictures showing people thinking and reacting. How can you tell? This is a step towards seeing that thinking is a solution to reacting.

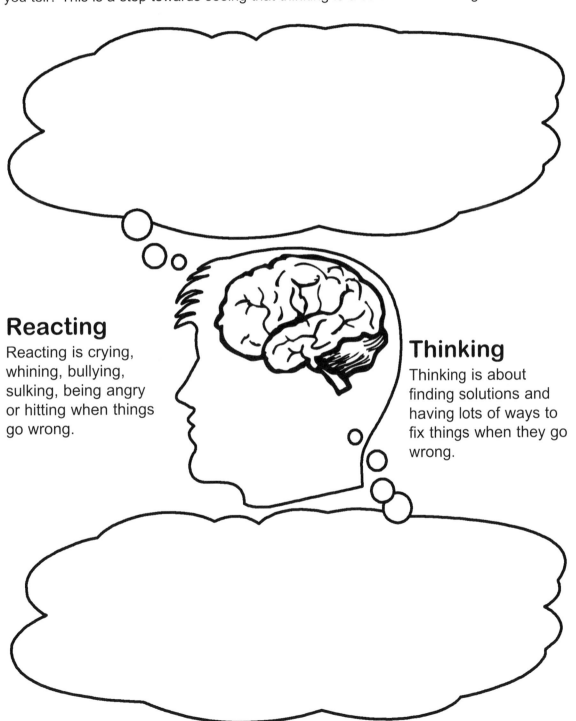

Reacting

Reacting is crying, whining, bullying, sulking, being angry or hitting when things go wrong.

Thinking

Thinking is about finding solutions and having lots of ways to fix things when they go wrong.

Logging your high and low energy times

How alert are you at different times of the day? Did you know that your mood, behavior and how well you learn depend on how much energy you have? This changes throughout the day. Record your high and low energy times with a dot an the column for each time, and join the dots with a line to discover your best learning times.

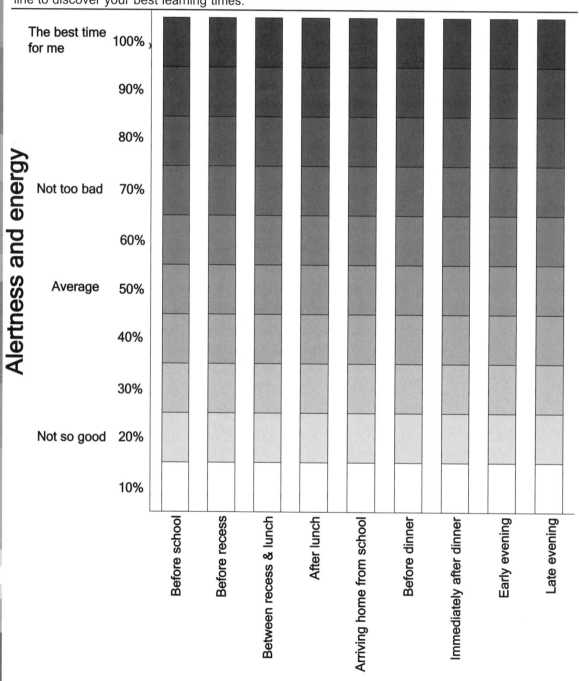

Alertness and energy

The best time for me	100%
	90%
	80%
Not too bad	70%
	60%
Average	50%
	40%
	30%
Not so good	20%
	10%

- Before school
- Before recess
- Between recess & lunch
- After lunch
- Arriving home from school
- Before dinner
- Immediately after dinner
- Early evening
- Late evening

Times

When you've got a problem

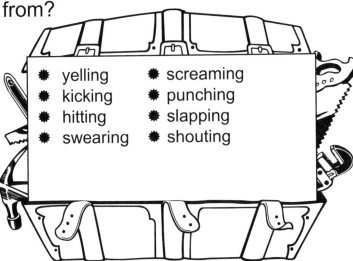

Which tool box do you naturally grab from?

about you

Inspired by Lindy Petersen's STOP THINK DO program.

- ✸ yelling
- ✸ kicking
- ✸ hitting
- ✸ swearing
- ✸ screaming
- ✸ punching
- ✸ slapping
- ✸ shouting

The aggro tool box

When you choose tools from this tool box, you will get angrier and others usually get angrier too.

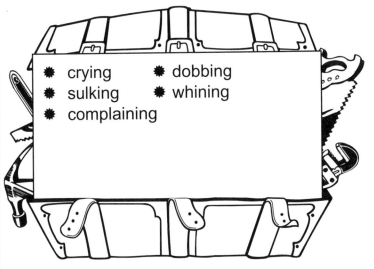

- ✸ crying
- ✸ sulking
- ✸ complaining
- ✸ dobbing
- ✸ whining

The weak tool box

Using the tools from this tool box does not really help the problem. The problem will stay with you, and you will feel bad.

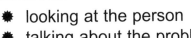

- ✸ looking at the person
- ✸ talking about the problem
- ✸ saying 'I don't like it when you ...'
- ✸ ignoring it or walking away
- ✸ making a deal: 'Ok, you can do that for a while if I can ...'

The cool tool box

When you choose a tool from this tool box you choose to start thinking. Once you start thinking, you'll find there are millions of ways to solve problems.

'What if I ...?'

What is likely to happen?

What is likely to happen if you were to behave like this most of the time?

What is likely to happen if you were to behave like this most of the time?

What is likely to happen if you were to behave like this most of the time?

What is likely to happen if you were to behave like this most of the time?

On loan to you:
The recipe for success

Use it. Enjoy the difference it makes.

Checklist of ingredients

* Punctuality: arrive on time.
* Get assignments in on time.
* Cooperate.
* Look friendly.
* Show enthusiasm. Look keen. Be interested.
* Say good things to others.
* Be honest.
* Be reliable.
* Be flexible. Do deals rather than argue.
* Speak up for yourself.
* Listen more and talk less.
* Show initiative.
* Be polite.
* Smile.
* Use positive body language.
* Try new things.
* Stick with things, even if they're tough.
* Ask for help when you need it.
* If in doubt, say sorry.
* Use a planner, an organizer or mobile phone to help keep your life under control.

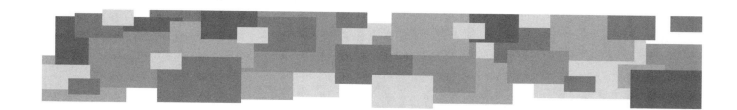

Chapter 3
Creating vision, setting goals and monitoring progress

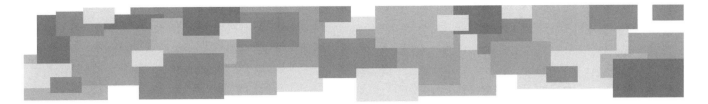

Creating vision

Before anyone can set a goal and work towards it, they have to have an idea about the bigger picture, a vision of what they want. Ascertaining what an individual wants, and the advantage of achieving it, initiates the process of change. Without consciously setting goals and thinking about how the future might be, even at a simplistic level, individuals choose to accept a future that a system or someone else will decide for them.

A good starting point may be simply identifying a bad habit or two a student might be ready to move from, then setting up ways to create new actions, new thoughts and new habits. The responses from the 'About you' exercises will provide information for students to develop their individual goals: what could be improved in the future.

These exercises aim at placing the student and mentor (parent, educator, clinician etc.) in a position where they are heading in the same direction. Otherwise, if the student can not see there is a benefit in making changes, it is nearly impossible to successfully build visions, effectively set goals and participate in achieving them. Once a goal is mutually agreed on, even if the understanding is more like a tenuous pact in the beginning, individuals are far more open to negotiating changes. And never underestimate that their tenacity in making changes is linked to your belief in them.

Make a wish list

The emphasis has to be to talk with and listen to students. Encourage them to generate wish lists of things that could make a difference to their learning, behavior, confidence, emotion and motivation. Examine what is feasible. Prioritize a list to work through, and begin by choosing one thing that can be quickly put into place at the classroom level to spark momentum. It is in the student's best interest to experience change as soon as they identify a way it might work. Link your efforts to systems and the interests of others who are able to help sustain the student's developing wish to make changes.

The one-page miracle

It is helpful to list, draw or write the things students want to achieve. Reinforce that whatever is done, or is not done, today will affect their choices for tomorrow. Work with the student's vision so it becomes tangible, touchable and physical.

The 'one-page miracle' is useful for developing goals with a class or individual (Amen 2002b). On the page, under the headings friendships, relationships with teachers and parents, academic achievement, school, work in the future, money and fun, encourage students to write exactly what they want for themselves in that area of life. Elicit discussion and encourage students to share their goals with one another. Ask, *Will your current behavior get you want you want?* Invite students to explain how their behaviors are likely to make their vision materialize. For students whose behaviors create doubts about this, the scene is set for further exploration. Suggest students display their goals somewhere they can frequently see them. This exercise helps individuals to stay focused in the now in order to strive for the things they want in the future.

Is success about making good choices?

Pose the questions: *To what extent does each of us have choice over our life? And is what happens to you your choice, or is it determined by someone or something else?*

Present students with a number of controversial or difficult scenarios, and discuss possible consequences depending on an individual's choice at particular moments. Discuss, argue and hypothesize about the extent to which the individual had choice or control over the situation. Have the students record the choices they have made in the past which have helped them. Ask, *Is it possible to exercise choice and make a difference, or is fate, difficulty or bad luck destined to be master?*

Teach children to recognize opportunity

Time spent discussing opportunity is invaluable. Begin by relating your own story, either a time you grabbed an opportunity or lost it. Recount a story about someone who seized opportunity and made life-altering gains. Ask: *What is opportunity? Do all opportunities suit all people?*

Examine and list different types of opportunity.

- *Who's never had opportunity?*
- *Who's had an opportunity in the past and grabbed hold of it? What was the outcome?*
- *Who now realizes they had an opportunity and let it go? Do they have regret? What would they do differently next time?*
- *Why is it that some people can see an opportunity, grab it and do really well; yet, that same opportunity can be missed by others?*
- *Do you know of someone who has had fantastic opportunity?*
- *Does opportunity just come along, or can it be made?*
- *Does opportunity, as the saying says, only knock once?*

Take it further. Investigate people who have seen and seized opportunity in the face of dire hardship and challenge.

Investigate the importance of attitude

What is attitude, and how important is it? Who is in charge of our attitudes? Examine and discuss Charles Swindoll's poem, 'Attitude' (available at <http://www.broadcast-live.com/music/life.html>). *Do you agree that 'life is 10% what happens to me and 90% how I react to it'?*

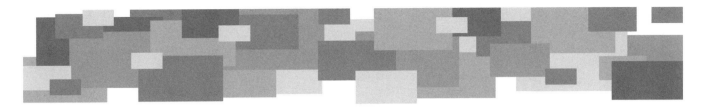

Play 'You decide the future'

Present case studies to the class. These might be fictional or based on the profile of several students you know. In any case, present them as fictional case studies. Each case study begins with the individual's specific job or career aspiration. Then, the individual's strengths, weaknesses, behaviors, attitudes, personality and special talents are presented. Next discuss whether the person's goals look achievable, based on what they have just heard about them. Ask, *What changes might they need to make to achieve their ambition? What are the minimum changes they should make right now?* (Raskind et al. 2002).

Linking now to the future

Develop lists of careers students feel best match their abilities and interests. Encourage discussion between students, sharing why they made their choices and what the careers entail. Search online, call a local college or go to the library to discover more about careers of interest and the prerequisites needed for the chosen fields.

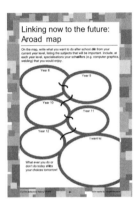

Discuss the step-by-step process necessary to get students from where they are right now to where they want to end up. Help students to link the present to the future by mapping a year-to-year and term-by-term plan. Make a map with labels, dates and ways to do this. Make maps showing preferred and alternative routes. Encourage students to display it, and use it like a road map to get to where they want to go.

Collect pictures that stimulate an appreciation of the career. Arrange for people in the selected careers to visit, to discuss the career and the journey they took to achieve their goal. Ensure they are enthusiastic. Sometimes arranging for a young speaker new to their career helps students to feel their vision is worth holding. Visit a location involved in this kind of work - it enthuses and motivates.

Borrowing from the future

Encouraging a student to write a mid-year or end-of-year report that they might want in the future is a cathartic exercise. The exercise, useful for middle primary students upwards, takes about a lesson and is best done in a one-to-one situation. Prerequisites include a trusting relationship, a mild willingness by the student to goal-set, and a copy of a previous school report. While the activity can provide plenty of chuckles, it compels students to confront criticisms, consider new goals and decide how to convert new goals into reality. This approach allows us, the adults, to participate in proactively nudging students to make attitudinal shifts and behavioral changes.

Jaxon's new vision

Case study

Jaxon's difficulties climaxed during the second semester of eighth grade. These prompted a psychological assessment which revealed he was very bright, but battling a mild learning disorder in combination with Attention Deficit Disorder, a handwriting difficulty and depression. The assessment provided new understandings about his complex mixture of difficulties. It became a catalyst to exchange ideas and develop new adjustments and supports.

Initially, Jaxon was annoyed by his ADD diagnosis. 'I've seen them on television. They're psycho! They yell, kick, hit and punch. I'm not like that!' Jaxon's misconception about ADD is common. It seems sensationalizing a few deliberately selected behavioral aspects, sometimes associated with ADD, attracts good prime-time television ratings. With more information, he learned that his ADD diagnosis was more about identifying a collection of temperament traits: his propensity to daydream, his habit of starting things with best of intentions but not finishing them, his poor organization and forgetfulness. Jaxon now had a name for what he already knew about himself. One of his interests was reading, and soon reading about prominent or famous adults also diagnosed with ADD became a pastime. Some of their lives were inspiring. If they could do it, so could he.

As we constructed a new report, by borrowing from what the future could be, Jaxon was confronted by an array of criticisms from his most recent report: talking in class, distractibility, indiscriminate scribbling in his exercise books, unfinished assignments and lack of commitment to complete written work. These pricked at his pride.

In completing this exercise Jaxon moved his thinking from 'it's too hard to change anything' to a more proactive position. He wanted to achieve better marks, show better application, look more attentive and demonstrate higher levels of motivation and organization. This first step helped determine the vision he had for himself. The next step was to set goals to reinforcement this vision.

Jaxon's original report		
Subject	Grade	Comment
Religion	A	Jaxon is a quiet student whose participation levels have fluctuated. Ongoing and focused supervision has been necessary to ensure his participation.
English	F	Jaxon has failed to hand in any work, focusing his efforts at socializing. There is no reason why such a bright young man can't be successful socially and academically.
Humanities	D	Jaxon's grade reflects his failure to submit a number of assignments. He was granted several extensions of time, but to no avail.
Mathematics	D	Jaxon continues to struggle. He would work when I stood alongside and encouraged him, but lost concentration when I moved on. These marks do not reflect his ability.
Science	C	Jaxon lacks motivation is, disorganized and not prepared to make the effort required.

Jaxon's self written report		
Subject	Grade	Comment
Religion	A	Jaxon is a quiet student whose participation level has been high. Ongoing supervision has not been necessary.
English	B	Jaxon has managed to hand in every piece of work assigned and has achieved a satisfactory mark. His concentration has improved dramatically.
Humanities	C	Jaxon's grade reflects his success to submit most of the assignments set this term. He has achieved a satisfactory mark by doing so.
Mathematics	B	Jaxon strives to reach his potential in mathematics and his efforts are beginning to pay off. He should be congratulated for his efforts so far.
Science	B	Jaxon's results this semester have been very pleasing. He possesses motivation, is organized, and prepared to make the effort required.

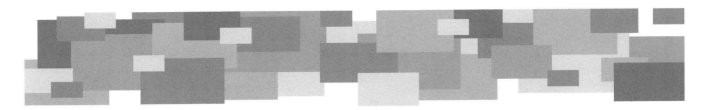

Setting goals

Goals do several things. First, they narrow the attention span to the task at hand. Second, they can provide hope of reaching the goal; the anticipated pleasure. This often triggers the release of the body's feel good chemicals, the endorphins.

(Jensen 2000a, p.155).

The vision a student holds can be turned into reality through collaboratively designing small step-by-step solutions. Achieving small goals, accomplished lesson-by-lesson, day-by-day or week-by-week, provides evidence of change. A good beginning may be as simple as asking the student, *What do you want?*

Sometimes they may not know what they want, yet this simple question can dissolve barriers. The truth is, tips, techniques, ideas and strategies rarely live up to expectations if the child does not trust in the relationship. Listening, appreciating, empathizing and getting on the same side of the fence as the child is critical. Explain to students that their difficulties will improve with time, and there are things that can be targeted now that will help. Healthy relationships, reinforced by mutual negotiation, invite success and sometimes gains occur surprisingly easily.

The code of practice

Cognitive behavioral training brings positive changes to individuals by linking predictable outcomes to each of their behaviors. It demonstrates that appropriate behavior attracts good things, and inappropriate behavior consistently attracts reinforcers that are inconvenient or unpleasant. This technique represents a vote of confidence in individuals to make better choices, and does best within a structured climate of collaboration and positivity. Managing behavior in this way helps us to remain objective and focus on changing behavior, rather than seeing the child as the problem, which invariably leads to heightened emotional levels, blame and conflict (Barkley 1990; Glasser 1999).

The reinforcers

Having effective and easily accessible reinforcers to draw from is essential. Wise teachers discuss, develop and display likely positive and negative reinforcers at the time of designing expectations. They know healthy relationships with students, alongside well-developed positive and negative reinforcers, influence behavior. Positive reinforcement may be a bonus of some kind given after the performance of a desirable behavior. Negative reinforcement works on decreasing an undesirable behavior by taking something away following a behavior that has been jointly defined as undesirable. Similarly, insightful parents have positive and negative reinforcers displayed on the fridge or bulletin board at home.

Positive reinforcers

Positive reinforcers are used to strengthen desired or target behavior. It is the art of observing, commenting on and providing social or concrete rewards for appropriate behavior. It may be as simple as catching a child doing something worthy and pointing it out. This encourages compliance and also lifts us from what, sometimes, can be an unwitting negative cycle we may have fallen into while wrestling with undesirable behaviors.

Social reinforcers

To effectively reshape behavior, the social reinforcer should immediately follow the new desired behavior. For most children a smile, a wink, a pleasant comment, a tussle of the hair, a stamp, a sticker, a certificate, having their name mentioned at assembly or being chosen to be a leader are highly motivating (van der Kley 1991).

Concrete reinforcers

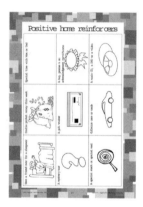
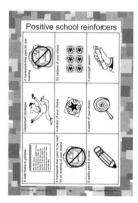

Others require more powerful reinforcers. Praise alone is not enough. Initially, these individuals benefit from more frequent and more immediate reinforcement. Positive reinforcers do not have to be expensive. Consider bonus time on the computer, special snacks, toys, a trip to the library, collector cards, cars or items, CDs, tokens (for example fake money, points or tickets which may be traded for additional television or computer time), gift vouchers and selecting something from the prize box. Artful teachers and parents use influential concrete reinforcers to motivate children to begin or finish work, or to comply. It is surprising how influential inexpensive plastic toys are! In other instances, it is best that the reinforcer is not given immediately. In a token system, stars or points are awarded for targeted positive behaviors, and can later be exchanged for a reward. This form of encouragement, well managed over time, usually leads to internal motivation, which, of course, is the ultimate goal. (Cameron & Pierce 1994, 1998; Fabes et al. 1989; Lepper, Keavney & Drake 1996; Maag 2001; Pfiffner, Rosen & O'Leary 1985; Weiner 1998; Wiersma 1992).

Negative reinforcers

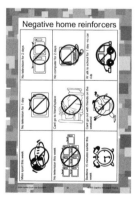
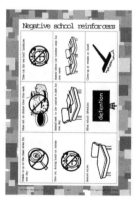

Negative reinforcers are used to reduce unacceptable behavior. These may include the temporary loss of a privilege, missing out on something anticipated, reduction of pocket money, being grounded, time out, reflecting on an action and writing an apology, moving to a less desirable place in the classroom or undertaking additional chores; something the child will seek to avoid in the future. When an undesirable behavior is consistently followed by a negative reinforcer, the undesirable behavior usually diminishes.

Unlike positive reinforcers, use negative reinforcers sparingly, and avoid them unless you are prepared to follow through. When you fail to follow through the child wins, learns how to persevere to get their own way, learns to

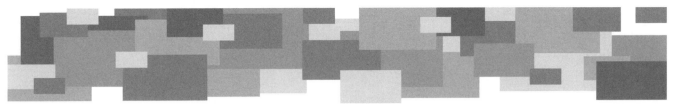

ignore your cues, to ignore basic expectations and to manipulate at a very sophisticated level. Poor management unintentionally teaches children and adolescents how they can effectively control their parents, teachers and others (van der Kley 1997).

A 'way-to-change' plan

When praise and occasional social reinforcers are not enough to bring about a negotiated behavioral change, a cognitive behavioral training program which relies on greater scaffolding and more powerful reinforcers is best suited. Introduce the program by whatever term best suits your situation: a contract, a learning plan, an improvement plan, a behavior plan or a stepping-up plan. My personal preference is a way-to-change plan.

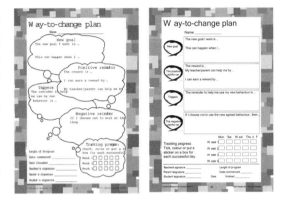

This clever, mutually designed strategy helps students to remember and reach new goals by increasing their accountability. It is optimistic and encourages pro-social participation. View the reinforcement system as a catalyst: an investment to kick-start students' intrinsic motivation and to strengthen their desire to do better for themselves.

Attention reinforces behavior

Assess the behaviors you instinctively respond to. Does your automatic response reinforce the behaviors you value? It should. Question which behaviors are worthy of your response and consider exercising the 90 per cent/10 per cent rule. In other words, allow 90 per cent of behaviors and comments to slip by, and only pick up on the 10 per cent that really matter. It is a sensible rule of thumb ensuring a healthy balance (Petersen 2002). Experienced classroom teachers know that specific positive comments always have to outweigh comments to refocus behavior in a ratio better than 3:1. Prioritize according to what you see as important within your own situation.

Collecting baseline information

Behavior always tells us something. Our task is to find out what it's saying, and observation is our greatest tool. For example, how often does the student call out, lose their temper or not finish work? When and where does this happen? Coming to grips with the ABCs of behavior is useful (Beamish, Bryer & Wilson 2000).

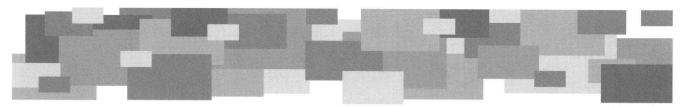

Antecedents: what situation, event or individual seems to prompt this behavior? Might the behavior be the result of a neurological difficulty, bullying, sadness, anxiousness, depression, immaturity, size or composition of the group, excitability, egocentricity, inflexibility, poor planning or poor explanation, cultural or language difficulties?

Behavior: specify what the behavior is. What does it look like? What does the student say or do?

Consequences: what usually happens in response to this behavior?

Structuring the plan to achieve success

You need to approach the plan determined to make it a successful experience. However, accept that at first the situation may become a little more challenging. What is pivotal is to get the child on side. Goals are always easier to accomplish if the child can see the value in them. Psychiatrist William Glasser, author of *Reality Therapy* (2000), believes no-one can make someone do something they don't want to do. Finding ways for individuals to explore what they are doing, to look at what they want, and determine how to achieve what they want must be most highly prized.

Redefine old behaviors in positive terms

Begin with ample discussion. Together, define one or two behaviors worth changing, and redefine them in positive terms. For example, the undesirable behavior might be that the student constantly interrupts in class. The behavior can be redefined positively as, *Raise your hand when you want something* or *During class discussions, count that four other people have had a turn before you do.*

Be specific about the new behavior and be sure the child is clear about how they need to look and sound (Marron 2002). Emphasis is best placed on strengthening the new positive behavior, as research consistently shows that a blunt attempt to stamp out a negative behavior is far less successful than structuring an increase in the frequency of the more desirable behavior (Barkley 1990). Ask yourself, *Is the expectation reasonable for this child?*

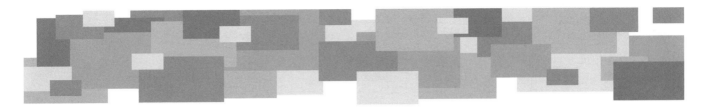

Reinforcements for the new behavior

Children need to know what reinforcements are to be offered and how they can be earned. Let the child participate in choosing the reinforcers (positive and negative) as it makes making changes all the more powerful. Make a list of a number of things they wish to earn as positive reinforcement and seize on what naturally motivates them. The Bulletin board provides a beginning to discuss and select goals.

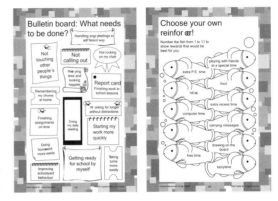

Occasionally provide surprise reinforcement. This tends to heighten awareness and feeds impetus. Also ask the child to participate in selecting negative reinforcers. Explain these will be used only when their old behavior gets in the way of their new thinking. Agree exactly when the negative reinforcer will be used. Decide together whether a signal might be used as a first reminder; but once their unthinking behavior takes over, a predetermined negative reinforcer becomes a non-negotiable consequence.

Ensure adequate social rewards are built in to the program, keeping in mind that children at different ages respond best to different systems. Quite young students, and those with ADHD, respond best to immediate incentives and feedback. This helps to keep the goal fresh in their mind. A consistent drip-feed, nurturing

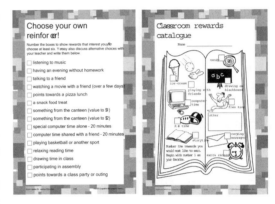

compliance and small changes, is best, as opposed to, *If you've been good all week, you can have a reward*. Older children are able to respond to more complex systems, or systems which have longer delays built in between behavior and reinforcement.

Filling in the way-to-change plan

A written promise helps steer the change way-to-change plan. The greater the child's involvement the more likely they are to succeed. The key to success in this system is tapping into the child's internal sense of pride, and trusting this will help carry their behavior forward (Marron 2002).

Fill out the new positive target behavior. Record the goal specifying exactly how often and how much of this behavior is required to achieve the positive reinforcer. Complete the positive and negative reinforcers agreed on, and record precisely how each reinforcer will be attracted. Formalize the plan by asking the student to sign it. The addition of your signature to the plan is a reminder that your role has to be inspirational in reinforcing successful change.

Select a place to keep the plan. You might take several photographs of the new target behavior agreed to. Once printed, the photographs can be attached to the way-to-change plan as a reminder of the new behavior being strengthened.

Go visual: Methods to monitor progress

To monitor behavioral change and record progress a persuasive visual means is effective. Traditionally, this is where star charts have been employed. They provide a motivating, easy to follow representation of success in relation to the goal set and the length of the program. In truth, any creative visual device will serve this purpose, particularly if it appeals to the child: gauges, clocks, thermometers, photographs of high-rise buildings where stickers can be placed on

 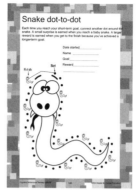 

windows as a child works successfully on their way-to-change plan - the potential is limitless. Lively visual monitoring devices help students to stay excited about their goal, but remain secondary to a well developed plan.

Place the chart and the way-to-change plan where they can be seen as often as needed. Ideal places are on the fridge, on the bedroom door, the pin-up board, contacted to the desk or, at school, stapled to the inside cover of an exercise book used daily. Each lesson or each day a sticker, a color, a move or whatever has been negotiated is added to the chart.

When things go wrong

If things go wrong, invent ways the student might disagree, express their frustration or escape the situation with their dignity intact, without threatening their chances of success. Discuss this and role-play how to do it if need be. Determine and visit safe places they can retreat to if they are feeling overwhelmed, overloaded or explosive. **Never take away privileges they have already earned.** They have been worked for and remain earned. Instead, a negative reinforcer is attracted, and it will take longer to achieve the concrete reinforcer. This helps students to experience the concept of meeting expectations. This is life education and practice at getting it right and wrong is invaluable. Allow for a restart without the connotation of failure.

Allow frequent reminders

Give frequent reminders about what is expected and about the positive reinforcer. Barkley's unifying theory of ADHD, *Inhibitions, Self-Control and Time* (2001), fits with what has long been suspected by teachers and parents. ADHD students cannot anticipate the future. Our planning has to do this for them. Incentive and reinforcement systems have to be palatable, manageable and win-win for both children and adults.

Be consistent and add interest

Be consistent. Follow through on what you say you will do, and once the program is initiated use it each day. Meet briefly every day to review progress. Praise effort as well as success. Over time, extend the standard required to achieve a concrete reinforcer. If they're doing it for an hour, try it until recess. The next week try until midday. Push

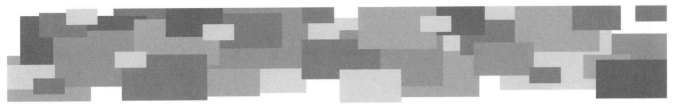

it out. Be prepared to move to new short-term goals once the initial goal has been achieved and never hesitate to change the physical appearance of the way-to-change plan to add interest. Aim to remove the rewards when praise begins to make a difference, otherwise the risk of converting students into reward addicts may materialize.

A common slip is to keep working at a behavior once the initial goal has been attained. The plan is not about achieving perfection; it is about behavioral normalization and developing flexibilities through thinking.

Designing a plan using a flow chart

Designing a way-to-change plan using flow chart construction delivers a strong visual representation about how the plan works, what is to be achieved and what stage the student is at within the plan. At a glance, it lets everyone involved know precisely how the system works and the negotiated steps that need to be followed. This is particularly important for staff who have difficulty in responding to students with challenging or different behaviors, or when new staff members suddenly find themselves on the scene and may be unsure how to respond.

As always, best outcomes are achieved when the student is on board and working collaboratively with a teacher, counselor and parents to develop the way-to-change plan. Developing the plan in the context of a supportive, proactive team that allows the student strong input ensures the student feels as though they own it, understand it and have greater internal drive to make it work. The following example is typical of what is used for elementary to middle school students. It can be very easily simplified to support much younger students.

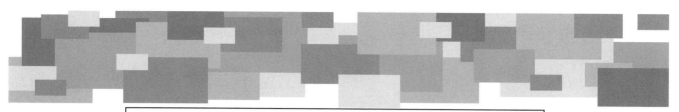

A way-to-change plan: Flow chart

Student: Seb
School: Fielton P.S.
Date commenced: 15th March 2005
Date to be reviewed: 2005
Target behaviors:
1.   For Seb to be happier and more successful at school
2.   To create a way for other children to let Seb pay with them
3.   For Seb to be able to learn better
To do behaviors:
1.   'Try not to go mad at people,' instead I can walk away or tell them what is wrong.
2.   'Not to swear or hit kids,' instead, I can sing my funny song and do something else.
3.   'To stop calling out in class and refusing to do any work,' instead I can make deals with my teachers.
Flow chart: How the plan works

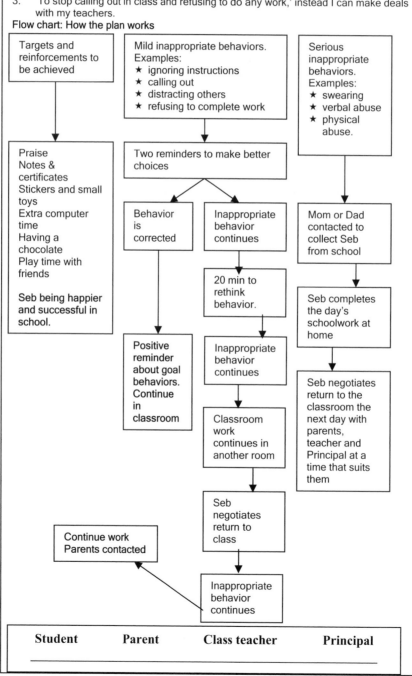

Student	**Parent**	**Class teacher**	**Principal**

Increasing Brett's daily exercise and compliance

Brett was fifteen years old and attended secondary school on a part-time basis. Although he was an engaging, entertaining adolescent, he was completely self-absorbed by his current topics of interest. It was nearly impossible to steer Brett away from what he wanted to talk about. Try as one might, he would resolutely pull the conversation back to his absorption. His interests included Warhammer, imaginative weapons of the future, money and the Discovery channel.

Brett had developed an opinionated, dogmatic conversational style about these which set him up as a regular target for ridicule and mimicry from peers at school. His obsessions made any learning outside his narrow interest areas virtually unachievable. He could intellectualize his difficulties, and in safe, calm moments even verbalize strategies to step away from conflict at school. However, once at school, he found his position unalterable. Instinctively he would engage in his predictable discourse, attract negative comments and feel frustrated, but persist, which attracted further antagonism. This resulted in Brett swearing, shouting and sometimes hurting others.

At home, Brett's intense single-mindedness meant he would spend his days lying on the couch watching the Discovery channel or surfing the net for interesting new 'weapons-of-the-future' sites. His strong natural tendency was to do what he wanted. When he was asked to help around home he would ignore the request or refuse. When pressed he would become angry, dictatorial, abusive and occasionally violent. Brett's physical inactivity had seen him gain 15 kilograms over the last twelve months, so increasing his mobility had become a priority to his parents.

To promote physical activity, a way-to-change plan was implemented, and Brett could see the value in it, as he did not like being overweight. He participated in formulating the plan and approved a 'check the list' idea to help monitor changes. One check, for compliance, would represent a 2-dollar gain, and noncompliance incurred the loss of a potential 2 dollars. (Brett was a keen financial manager and hated the idea of squandering potential income.) He negotiated to complete a minimum of one and a maximum of two tasks per day: walking the dog around the block, going for a twenty-minute bike ride, walking to his friend's house, walking to the local shops to do an errand, collecting and disposing of the doggie doo from the back lawn, mowing the small back lawn, cleaning three windows (Brett quite enjoyed cleaning windows!), washing the car or taking letters to a nearby post office box.

The money could be taken in cash at the end of the week, or could accumulate to buy books on futuristic weapons. Thankfully, Brett's obsession provided effective leverage. A similar plan had been running to prompt Brett to go to school more regularly, so trying this did not seem too different or daunting for him. The plan was constructed and displayed on the fridge.

His parents were crafty. When he needed reminding they would walk over the chart and say, 'Brett, it is three-thirty; if you haven't done your part of the bargain for the day by four-thirty then you will lose your check today.'

This was usually enough, and slowly Brett developed a new routine of doing one or two activities a day that fell outside his very rigid comfort zone. Progressively, his physical activity was extended to making the bed, emptying the rubbish, even moving furniture while his mother vacuumed. Small steps helped Brett to become more active and

Cognitive Behavioral Training

compliant. The way-to-change plan delivered an outcome far more powerful than wishing Brett's old habits would change.

Preventing Will's touching

He knew he did it, but said he couldn't help it. He had lightly rubbed his mother's cheek with the back of his fingers for as long as he could remember. Nine-year-old Will said it was because he liked the softness of her face. Annette, his mom, thought Will's habit had evolved because he found reassurance in doing this. She remembered him doing it when he was much younger in situations he felt uncertain about. It was part and parcel of a package of repetitive habits linked to his Asperger Syndrome diagnosis.

Annette explained to Will that it wasn't a thing that boys his age did any longer. The habit had come under scrutiny when his soccer coach snapped at him while he was rubbing his mother's cheek at the half time break. This delivered a jolt to Annette too. She realized it was time to make changes. She told Will it didn't look cool and needed to change. Despite possessing an array of rigid, ritualistic ways, Will always presented an engaging, sunny and compliant nature. He was well-accepted by peers and it was important to him to look cool. Being told that this behavior needed to change because it wasn't cool was motivation enough to start thinking about it. This was his incentive.

Annette and Will designed new rules to change this old unwanted behavior. They wrote them up on a way-to-change plan. Now Will could brush his fingers gently across Annette's cheek, but only at home during his favorite television show, which they sometimes watched together, and when she read to him at night. At all other times, if Will went to put his hand up, the agreement was that Annette would take his hand and hold it gently at her side or put it back down by his side and move away. Additional incentive to reinforce the new habit came from charting his progress on a 'Keep the hand down' chart they made together. Will knew if he could get this right day by day over four weeks, then together they would break the old habit he no longer wanted.

Each day over the following four weeks Will made a point of placing a hand sticker they had bought on the chart. Occasionally he would forget and would rely on Annette to take his hand and put it down by his side. The memory lapse didn't matter because he was rewarded for developing better habits. Gradually, this old habit faded leaving Will feeling he looked as cool as any of his friends.

Reducing Juan's demanding behavior

Excerpt from a letter written to Juan and his mother following a consultation.

Dear Juan,

I really enjoyed meeting you, your mom and your little brother yesterday. I know you're keen to start this 'way to change' plan, so here it is.

What is the bad habit we have decided to change?

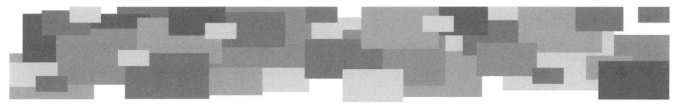

Interrupting your mom when she is speaking with other people, and especially when she is speaking on the telephone.

What is the new way to get your mom's attention when she is on the telephone or in conversation?

First, we agreed that no words are to be used. Walk up to mom and put your open hand gently on her shoulder, just like we rehearsed. Resting it gently is the cue that you need her attention as soon as she can. Wait. Don't speak. Look at your mom's face and wait for her response. She may excuse herself from the conversation and speak with you, but most likely she will put her finger up and smile. That will mean, 'I have heard you, and as soon as I have finished this conversation you will be my priority.'

You need to move away and do something else until she is ready to help. In the meantime you may be able to work it out for yourself.

You asked whether you could interrupt if it was an emergency.

YES! If it is a genuine emergency you do anything you want to make sure the emergency is attended to, and everybody is safe. Thankfully emergencies do not happen often.

What if you forget to use the new way? How many chances do you get each day?

You get just one chance each day - seven days a week. This is fair because we are trying to break an old behavior pattern and old habits can be tricky to change. Chances are that you will fall back into the old pattern sometimes. If you do that, your mom just turns around and says, 'Juan, that's your one chance and now it's gone'. Then she turns her back to you and you must walk away. Stay away for ten minutes. You must not expect your mom to respond to the old habit. She must ignore you. This is really important, and she has to get this right. To get her attention while she is on the telephone or with other people, you need to use the new behavior.

What is your positive reinforcer?

Mom and you have decided on a DVD you've been trying to save up for. It will be yours after a successful two-week trial.

How can we keep you excited and track your progress?

Reminding you about your reward will help, so your mom is going to photocopy the front cover of the DVD and cut it into fourteen pieces. Each day, when you are successful, she will return a piece, and you can glue them to a cardboard sheet, just like a jigsaw. When all fourteen bits are back together you have achieved your DVD, and you know you really can control your old interrupting habit.

What if you mess up? Will you still get the DVD?

Yes, eventually. You will never lose it. It will just take longer.

Remember the negative reinforcer too!

Each time you break the new way, after the daily chance has been given, you lose fifteen minutes of potential playing time on your computer game. Mom can do this whenever she chooses. She may even choose to do this when you have friends over.

Why are we doing this?

We are doing this because most 11-year-olds have this behavior under control. So to help you feel better, and look better in front of people, it is time to target this behavior. It looks unthinking, uncaring and demanding ... and that's not what you are like on the inside!

Do I think you can achieve this?

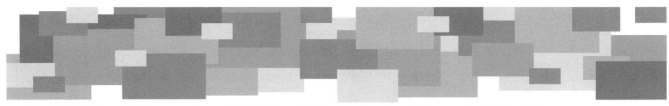

Absolutely! I wouldn't suggest we do it if I thought this was too hard. I know the DVD will be yours because you already know that interrupting mom in front of others makes you look different to the way you want others to see you. So apart from shaking off an old habit, you are well and truly ready for it.

Good luck!

Case study — *Improving Michael's school behavior*

Michael was twelve years old and described by his teachers as excitable, silly and smart-mouthed. He presented a barrage of low-level annoying behaviors. He had received fourteen 'bad behavior cards' from his school during a term and there were rumblings that a similar performance next term might result in his expulsion. Most of the cards were for thoughtless, impulsive behaviors - saying things without thinking, becoming carried away with the moment and upsetting others when he became overexcited, frustrated or annoyed. He also received bad behavior cards for not bothering to attempt homework.

Michael and his mother hit on an idea. They decided to use the number of bad behavior cards he received in the previous term as a measure for changes to his behavior in the coming term. Michael's goal for the new term was to halve the number of bad behavior cards. So, to be successful he couldn't receive more than one bad behavior card each week.

Michael, his teacher and the school counselor set up an improved homework system, and this supported Michael's mother in taking a renewed interest in organizing the homework routine. His teacher and counselor worked with Michael to create a way-to-change plan flow chart. This assisted him to understand that his previous behaviors were genuinely of a low-level irritating nature. Knowing this gave him an incentive to make changes, rather than seeing himself as all bad. Understanding, and being able to see, what consequences particular behaviors would attract was also a steadying influence.

Michael and his mother kept track of successful days by sticking a small hamburger on an incentive chart for each one. When Michael accumulated four consecutive hamburgers they went to a fast-food outlet to celebrate. The chart at home helped Michael to see how he was going, and the closely spaced rewards buoyed his enthusiasm. By the end of term, he had four bad behavior cards. Michael had been successful. His short-term planning had helped him to achieve his long-term objective.

With supportive intervention, which allowed him to think more about his behavior, Michael was able to control his behavior better than ever before. His confidence and ability to acquire improved behaviors had changed.

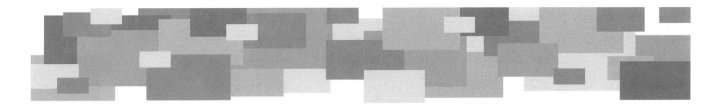

Easing Robert's calling out and roaming

Case study

Robert had just entered sixth grade. He was tall, wiry, good-natured and very likable, but always on the move, wanting to share his every thought. His two psychological assessments had revealed that ADHD was at the root of his overactive, highly verbal and impulsive behaviors. While Robert's dynamic behavior worked in his favor on the soccer field, and had gained him respect, it ran counter to the sorts of behaviors expected in the classroom. School had been a long, exacting journey for Robert, as it did not easily accommodate his natural exuberance and lightning impulses.

Mr. Bowden, Robert's new teacher, was known as 'a man of few words'. He decided it was time for Robert to step up by being offered more choices than were naturally available to him. So, in one short session after school, he explained to Robert what was to happen.

'Robert, you've been with me for three weeks now, and I've decided I like you, but some things have to change. If they don't there are big problems ahead for you. I want this to be the year you learn to stay in your seat and get control over calling out! At the moment you're up and wandering about before you've even thought about it. It's time to start thinking about what you do. First, we'll work on you staying in your seat. As far as your calling out goes, I'll ignore it for the moment!'

Mr. Bowden cut a picture of a chair into nine pieces. He explained, 'At the beginning of the day, I'll make sure there are puzzle pieces in the box on my desk. When you remain in your seat for a lesson, you can take a piece from the box. It won't be for every lesson, but you'll know when because I'll give you a wink. When you have all nine pieces and can show me the entire picture, you can select a reward.

Each lesson I'll give you one warning to stay in your seat, but if you choose not to think about staying in your seat after the warning, I'll exercise a negative reinforcer. You will lose the privilege of your extra recess for the day.' Mr. Bowden had arranged for Robert to join an additional afternoon recess with another class to satisfy his exuberance and enjoyment in this area. 'Once you have four class rewards, you'll earn a much bigger reward that your parents and I have discussed, and once you've achieved this you'll know you have stretched your self-control. It gets easier, Robert!'

Mr. Bowden and Robert negotiated two other places in the classroom that Robert could move to, as staying in one place for too long was tricky for him. Mr. Bowden promised that if Robert asked he would be allowed to move, because asking meant Robert had thought about what he wanted to do. Together, they worked on the plan over two school terms. Robert made good progress, but sometimes attracted the negative reinforcer. Within three months, staying in his seat was no more than a minor problem and calling out had completely ceased.

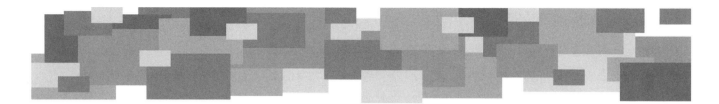

Helping Kim find a better balance

Kim was in ninth grade and possessed an IQ within the top 1 per cent. Yet, her behaviors always indicated her struggle with emotional intelligence. Her school history was punctuated by poor work performance, niggling noncompliance, mild behavioral difficulties and poor motivation. Her best performances occurred when they were on her terms or there was something obvious for her to gain. At home, the struggle was the same. Her parents worked hard to maintain a positive, balanced relationship, but she subtly and overtly pushed and manipulated to have things her way. Compromise and empathy seemed elusive qualities for Kim. The past six months had seen marginal gains at school, but home behavior demonstrated an increasing absence of courtesy and family thoughtfulness. Everyone felt on edge around Kim. Her parents decided to take an unruffled stand. They needed Kim to make a few basic attitudinal changes. Her parents explained what they were seeing at present and what they required from now on. Kim's way-to-change plan was simple. First they listed the new required behaviors. These included:

- saying thank you
- saying I'm sorry
- giving a hug
- giving a kiss
- setting the table
- clearing the table
- helping with the dishes rather than disappearing
- doing something thoughtful
- asking her mother or father if they needed help
- asking a family member how their day had been
- making others in the family laugh
- helping her brother and sister with their homework
- spending some happy time with her brother and sister
- feeding the cat
- taking out the garbage
- making her bed each day
- straightening her room up once a week
- self-initiating her homework
- getting up in the mornings without fuss and on time
- smiling
- telling a joke.

Each day Kim had the opportunity to earn about twelve checks. One check was recorded each time her mother or father noticed one of the new targeted behaviors. If, by Thursday morning, Kim had achieved fifty checks she was entitled to spend time with her friends on Friday after school and enjoy a weekend outing with them. It was no longer her right to automatically expect to go out with friends over the weekend. After several weeks, Kim's mother

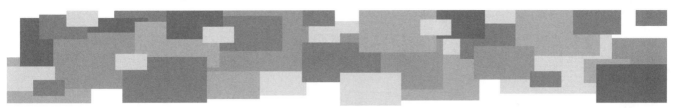

commented, 'Kim, have you noticed how much happier it's been around here for everybody, including you, lately?'. Kim quipped, 'I thought it was stupid doing this. It's been okay.' The plan continues to work in this household as a way to visibly reinforce caring, cooperative behaviors. Sometimes cooperative behaviors just disappear in the bustle of busy family life.

Blackline masters

- Vision building
- Linking now to the future: A road map
- Mouse help
- Goal-setting: Hitting the target
- Positive home reinforcers
- Positive school reinforcers
- Negative home reinforcers
- Negative school reinforcers
- Way-to-change plan 1
- Way-to-change plan 2
- Way-to-change plan 3
- Way-to-change plan 4
- Way-to-change plan: Flow chart
- Identifying the ABC's of behavior
- Bulletin board: What needs changing
- Choose your own reinforcer! (elementary)
- Choose your own reinforcer! (upper elementary/middle school)
- Classroom rewards catalog
- Wiggling your way to success!
- Panda progress
- Go for goals with Gerald
- Snake dot-to-dot
- Skull dot-to-dot
- Australian dot-to-dot
- Duck dot-to-dot
- Gauging progress
- Get to the top
- How hot can I get?
- Star chart (three moves)
- Star chart (four moves)
- A quick goal!
- Staying in my seat
- I don't have to yell out

Vision building

Linking now to the future maintains motivation!

List careers you are interested in knowing more about.

1. _____

2. _____

3. _____

Choose one from above and complete the following.

Picture showing aspects of this career

List the sorts of things to do in this career

1. _____

2. _____

3. _____

Career

Where do you train for this career?

Place: _____

Phone: _____

Contact person: _____

_____

What are some associated careers? Where could you find employment?

_____

_____

_____

_____

Contact of possible guest speaker

Name: _____

Phone: _____

_____

Linking now to the future: A road map

On the map, write what you want to do after school. Work from your current year level, listing the subjects that will be important. Include, at each year level, specializations your school offers (e.g. computer graphics, welding) that you would enjoy.

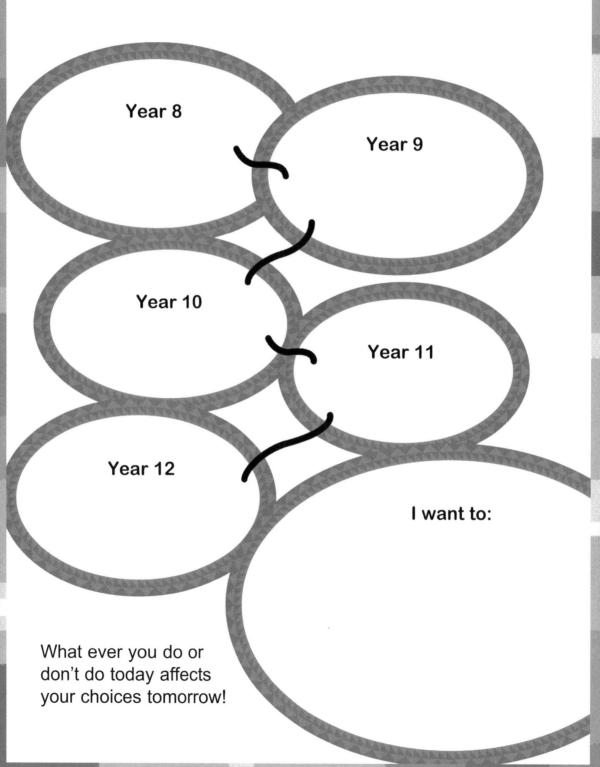

Year 8

Year 9

Year 10

Year 11

Year 12

I want to:

What ever you do or don't do today affects your choices tomorrow!

A short-term goal that helps get you to your long-term goal.

A short-term goal that helps get you to your long-term goal.

A short-term goal that helps get you to your long-term goal.

The long-term goal

A short term goal that helps get you to your long-term goal.

Mouse help

short term

If you can't reach your goal the first time, don't give up! Simply restart. It's important to pick yourself up and keep moving towards your long-term goal.

long term

Short-term goals: For the next week or two

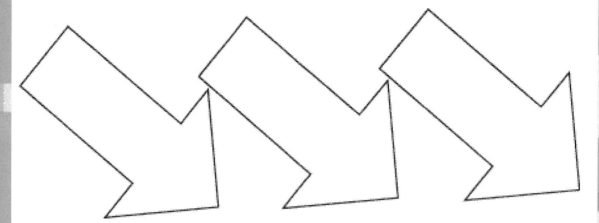

Goal-setting

Hitting the target

Name _____

Long-term goals:
The term or year ahead

If you can't reach your goal the first time, don't give up!
Simply restart. It's important to pick yourself up and keep
going towards the long-term goal.

Positive home reinforcers

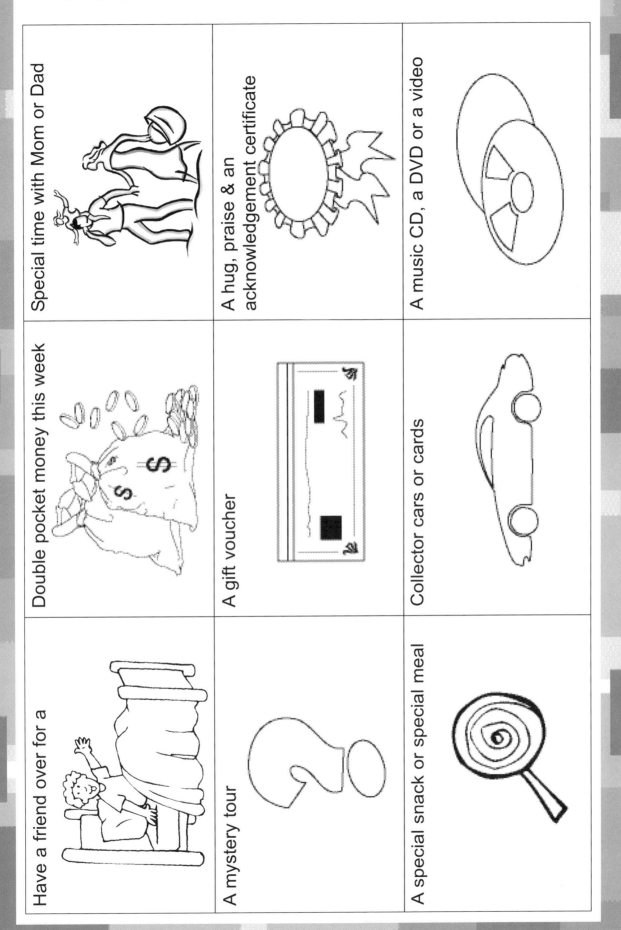

Have a friend over for a	Double pocket money this week	Special time with Mom or Dad
A mystery tour	A gift voucher	A hug, praise & an acknowledgement certificate
A special snack or special meal	Collector cars or cards	A music CD, a DVD or a video

Positive home reinforcers

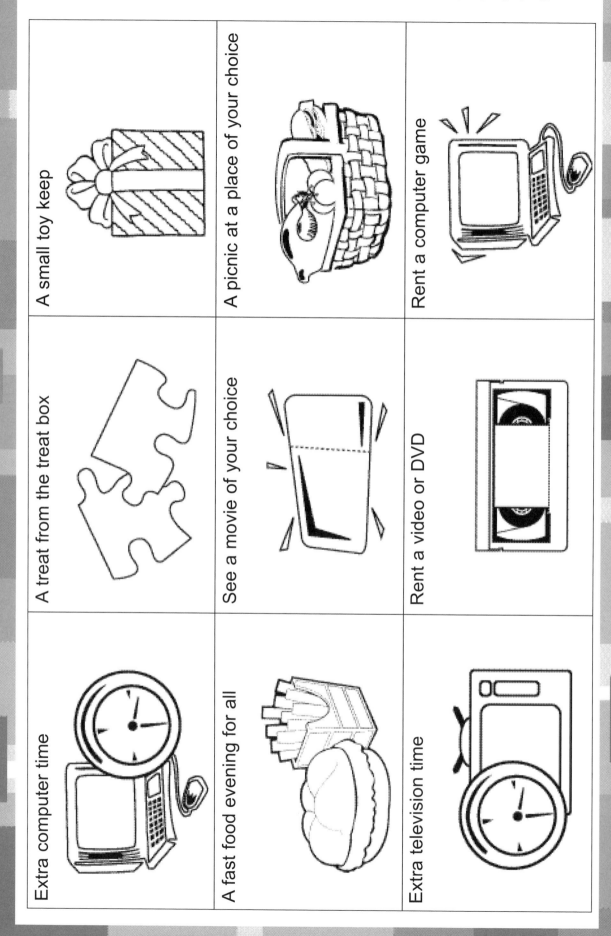

A small toy keep

A picnic at a place of your choice

Rent a computer game

A treat from the treat box

See a movie of your choice

Rent a video or DVD

Extra computer time

A fast food evening for all

Extra television time

Positive school reinforcers

A note home to parents	Classroom privileges	A homework-free pass for one evening
Dear Mrs. Green, Tony has been a delight to have in the classroom today. He finished all his work on time, and was extremely helpful in pack-up at the end of the day. Keep up the good work, Tony! From Mrs. May 		
A homework-free pass to be used for an evening of your choice	A sticker of your choice	Six stickers of your choice
		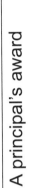
A wacky pencil or marker	A sweet of your choice	A principal's award

Positive school reinforcers

Fifteen minutes of free time on the playground with a friend

The choice of your favorite game for P.E.

Be dismissed from class a few moments before anyone else

Bonus time on the computer

A lesson helping younger children in another class

Be teacher's helper for a lesson

Something for free from snack box

First in line

Take your work to a teacher of your choice

Negative home reinforcers

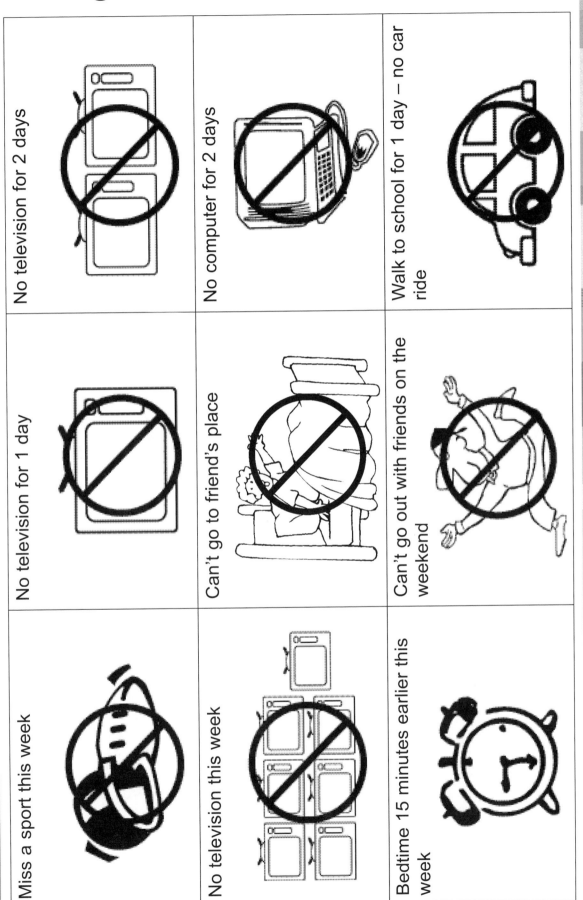

Miss a sport this week

No television for 1 day

No television for 2 days

No television this week

Can't go to friend's place

No computer for 2 days

Bedtime 15 minutes earlier this week

Can't go out with friends on the weekend

Walk to school for 1 day – no car ride

Negative home reinforcers

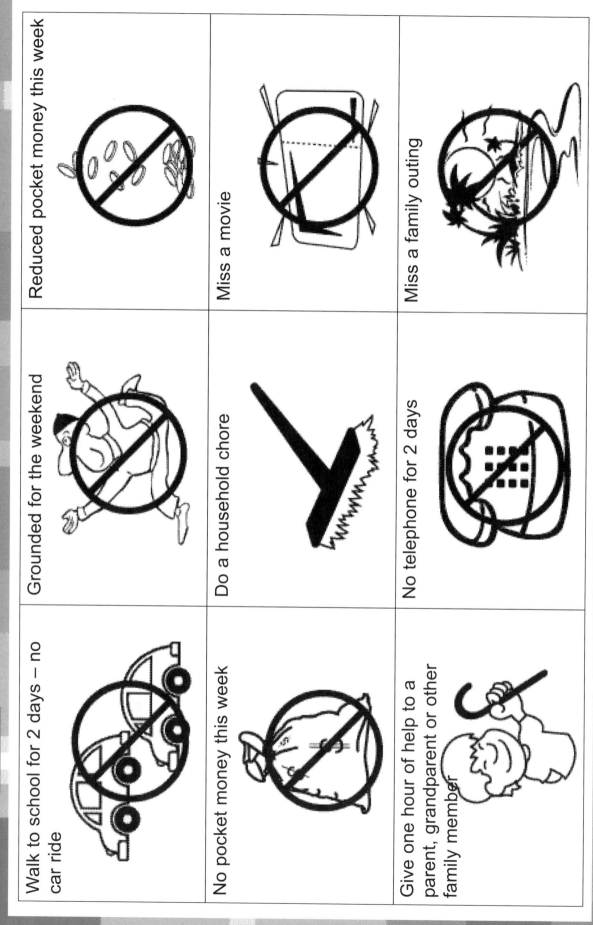

Reduced pocket money this week

Miss a movie

Miss a family outing

Grounded for the weekend

Do a household chore

No telephone for 2 days

Walk to school for 2 days – no car ride

No pocket money this week

Give one hour of help to a parent, grandparent or other family member

Negative school reinforcers

Time out for one half lunchtime

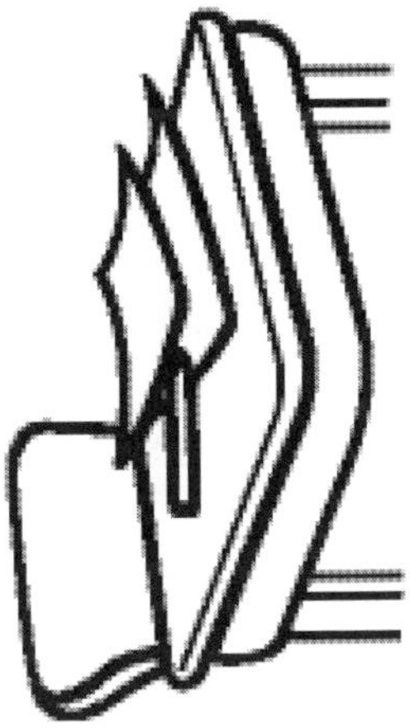

Seated where the teacher says for one week

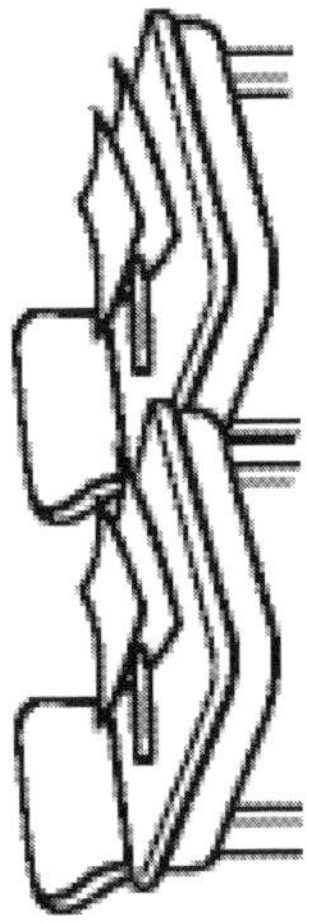

Clean-up at recess or lunch

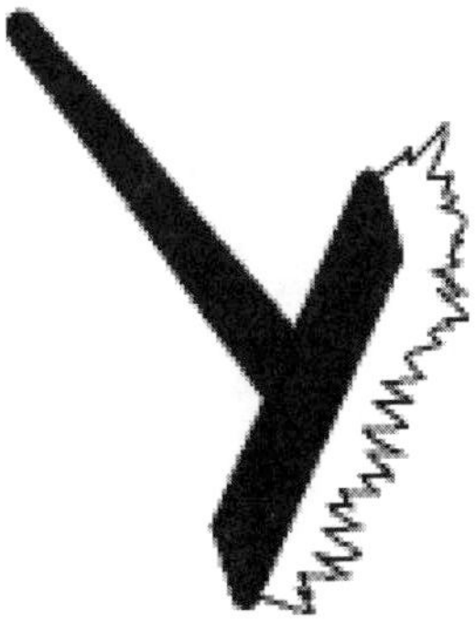

Miss out on choice time this week

Seated next to the teacher's desk for one day

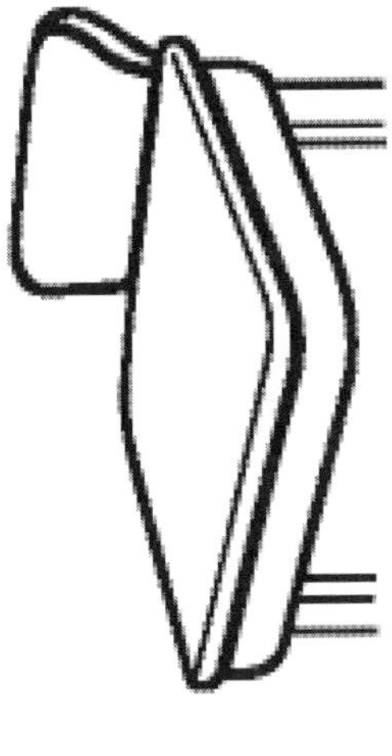

After school detention

detention

Unable to go to the class store for one day

Time out during lunch or recess

Seated alone

Negative school reinforcers

Complete a task requested by teacher (e.g. clean up classroom) 	Write a letter of explanation 	Re-do your work in your own time
Miss a lesson of your teacher's choice	No recess	Work without a seat for a while
Pick up papers, work in the lunchroom or clean the 	Be delayed 10 minutes after	No drama this week 

Way-to-change plan

Name _____

Date commenced _____ Date finished _____

New goal: The new behavior I want to use is …

My new behavior can happen when I …

Triggers: The reminder to help me use my new behavior is …

The positive reinforcer:
The reward is …
I can earn a reward by …

My teacher/parent can help me by …

Negative reinforcer: If I choose not to use the new behavior, then …

Tracking progress: place a sticker on a dot each successful day
• • • • • • • • • • • • • • • • • •

Parent's signature _____

Teacher's signature _____

Student's signature _____

Way-to-change plan

Name _____

New goal: The new behavior I want to use is …

This can happen when I …

Positive reinforcer:

The reward is …

I can earn it by …

My teacher/parent can help me by …

Triggers: The reminder to help me use my new behavior is …

Negative reinforcer: If I choose not to use my new behavior, then …

Date commenced _____ Date finished _____

Student's signature _____

Parent/Teacher's signature _____

Way-to-change plan

Name _____

New goal

The new goal I want is ...

This can happen when I ...

Positive reinforcer

The reward is ...

I can earn a reward by ...

My teacher/parent can help by ...

Triggers

The reminder to help me use my new behavior is ...

Negative reinforcer

If I choose not to work at the new goal, then ...

Length of Program

Date commenced _____

Date finished _____

Teacher's signature _____

Parent's signature _____

Student's signature _____

Tracking progress:

Check, color or put a sticker on a box for each succesful day

Week 1 ☐ ☐ ☐ ☐ ☐

Week 2 ☐ ☐ ☐ ☐ ☐

Week 3 ☐ ☐ ☐ ☐ ☐

Way-to-change plan

Name _____

New goal

The new goal I want is …

This can happen when I …

The reward is …

The positive reinforcer

My teacher/parent can help me by …

I can earn a reward by …

The reminder to help me use my new behavior is …

Triggers

If I choose not to use the new agreed behavior, then …

The negative reinforcer

	Mon	Tue	Wed	Thu	Fri
Week 1					
Week 2					
Week 3					
Week 4					

Tracking progress
Check, color or put a
sticker on a box for
each successful day.

Teacher's signature _____

Parent's signature _____

Student's signature _____

Length of program

Date commenced _____

Date finished _____

Way-to-change plan: Flow chart

Student _____   Date commenced ___/___/___
School _____   Date to be reviewed ___/___/___

Target behaviors

1. _____
2. _____
3. _____

To-do behaviors

1. _____ Instead, _____
2. _____ Instead, _____
3. _____ Instead, _____

Flow chart: How the plan works

| Targets and reinforcements to be achieved | Mild inappropriate behaviors
Examples:
* ignoring Instructions
* calling out
* distracting others
* refusing to complete work | Serious inappropriate behaviors
Examples:
*unacceptable language
*verbal abuse
*physical abuse |

Two reminders to make better choices

Behavior is corrected

Inappropriate behavior continues

Student   Parent   Class teacher   Principal

_____   _____   _____   _____

Identifying the ABC's of behavior

Behavior
WHAT Is the behavior

Antecedent
WHY does it occur? What seems to set it off?

Consequence
HOW intense is the behavior?

Circle the number thst represents the intensity of the behavior.

1 2 3 4 5 6 7 8 9 10

Low intensity → High intensity

Antecedent
WHEN does it occur?

Bulletin board: What needs changing?

Handling angry feelings in a different way

Not touching other people's things

Not calling out

Not rocking on my chair

Worrying less and looking happier

Report card
Finishing work in school lessons

Remembering my chores at home

Finishing assignments on time

Doing my daily reading

Working for longer without distractions

Starting my work more quickly

Doing homework more easily

Getting ready for school by myself

Taking turns more easily

Improving schoolyard behavior

Choose your own reinforcer!

Number the fish from 1 to 11 to show rewards that would be best for you.

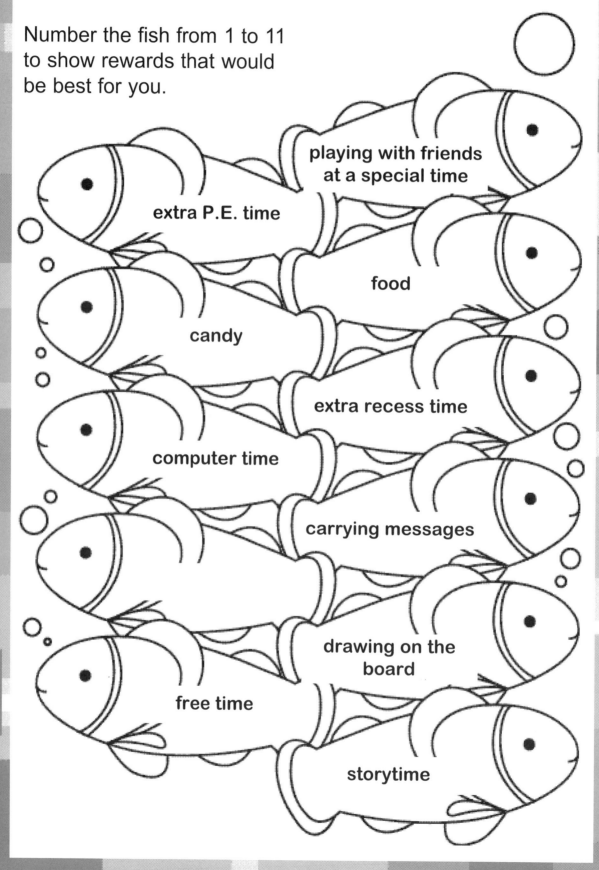

playing with friends at a special time

extra P.E. time

food

candy

extra recess time

computer time

carrying messages

drawing on the board

free time

storytime

Choose your own reinforcer!

Number the boxes to show rewards that interest you. Try to choose at least six. You may also discuss alternative choices with your teacher and write them below.

☐ listening to music

☐ having an evening without homework

☐ talking to a friend

☐ watching a movie with a friend

☐ points towards a pizza lunch

☐ a snack food treat

☐ something from the reward box (small item)

☐ something from the reward box (large item)

☐ special computer time alone – 20 minutes

☐ computer time with a friend – 20 minutes

☐ playing basketball or another sport

☐ relaxing reading time

☐ drawing time in class

☐ participating in extra-curricular activities

☐ points towards a class party or outing

Classroom rewards catalog

Name _____

ice-cream

playing with friends

computer time

P.E. time

storytime

candy

drawing on blackboard

free time

other

carrying messages

extra recess

Number the rewards you would most like to earn. Begin with number 1 as your favorite.

Wiggling your way to success with Wally

Wally the worm is trying to get to his friend's wormhole. Help him by coloring in one of his body segments each time you achieve a target (each lesson or each day). Every fourth segment you color in will earn you a small reward. When Wally has been colored in completely, you have achieved your goal and earned the reward agreed on!

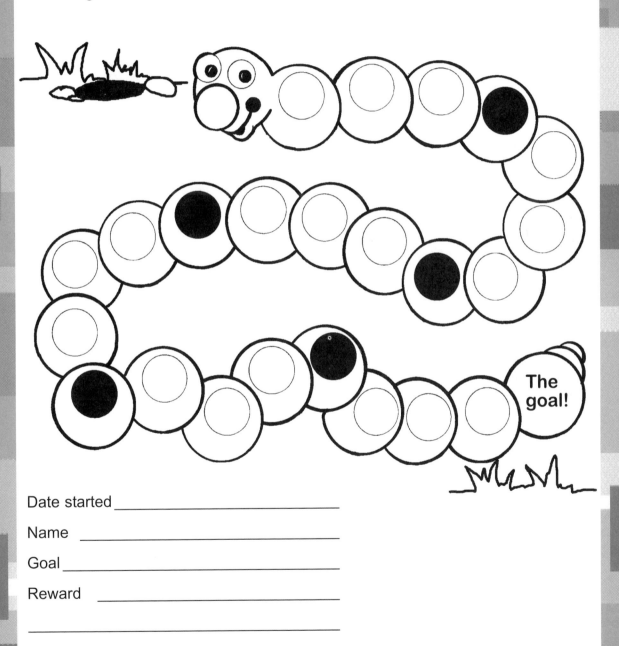

Date started _____

Name _____

Goal _____

Reward _____

_____

Panda progress

Each time you achieve a target, color in a pair of panda footprints. When the colored footprints reach the panda, you've achieved your goal and your reward!

Date started _____

Name _____

Goal _____

Reward _____

_____

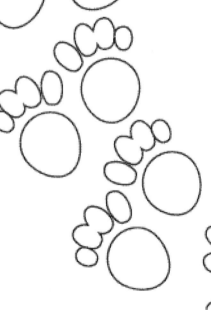

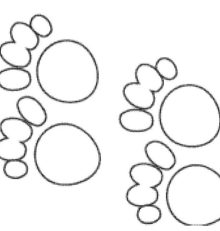

Go for goals with Gerald

This is a bug. His name is Gerald. Each time you finish an agreed task, at home or at school, put a sticker on one of his spots. When all six of Gerald's spots have a sticker on them, you'll get your reward because you've achieved a goal!

Date started _____

Name _____

Goal _____

Reward _____

_____

Snake dot-to-dot

Each time you reach your short-term goal, connect another dot around the snake. A small surprise is earned when you reach a baby snake. A larger reward is earned when you get to the finish because you've achieved a longer-term goal.

Date started _____

Name _____

Goal _____

Reward _____

_____

Finish

Start

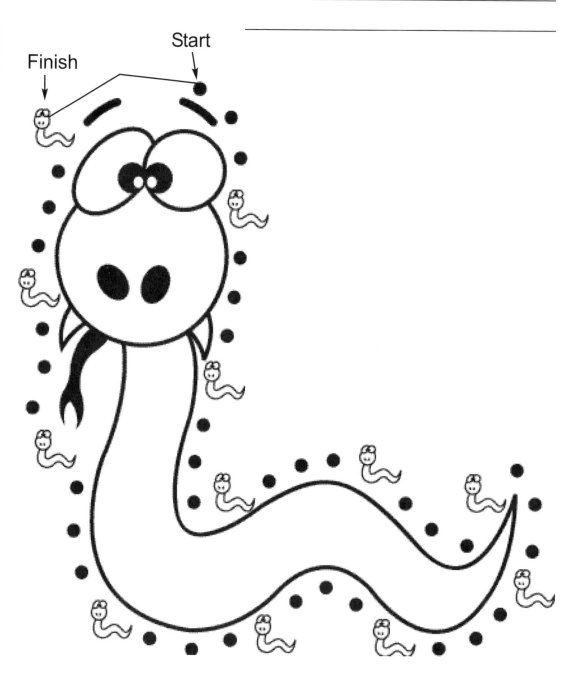

Skull dot-to-dot

Each time you reach your short-term goal, connect another dot around the skull. A small surprise is earned when you reach a pumpkin. A larger reward is earned when you get to the finish to celebrate achieving a long-term goal.

Finish   Start

Date started _____

Name _____

Goal _____

Reward _____

_____

Australian dot-to-dot

Each time you reach your goal, connect another dot around Australia. Remember, you earn a small reward when you reach a dot that is circled. A larger reward is waiting for you when you get to the finish.

Date started _____

Name _____

Goal _____

Reward _____

_____

Duck dot-to-dot

Each time you reach your goal, connect another dot around the duck. Remember, you earn a small reward when you reach a puddle. A larger reward is waiting for you when you get to the finish.

Date started _____

Name _____

Goal _____

Reward _____

_____

Finish   Start

Name _____

Goal _____

Comments

Gauging progress

Monday

Tuesday

Wednesday

Thursday

Friday

Get to the top

Name _____

Goal _____

Keep track of your progress. Check off a square or cover it with a sticker each time you achieve your goal. Decide on what awaits you once you reach the top.

How hot can I get?

Name _____

Goal _____

Keep track of your progress. Color a square or cover it with a sticker each time you achieve your short term goal. Decide on what awaits you once reach the top.

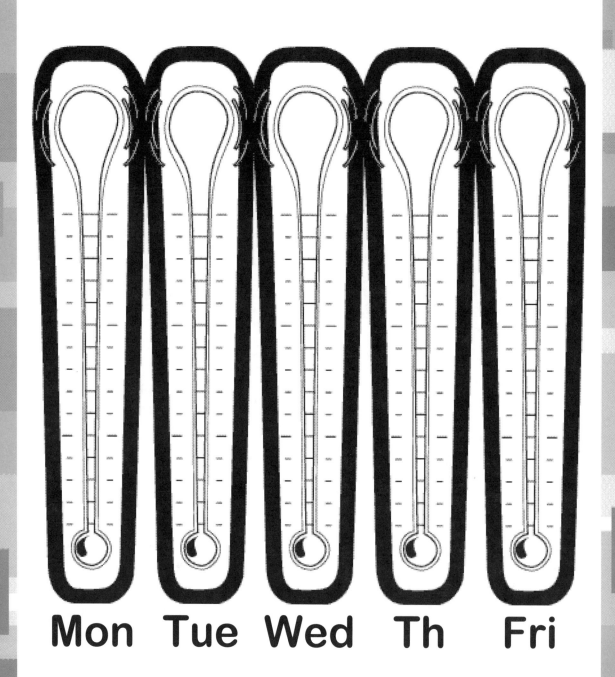

Mon   Tue   Wed   Th   Fri

Star chart

Name _____

Goal _____

Every time you reach your goal, put
a sticker on the circle next to it.

Star chart

Name _____

Goal _____

Every time you reach your goal, put
a sticker on the circle next to it.

A quick goal!

Date ___/___/___

Today's goal is _____

_____

_____

Time	Student rating /10	Teacher rating /10
Morning		
Lunch and recess		
Afternoon		
Total	**/30**	**/30**

Keep a tally of scores. Average the teacher and student ratings. If over a day, scores reach an agreed average, you will get a reward

Staying in my seat

Of course I can, I just
need some quiet
reminding!

I don't have to yell out

Because I'm
the boss of me!

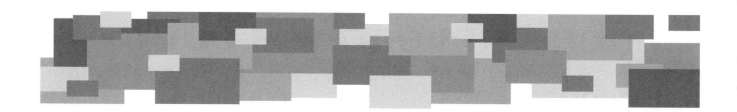

Chapter 4
Fostering emotional resilience

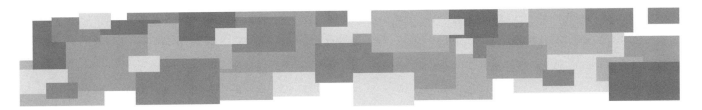

Setting the emotional tone for students

Successful teachers instinctively interpret problems as challenges, rather than seeing them as setbacks, losses or threats. They speak to their students optimistically, appreciating that their positive talk and behavior plunges students into a world of promise, practice and progress. They recognize that the habit of optimistic thoughts and talk can be cultivated.

The best disaster recipe for emotionally vulnerable students is when their reactive, dogmatic and inflexible response meets a teacher with the same attributes. These are teachers who are perceived as commanding students to do things. Backing students into a corner without providing a dignified or private way of exiting is motivation for students to say and do things they would not dream of saying or doing in the normal course of events. The truth is that when tempers heat up and emotions become overloaded, demanding instant reform from any individual in any circumstance can result in disastrous consequences. It also helps to know that the processing and response speeds of some are likely to be longer when under emotional duress. This makes instant compliance very difficult, or impossible.

These students are reliant on mature, poised teachers who treat them with respect, who speak quietly or privately when reprimanding, who give time and opportunity for responses, and can cleverly sidestep until the heat of the moment subsides. They know their students' emotional stability is keenly connected to theirs, and to remain effective they avoid being caught up in the vortex of emotional chaos which often surrounds these children.

Consciously and subconsciously students gauge the emotional climate of the classroom by asking themselves:

- Is my teacher moody?
- Is my teacher short-tempered?
- Does my teacher shout?
- Does my teacher like me?
- Does my teacher prefer the smarter kids?
- Do the rules keep changing?
- Is it safe to make mistakes?
- Is it safe in my classroom?

The emotional safety of the classroom is a direct result of the teacher's interpersonal skills, and this is what often dictates success or failure. The influence of the teacher's interpersonal skills transcends the quality of a task or curriculum. These skills truly determine whether or not students can persevere and remain engaged.

Cognitive Behavioral Training

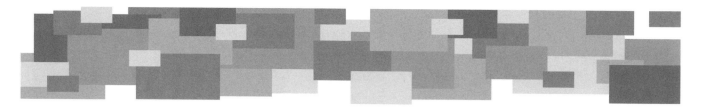

Celebrate similarities and differences

These exercises lead students to see it is normal and healthy for individuals to have different reactions, attitudes, attainments and perspectives. They strengthen the notion that we operate at different rates and can feel differently over remarkably similar events. They reinforce that human development is truly uneven in nature.

Begin by asking students to list ways in which they are more or less developed than others their own age. Compare and discuss sporting abilities, reading abilities, friendships and academic abilities, and emphasize how so many of these differences successfully resolve themselves over time. Not only are students reassured by discovering it is normal to develop at different rates, but they find it reassuring that their teacher embraces diversity too.

A recent study found the incidence of depressive symptoms in youth with Asperger Syndrome (the sample included ages ranging from ten to sixteen years) running at an overwhelming 25 per cent (Hedley & Young 2003). Their recommendation to combat depression and improve general well-being is to promote activities that reduce the negative perception of difference. Simple graphs are a powerful visual means to highlight and compare diversity.

Seeing and feeling differently

To highlight differences in intensity of feelings, have students rate their feelings concerning common school experiences: friendships, general acceptance, sporting success, bullying, academic success or failure, being 'put down', subject success and so on. Plot each response and connect them to make a line graph. What an eye-catching way for students to see that everyone has different attitudes to similar experiences. It is part of being a human being.

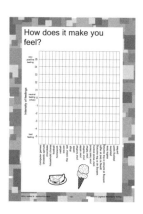 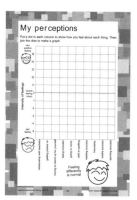

Similarities and differences: When did they happen?

Send home a survey asking parents to give indications of when their children sat up independently, started to walk, first talked, when their first tooth arrived, when they lost their first tooth, first slept in 'big bed', rode a bike, learned to swim and so on. Create graphs which observe these differences and display them. They are good visual reminders that some students learn earlier than others, some learn more smoothly, some are hungry, eager learners, while others need to be led. What matters most in the end is being in a place where conditions favor acceptance, learning and change. The obvious conclusion is that it is far less important when someone learns to do something; most importantly it is that they learned (inspired by Taylor-Neumann 2002).

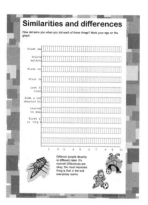

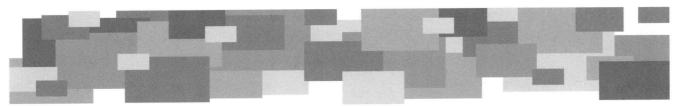

What is fair in the face of differences?

This activity presents an opportunity to develop ethical concepts. Pose the question, *How can I be fair to two sorts of students? One of them cannot keep to the rules very well and the other obeys the rules almost all of the time.* Even the youngest of children are quick to point out that some find it easier to follow rules than others. They have already identified these differences because they live with them on a daily basis. For older students it is possible to take it a step further. They have rudimentary understandings about impulsivity, anger control, inflexible personalities and emotional overload. Explain that for some these are genuine problems, and affect their self-control. Students with these difficulties behave in this way because their difficulty makes them react like this, not because they set out to be naughty. Ask, *Who has ever had trouble keeping rules?* Encourage students to speak about their mistakes and how they felt about them. Ask, *What helped you best to remember the right way?*

Draw a continuum along the board, with 'Cool Carl' who always waits for his turn at one end and 'Talking Todd' who hardly ever remembers to wait for his turn at the other. Ask, *Should Cool Carl and Talking Todd have the same consequences if they break the wait-for-your-turn rule?* The response from the group is universally no, because the students appreciate the fundamental self-control inequality. They, at their formative age, can see that Talking Todd cannot remember and punishing him is not likely to improve his memory.

Then how can we manage this? Listen to what students suggest. They will amaze you with such ideas as: reminders, using reminder buddies, changing seating arrangements, providing rewards and incentives, giving second chances, giving easier rules, teaching them how to stop, teaching them consequences and so on. For older students, it is possible to sensitively take these understandings a little further. Explain to the class to imagine the same continuum running across the front of the classroom. Cool Carl is at one end and Talking Todd at the other. Invite your students to walk up and place themselves at a point on the continuum according to how they see their self-control at school. Bravely, place yourself on the continuum too. This exercise provides scope for inspiring discussion and certainly addresses the issue of fairness and differences (inspired by Taylor-Neumann 2002).

Islands of competence

Giorcelli (2000) reminds us that there are areas that children and young teens feel successful about; however, these are often not acknowledged in the day-to-day activities at school. Consider developing an 'Islands-of-competence inventory' for every student in class. Create a display for students to showcase their talents, especially talents that do not comfortably fit into the school curriculum.

Arrange for students to regularly update their display and share new opportunities, wins or milestones with the class or school. Work through the inventory, giving several students each week a chance to speak about or demonstrate their island of competence. 'Student of the day' or 'student of the week' is an excellent way to spotlight this. On a simpler level, make it a daily habit to engage a student about their interest or talent. Developing and maintaining an islands-of-competence approach helps students know that their abilities are acknowledged within an environment where to achieve an average level of competence might be difficult. This helps to compartmentalize school difficulties, and puts balance into their lives. Without it, it is too easy to allow school difficulties to become continents of

Cognitive Behavioral Training

incompetence for struggling students.

Uncovering and dealing with stresses

Arrange for students to discuss situations that create the greatest stress in their lives. Have them share how their bodies feel when they begin to feel stressed, and the sorts of coping mechanisms they use to counter stress. Make a list of common stresses in student's lives, and record the stress indicators and useful solutions they have invented. Set plans in place so students can use them automatically if they become overwhelmed or angry.

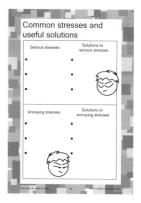

Dealing with emotional crisis: Meltdown cards

Cool-down or meltdown cards work for students at any age level. The idea is that several sit on the teacher's desk. In times of emotional crisis a student takes a meltdown card and goes to a cool-down area to unwind, rather than alienating themselves by repetitive spills of anger in front of their peers. Places like the school garden, the resource center, a quiet courtyard, a copse of trees or a student retreat room are often used. The meltdown card conditions are explained on the cards themselves. Walking away releases the child from the pressure of immediate reform, which of course can push distressed students over the edge. In this way they have a chance to regain poise and regroup their emotions. It is an honor system; students are expected to make a choice as to which area they go to rather than wandering. In most situations it is used honestly and effectively. An alternative, as heat begins to creep into a situation and loss of control looks likely, is to use a rehearsed key word, phrase, touch or signal to indicate it doesn't have to end in anger or tears, and

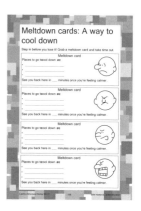

it's fine to withdraw. Sending students on a message, any message, to avoid the inevitable blow up is a sensible distracting option. In more extreme situations suggest to parents they give the student time out to regroup by creating a long weekend or a midweek break. This needs to be subtly and cleverly orchestrated.

Refining behavior management strategies

Sometimes the basic behavior management approach, effective for most, actually inflames difficulties for asynchronous students - the 'out-of-balance' students who display dogmatic, rigid and highly egocentric behaviors. Accepting another style of management, which attracts different positive and negative reinforcers, can be very productive.

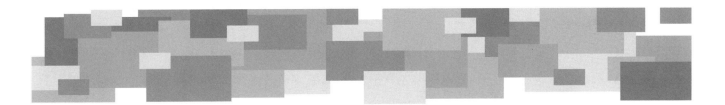

Managing behavior differently

Case study

Educators and school systems who choose to identify, highlight and appeal to the unique interests of students do best in effecting positive behavioral changes. Nine-year-old Nu found it difficult to keep her easily overwhelmed emotions under control. It didn't take long for her teachers to discover a compelling reinforcer to help keep them in check, and propel her motivation to take advantage of the cool-down systems in place. Nu and her teacher developed a series of basic strategies to use when she felt overwhelmed, unsure, scared or angry. These included leaving the room and going for a walk, running an errand, taking time out from what she was doing to read her book, or moving to sit near a friend she trusted.

Over time, with these support structures in place, the frequency of Nu's loud attention-grabbing outbursts decreased. Her calmer, more predictable demeanor also improved her acceptance by others, which in turn helped Nu feel more settled. Nu had a passion for plants, gardening and being outdoors. The truth was that she was invaluable in the outdoor situation! Success at meeting improved self-control targets resulted in her spending the last hour on Wednesday and Friday afternoons with the school grounds person. The motivational edge this simple plan gave to Nu eclipsed a string of behavior plans and negative consequences previously trialed.

Prioritizing to enhance emotional stability

Work out priorities. How often are you stalled or completely derailed by unnecessary low-priority issues? Allow yourself to step away and determine the significance of issues. There are battles that should not be fought, that really are not important. So often we only realize their unimportance after the event. When making a judgment over whether an issue is truly priority-worthy, ask yourself, *Is this worth tackling? Is it a prime indicator of how successful or unsuccessful this student will be?*

Setting the emotional tone for parents

The emotional climate teachers generate for parents falls squarely in the domain of a teacher's choice. What a teacher says, and how they say it, is as powerful as what they choose not to say. The look they choose to deliver, or the distance they choose to put between parents and themselves is a definitive act. Teacher attitude either extends an invitation to parents or signals alienation.

Developing warm communication links, displaying a willingness to disarm worry, and delivering small, thoughtful kindnesses contribute to an integrated classroom community (Brock & Shute 2001). Breakfasts, returning to school for an evening meal, inviting a motivational speaker, meeting at a local restaurant for dinner, arranging a working breakfast where the class plans for the coming term, or a working bee with parents and students make an inspirational impact on class moral and parental relationships. Initially, the extra effort may seem bothersome, but parents are always willing to help with the organizational tasks. A further spin on this is parents getting to know one another. This, in turn, creates links which extend to children's friendships.

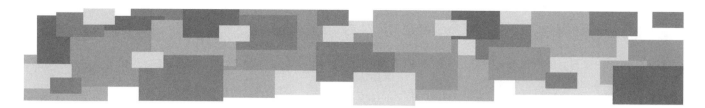

Parental anxiety and student emotionality

Naturally many parents of children with difficulties or delay hold a heightened state of anxiety about their child's progress and success at school. Involving them and inviting their opinion on ways to support their child will help disarm their worry. This can directly and indirectly stabilize the student's emotional state. Make a start by asking: *What worries you most? What would you like me to do to help? What has worked best in the past? How can we work on this together?*

Working with student helplessness

Many students with learning or developmental difficulties have had considerable input from others to help them keep up. By the middle primary years, parents may gradually begin to discriminate between their child's learning performance and emotional performance. They may begin to see that their child has developed apathy and disengagement which impedes their basic functioning and independence (Jensen 2000b). A range of simple, day-to-day problems emerge concerning forgetfulness, poor planning and time management, misplacing belongings (especially school-related items), failing to complete simple household chores and gross inefficiencies in the use of time. These parents have inched their way along a perilous tightrope. They knew at the outset that too little encouragement or intervention would erode skill acquisition and deteriorate their child's fragile self-esteem. Yet, too much or ill-placed support sees the child failing to internalize their part in the learning and performance partnership. While reasonable progress may have been achieved with the primary difficulty, they now face a debilitating secondary issue: their child's learned helplessness. It emerges surprisingly quickly, and in what seems a blink these children have their parents, especially their mothers, squarely in their service. The question, often avoided, that really needs to be asked of the student is, How can you help yourself? Until this question is asked, students do not take responsibility for anything, and expect their mothers to stay in an emotional flap, solving their problems for them. The healthiest approach is to counsel parents and students that students do best (regardless of learning or attentional difficulty) when they do for themselves. Turning a helplessness situation around is a gradual process. It means moving from providing abundant support to giving encouragement for independent efforts. Initially this new approach may result in failure, even though workload and expectations are tailored to smaller, achievable units. Nevertheless, failures should be tempered by a vote of confidence for independent effort. This requires an emphasis on negotiation, directness, consequential management, creativity, work adaptations, and above all consistency to reshape behaviors. Consistently steering students so they can see what they need to do promotes success within the classroom and family.

Emotionally supporting strategies

I love doing this!

Build something students enjoy into each and every day. Just as it does for us, this gives them a chance to come up for air and breathe in something safe and uplifting. Spend time brainstorming what students' 'heart and soul stuff' really is, and how it might be incorporated into the school day.

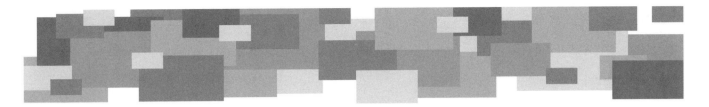

Develop outside-school networks for students

Some of our students suffer terrible isolation from peers and are vulnerable to depression and worry. Often their best friendships and connections take place outside school. Teachers are in a wonderful position to ask students what activities they get pleasure from outside school, what happens, why they enjoy it, and gather and distribute contacts so others may become involved. When students seize on an outside interest it helps to tip the emotional balance in their favor. In some instances, these interests lead directly or indirectly to future career paths. The achievement of friendship and peer acceptance provides a stabilizing emotional foundation that allows the academic component to fall into place more easily. We need to acknowledge this, and actively promote these links.

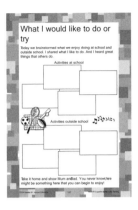

Guide students to do thoughtful things

Create situations to teach caring. Inspire students to send a thank-you card, an email, a note or make a phone call to someone who has been helpful, or needs their spirits raised. Occasionally, send students home on a secret mission to do a good deed for someone that night. Be instrumental in setting them up to deliver a kindness that they may not normally think of or show. This reaching out, taking an extra step, has more to do with the notion of performing a kindness than expecting something in return. This sort of practice positively influences relationships, softens attitudes and permits new doors to open. Teaching themes of care to our students reinforces what is at the core of human existence. Modeling how to care for others reinforces that they themselves are cared for (Noddings 1998).

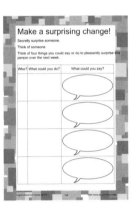

Maintaining connectedness and buoyancy

Mail a congratulatory or encouraging letter to students. Present or mail a small surprise, a certificate, a small trophy, or a revered sticker. Send a fax, text message or email; leave a congratulatory message on their answering machine at home; or have the principal present an award. There are a myriad of ideas to maintain their emotional buoyancy and connection to school.

Keep a journal of good things

Provide time for students to keep a journal of the good things that happen to them. Use a continuum to rate the days. This helps reinforce that although they may have faced difficulties during their week, there have also been some pleasant and enjoyable moments. There has been a balance!

Sunlight and aerobic exercise

At least once a day, for ten to twenty minutes, get students outside for fun and aerobic exercise. Not only does vigorous exercise burn off excess energy, but students collect their mandatory ten minutes worth of sunshine, providing an essential dose of vitamin D. The fun factor helps release endorphins, which helps ensure well-being.

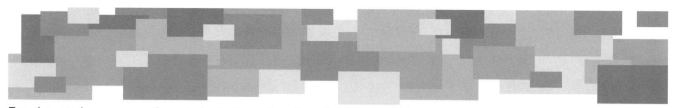

For the restless, overactive students there is often the bonus of improved attention and concentration when returning to classroom tasks. It is surprising how many parents report vigorous afternoon exercise as a wonderful homework aid, assisting their child to attend to the task more easily.

Program smile and laughing times

It sounds hackneyed, but smiling and laughing are good medicine. They lift the spirit and reduce tension. Laughing spreads happiness, goodwill and tolerance, and is often compared to a mild internal physical workout. As we laugh, the muscles in our face, neck, chest and diaphragm all work hard enjoying themselves. When we stop laughing these muscles relax, and we are more relaxed than we were previously. Begin by programming joke-telling sessions, or exchange real-life embarrassing moments!

Invite or engineer success nominations

Once or twice a week, ask the class to nominate someone (self-nomination is fine) who has made progress in a particular area. Ask the nominee if they know why this change has happened. Invite others to share their thoughts about the improvement. Impromptu heartfelt acknowledgment by peers is a powerful motivator. To this end, provide a letterbox in the room and arrange a time for children to write encouraging comments regarding things they have noticed about others: changed attitudes, helpfulness, kindness, improved concentration or behavior, improved work ethic, better organizational skills and so on. Read them to the class, or better still invite the author to do so. Keep a tally of weekly nominations throughout the term and reward these students in a more significant way at the close of term.

Mentoring partnerships

Students frequently talk about significant others (mentors) whose guidance and encouragement made a difference. Their mentor may have been a teacher, a school support officer, an older student, a school counselor or a principal, and in other circumstances mentoring may have taken place outside school through a friend, therapist, parent, relation or older sibling. What appears almost universal is that they felt their mentor believed in them, helped maintain their goals and helped them to discover more about themselves. They believe that the clear, realistic goals their mentors held for them reinforced their belief in themselves. Their mentors unemotionally mirrored back events impacting on them by asking:

- *Why do you think that happened?*

- *Was there another way you could have handled it?*

- *What may have happened if you had done it that way?*

- *You forgot again. What gives you the right to keep forgetting when the others have to remember?*

- *I agree, your work rate has to step up. Let's work on one idea to do this in the new term.*

- *Remember when you kept losing your task sheets and assignments? What's happened to change this? What are you doing differently?*

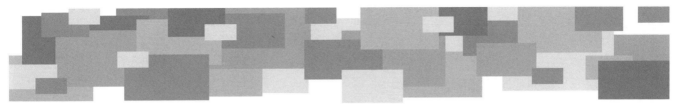

By depending on their mentor, the child began to flourish, accepting structures to develop routine, and strategies to build relationships and academic skills. As a consequence, their world became more predictable, allowing them to behave more proactively.

Within school systems, untapped resources exist for regular on-site pastoral care (mentoring). Starting may be as simple as a commitment to designate one individual - class teacher, home room teacher, school counselor, grounds person, secretary or volunteer - to sensitively work with an 'at-risk' student and liaise with affiliated teachers (Bisland 2001). One approach allows the student to check in with their mentor regularly to review the week, to make planning adjustments and organize for what is upcoming (Coenen 2002). This relationship acknowledges the extra effort students put into every piece of work they attempt, and that these small increments of work in every subject compound to make a big difference to their overall workload.

Many school districts have a teacher-student mentoring system in place. The teacher-student mentoring program assists students experiencing trouble with academics, organization and issues of a personal nature. The teacher-mentors work with students to build confidence, set goals, organize and develop learning plans (Goodfellow 2003). Effective mentors keep parents regularly updated within a framework of positivity.

Peer tutoring or 'buddy' support systems

The benefit a student can obtain from a peer as a tutor is remarkable. Increasingly, researchers are evaluating results from systems organizing peer tutoring. The outcomes are consistently powerful and encouraging (Coenen 2002). Systems may begin by simply designing time for an older student to work on a small task with a younger student. Higher levels of sophistication might incorporate building a regular time at the end of the day for a student to lend homework support to another, or arranging a small group of tutors to run homework support late in the day or after school for younger students. Another idea is to have a student regularly listening to and supporting a younger student facing emotional or friendship difficulties.

Traditionally, peer tutoring has been considered as a one-on-one arrangement, but small groups of one to three working on a task with an older peer are wonderfully useful. Such associations are far from one sided (Cohen 1986). The older students, the tutors, gain leadership skills, benefit from re-exposure to previously learned material, develop patience and find satisfaction knowing they have helped someone else. Meanwhile, those being tutored have the opportunity to complete more work, develop positive study habits, learn how to organize more effectively and are likely to have made academic gains along the way. In reality, peer tutoring and mentoring relationships have positive social and academic effects on all participants (Foot & Howe 1998). How students work together is only limited by our administrative imagination.

Disappointment and overwhelmed feelings

Most children deal with disappointment relatively well, but there are those who become severely upset. Their elevated sensitivities and lack of self-regulatory capacities make them vulnerable to public humiliation. In situations where disappointment is likely to cause an outburst, one idea is to use a rehearsal technique. Situations such as award presentations, tests or exams, public speaking and school assemblies are situations worth rehearsing or preplanning. Rehearsing helps students to intellectualize their likely feelings and think their way to remaining calm.

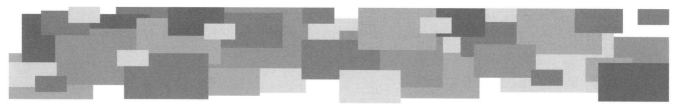

In one situation, a middle primary student, often overwhelmed by disappointed feelings on presentation evenings, helped his teacher write an article for the school newsletter. It explained that while winning a prize at presentation evening acknowledged the effort of a few, no-one could ever take away anyone else's personal best. The process of writing the article for the newsletter assisted him to intellectualize and contain his feelings during the presentation.

Ben's book

Case study

Ben was a lightly built, sweet eight-year-old, who several times a week would lose control. Mostly, this occurred when he became overwhelmed by social or learning situations, but sometimes he became agitated by the working noise within the classroom. He described the classroom noise as tickling his ears and the difference between ear tickling and his ears hurting was infinitely small. Ben could find himself uncontrollably upset within a heartbeat, and despite being good natured, was very difficult to console. Once reaching this state, the more others tried to pacify, the longer it took Ben to calm down.

His teacher decided on a new tactic. First he managed to arrange some special time with Ben. They discussed and planned a new arrangement. From now on, when Ben became upset, his teacher encouraged the other children to leave Ben alone, and he would not interfere either. He explained he knew Ben's good brain could think its way through the upset. Only if Ben asked for help would he help out. They agreed it would be best for Ben to go to a special spot (on the big cushions by the bookcase in the classroom) when he felt upset. Then, once he was feeling better, he could begin working in BEN'S BOOK and complete one activity.

During their sessions together Ben and his teacher searched out activities which appealed to Ben, and added them to BEN'S BOOK. There were dot-to-dots, math puzzles, crosswords, mazes, 'what's missing' activities, 'what's different' puzzles, drawing and coloring activities, and so on.

His mother helped by taking the book home and making a strong material cover on which she embroidered BEN'S BOOK. She stitched pockets for pencils, erasers, crayons, a glue stick and scissors.

Now when Ben becomes distressed he uses his book to independently settle before rejoining the group. Providing students with alternate ways to avoid full-blown emotional fallout and teaching them how to recover is vital.

Reframing thinking: 'Shifting the goal posts'

Case study

As a Dyslexic student, school had always been a challenge for Jordy. Not surprisingly, he had become accustomed to expecting difficulties and having to deal with problems. Six months ago he started secondary school. All began well enough, but things were beginning to unravel because of the requirement to take two years of a foreign language. 'It's not fair, he complained. 'I can't write in English properly and now they're asking me to write in Spanish. I can't remember it. I've tried. It doesn't make sense. It's stupid! Mom's been to the school and they say everybody has to do it. His school counselor explained that by the end of tenth grade most students

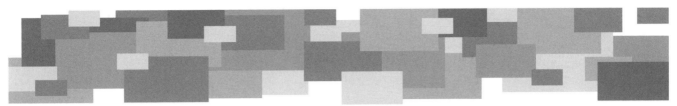

taking a foreign language chose to stop. 'As far as the big picture is concerned it just doesn't matter. Focus on what does matter,' advised the counselor.

'Yes,' Jordy complained, 'but going to Spanish class four times a week makes me angry. I can't remember it. It makes me feel dumb. Then I'm angry for the rest of the day.' After much discussion his school counselor and mother offered Jordy a challenge. The challenge was to shift his focus from academic outcomes to personal performance outcomes. Jordy was offered $50 at the end of semester providing he scored in the highest category for attitude, regardless of whether he failed Spanish. The focus needed to shift from the resentment created by his intractable language and symbols difficulty to enjoying hearing about the culture, the country and participating with greater enthusiasm.

Giving students permission to shift goal posts, or reframe their thinking, helps them feel safer, more connected and opens the way for learning. In contrast, unresolved angry, bitter feelings can pervade and erode performance in other areas.

Natural therapy

Case study

Lin had a terrible time each morning making the transition from home to school. By the time this delightful seven-year-old arrived at school she was almost defeated by anxiety, and found it difficult to leave the car. Her obsessive-compulsive disorder drove her to open the car door, take a few steps towards the school building and then return to the car. Without support she would repeat this a dozen times, becoming more and more distressed.

To help bring her back to a calmer state her parents (with the support of the school) arranged for Lin to have a foot massage by a professional masseuse almost as soon as she arrived at school. Lin was greeted by the masseuse in the parking lot and together they walked down to the room where she was given her massage in private using calming oils. This seemed to reduce her anxiety and assist composure. Shortly after, she entered the class without the stress previously experienced.

After four weeks Lin was gradually weaned off of her foot massage, and with continued verbal reinforcement and an older friend meeting her at the car each morning a secure morning routine was established (inspired by Spalding 2002).

Friendship and social development

Social-skill training programs

Formal cognitive behavioral social-skill training programs where children are taught how to solve social problems positively and how to act in pro-social ways are most effective. Lindy Petersen's internationally recognized STOP THINK DO program is a prime example (Petersen & Adderly 2002a, 2002b). It links feelings to behavior, and develops techniques to insert thinking between feeling and behaving. This approach develops self-control and communication skills primarily at STOP, cognitive problem-solving skills at THINK and behavioral skills at DO.

Cognitive Behavioral Training

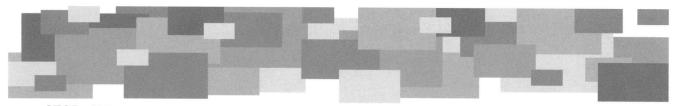

STOP: Children learn how to stop themselves from reacting impulsively and using their 'bad habits'. Instead, they look and listen to find out what the problem is and how people around them are feeling.

THINK: They are guided to think about options to solve the problem and consider the likely consequences of these options.

DO: Choose the option with the best consequences for themselves and others, and do it confidently.

Best outcomes are achieved with the continuing support of significant others, parents, teachers and peers, for maintenance and transfer of skills (Petersen & Le Messurier 2000). These students rely on the right prompts, the right language and cueing at their point of performance. They need support reinforcing what they can't do naturally, and this approach builds on what they already know. In addition, there is an definitive link between a good learning environment and a positive social one. When children are relating well and behaving in friendly ways to each other they tend to encourage each other's learning. Teachers who generate a positive social tone enhance student learning, inclusivity and social tolerance in the classroom (Church, Gottschalk & Leedy 2003).

Two other well-regarded cognitive behavioral programs which explicitly teach children and adolescents to understand more about themselves, the demands of social life and how to increase their social resilience and friendship building skills include Program Achieve and The Resourceful Adolescent Program (Shochet et al. 1997).

Informal social-skills opportunities

A less formal alternative is to encourage parents to involve their children outside school in activities such as Scouts, computer groups, science clubs, chess clubs, bowling clubs, drama classes, music groups, youth groups, rock-climbing groups, car clubs, swimming clubs, fishing clubs, role-play groups, ballet, tap dance, jazz, choirs, BMX clubs, church groups, tai chi, karate and so on. These situations create opportunities for children and adolescents to practice relationship skills which directly and indirectly lead to friendships. Meanwhile, keeping a more formal social-skills training program running in the classroom is a bonus for many students.

Build a friendship wall

Comparing the qualities necessary for developing friendships to the building of a wall is a tangible approach to an abstract concept. To do this, obtain twenty to twenty-five wooden blocks from the hardware store, and have them cut into cubes of about 10 centimeters. These are to become the bricks for the friendship wall. Ask students what qualities they prize most highly in friendships. Elicit typical qualities: good moods, predictable, truthful, forgiving, optimistic, likes the same things, sharing, kind, trustworthy, good reputation, popular, in the cool group, good-looking, tall, short, good at schoolwork, wealthy parents, good at sports, can stand up for themselves, fun, serious minded, smart and so on. Write one of the qualities given by students on each block, using a bold permanent marker.

Next, survey students to ascertain a ranking of the most important qualities they look for in friendships. Lay down the seven highest-ranked blocks as the friendship foundation. Lay the next six highest-ranked blocks on top just as bricks in a wall would be laid. Continue to lay the courses of bricks in decreasing order of friendship priority. The last

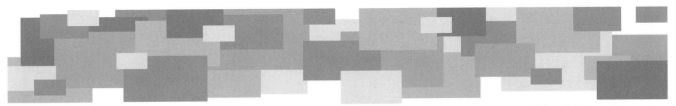

brick laid on the top of the wall represents the quality least essential in the maintenance of friendship as far as the survey is concerned. Once the wall is built, question individuals whether they would have built the wall in exactly the same way. In particular, target qualities along the bottom two courses. Ask if there are qualities here that should not be here because they are less essential compared to qualities on the blocks laid higher up. As discussion progresses slide out bricks from the bottom two courses identified as not worthy to be located in this position. Watch the gaps emerge and see how long the wall says together. This is a tangible way to discuss the qualities sought in friendship and to see how dependent each characteristic is on the other. (Based on an initial concept by Shine SA Inc. <http://www.shinesa.org.au>.)

Discuss and display the rules of friendship

It is startling how often teaching the rules of friendship is required. Students refer to these as recipes to follow, and soon uncover that it is one thing to meet new people in a successful manner, but is quite another set of skills to maintain friendships. Even if the rules of friendship provide little more than basic instrumental skills to hang new behaviors on, their place is invaluable. Kerry Armstrong, author of The Circles, adds an insightful dimension on how to deal with friendships (Armstrong 2003). She offers *The Circles* as a guide to help individuals sort through their feelings about others. Kerry suggests that by placing people within a concentric circle framework, it is easier to see how we feel about

them and ourselves. *The Circles* helps to make sense of friendship issues and provides a way to take objective control over them.

Teaching sorry and friendship repair

It seems obvious, but sorry counts. It can retrieve and revive so many situations. Yet, some find it difficult to utter, even once they have regrouped their emotional resources. Discuss with students what sorry means, when to use it and how it can be delivered. Role-play situations where sorry might be helpful. Try sorry with a smile, a touch, a wink, a handshake, a rub on someone's arm or a hug. Brainstorm the diversity of words and actions that mean sorry - there are dozens! Teach that sorry may not always be wholeheartedly accepted, but it is a very powerful repairing gesture and can make a difference in allowing each to move on with less resentment.

Teaching empathy

Teaching students how to behave empathetically and sharpening empathic perceptions is always helpful. Watch videos, role-play, listen to audio tapes, watch mock arguments and discuss why individuals thought, felt and reacted in particular ways. This helps to stretch the student's empathic awareness. Ask questions such as, *Is this disagreement as straight forward as it seems? Whose fault is it? So, who's wrong and who's right? Is one person more right than the other? Why? Who's the victim? How is each person feeling? How can you tell? What are the signs? What would you do? What would you say? How would you look? What tone of voice would you use?*

Cognitive Behavioral Training

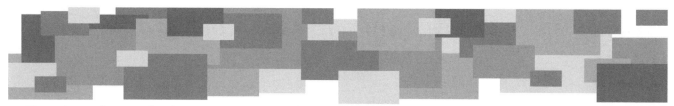

Empathy and sympathy does not come easily for some. However, in the final analysis, if they demonstrate the right look, the right action and use the right words, truly empathic or not, they pass the empathic test with flying colors! Empathy rates high on the priority list for successful socialization and relationships. In addition, having empathy, or knowing about it, alerts students to be less hasty in their judgments and more accepting.

Keeping a distinction between home and school

Many asynchronous students develop black-and-white attitudes about school and home. You will know when you meet them. Their rigidity shines like a beacon. School is for schoolwork, even though output may not be ideal, and home is strictly for home pursuits. These students resent additional work, even though it is intended as supportive intervention. The consequence is that sending unfinished class work home to be completed is likely not to achieve what was intended. In some instances a little negotiation can achieve a softening of attitude. For others with very rigid, intransigent attitudes unfinished schoolwork, or problems that occurred at school, should not become a parental responsibility. The solutions to these issues need to be found at school. Teachers who refuse to adjust their attitude on this subject might trial supervising the unfinished home chores of their students at school!

Relaxation and visual imagery

Relaxation and visual imagery techniques provide easy, reproducible ways to tame angry feelings, frustration and overload. Clever people have long used these approaches to help move their feelings and activity levels from one state to another. Relaxation therapy does not require the same sort of discipline as meditation, but has the scope to re-energize, calm, allow reflection and lift performance. So real are the benefits that many teachers use these combined approaches to support students during transition times. There is always a handful of students who experience difficulty adapting their behavior to the expectations imposed by the new situation, despite knowing what is expected. Classic transitional times at home and school are:

- entering the classroom following lunchtime play
- moving from a high energy lesson (for example physical education, drama or dance) to a more formal learning environment
- exiting school and returning home
- settling into homework
- winding down later in the evening, making the transition to bed.

Relaxation and visualization provide practice for children to develop the skill of converting words to images. Surreptitiously they encourage the art of concentration. These techniques offer practice at being still, focusing on one thing at a time, listening and responding. In the beginning, it is the children with concentration and learning difficulties who seem to struggle with relaxation. With guidance and persistence, they fidget less and become more settled. This calming technique allows students to harness their thoughts, rather than permitting their thoughts to be unproductively scattered.

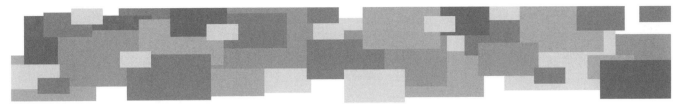

Introducing relaxation techniques

The accumulation of behavioral evidence has convinced most people of the benefits gained from relaxation. More recently though, brain imaging results confirm this (Amen 2002). Deep relaxation is easily achieved through diaphragmatic breathing and progressive muscle relaxation. To teach belly breathing ask students to lay on the floor and place a book on their tummy. As they breathe in filling their lungs with air the book will rise. Then, as they exhale the book falls. Teach students to take slow deep breaths, about six each minute.

The preferred approach is to employ relaxation as a diversion technique where benefits occur naturally and without the need for explanations. For example, a calming session for ten minutes or so helps pupils to wind down from high-energy lunchtime activities, ready for more formal activities. Alternatively, the technique can be used to explicitly target controlling anger, worry, insomnia, distraction, overreaction or dealing with sad feelings. Try this approach if the aim is to explicitly reshape or change a behavior.

- Explain that the technique helps to relieve bad feelings and bad habits. This is a way to replace these with something pleasant and refreshing.

- Establish when the behavior usually occurs. Knowing this alerts the student to their difficult time. Those with poor self-awareness are likely not to be able to identify this independently.

- Discuss this old behavior. You might ask, *What do you say and do when behaving in this way? What does it look like, can you show me? How do you feel when this happens?*

- Explain the problems this behavior causes.

- Begin using the relaxation technique when the bad habit occurs. With time and practice, the new behavior will replace the old unwanted behavior.

- Build a collection of relaxation stories on tape which appeal to the child or group. Assembling a tape, which can be easily accessed, reduces everyday input. Work to build it into the child's or class routine.

Making a relaxation tape

Turn off the lights and partly draw the curtains to reduce the light. Light a large candle to signal the beginning of relaxation. Ambience is important.

Find a comfortable place to lie or sit.

Wiggle a bit to get comfortable.

Now get ready to recharge.

Begin by thinking about the things that have been hard or unfair for you today. Think about the things that may have made you angry or annoyed. What we are about to do will help you let go of any bad feelings you might be carrying.

Be still.

Feel your body relaxing.

Cognitive Behavioral Training

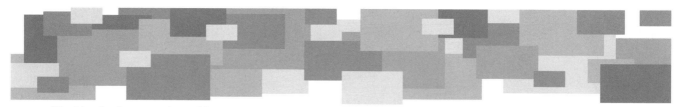

Start by feeling your breathing.

Take a deep breath as I count to three. One, two, three. Hold it in. Now begin to let it out as I count to three. One, two, three. Slowly breathe in again. One, two, three, and hold the new air and its energy. Breathe out slowly as I count to three. Out go the angry or unfair feelings. Wait for a bit. Breathe in counting to three. Wait. Breathe out counting to three. You continue with this gentle rhythm for two minutes. I'll let you know when to stop.

Listen and little by little parts of your body will begin to relax.

Lie still and stretch, keeping your back and legs on the floor. Make yourself as long as you can. Hold the stretch (pause). Let it go and relax.

Now do the same with only your right leg. Tense the muscles. Hold them tight (pause). Let the muscles relax. Do the same to the left leg now. Stretch and tighten the leg, then hold it (pause). Let go.

Go to your feet. Right foot first. Wiggle your toes. Now push your toes wide apart. Hold the stretch (pause). Now relax them. Let's do the left foot ... wiggle your toes and push them wide apart. Hold the stretch (pause). Then relax them.

Stop for a moment and check on your breathing. Keep to the rhythm. Breathing in one, two, three. Holding it for a moment. Slowly breathing out one, two, three.

Let the feeling of relaxation gently move from your legs, up your back and arms, and down into your fingers. Stretch your fingers wide apart, and hold them apart while you count ... one, two, three ... relax them. Do the same for your shoulders. Move your thoughts to your face. Close your eyes. Squeeze them tight. Let them relax. Do it again if you want. Relax your facial muscles because they've been talking and smiling all day. Then tighten your face again. Keep it tight to the count of three. Relax your face again. Now tell your mind to relax (pause). You can use this feeling of relaxation whenever you want to slow or calm down.

Keep your eyes closed if you can.

At this point begin reading a relaxation story, or part of a novel being enjoyed.

Sunshine shower: A rescue remedy

This technique builds quite naturally onto the relaxation and visualization technique described above. A colleague of mine uses the Sunshine shower successfully in the classroom with his upper primary students.

He explains to his class ... *There will be times when you will need to stop. When you need to put in a bit of thinking time before you react. This is the moment to let yourself be rescued by the Sunshine shower. It saves you from losing it or having a tantrum in front of everyone.*

When you know something has got the better of you, and you feel angry, use the Sunshine shower.

• *Go outside and sit by yourself at one of the quiet places we've agreed on.*

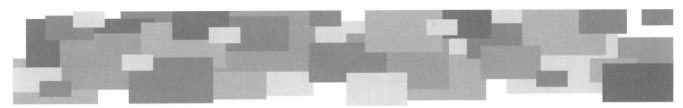

• Sit and be still. Turn your back to the sun.

• Close your eyes or choose something to stare at.

• Feel, or imagine, the sun on your back. Feel its warmth and energy. Enjoy it.

• Soak up the Sunshine shower for a few moments. It's okay, I want you to.

• Think of something you like. Rethink your favorite relaxation story, remember a place you enjoyed visiting, replay a good time you had in your head, or think of something you are looking forward to. Spend a few moments and see if your thoughts can make you smile.

Come on back to class. If you want, let me know you have just taken the Sunshine shower.

Visual imagery and concentration

Ask students, *What might happen when you can't concentrate, or find it hard to settle and finish schoolwork?* Here is an imaginative explanation that can support children. It turns the abstract into a practical understanding. This works well with young children diagnosed with concentration difficulties, especially if they have a creative mind.

Imagining the gremlins

Try this:

Your brain is made up of billions of cells. These cells send messages to each other with little electronic pulses. For you to be able to remember and do things, the electronic messages must travel through thousands of pathways. Imagine these pathways are sometimes blocked by little gremlins that are able to stop the concentrating messages from getting through. These gremlins like to sit right in the middle of the concentrating pathways and talk and talk and talk.

Luckily, you are about to discover the secret to manage your gremlins. Controlling the gremlins will become easier. You can make them do what you want them to do, but it takes practice.

The secret to gremlin-busting!

Imagine what your gremlins look like. They often look crazy or wacky. They're always noisy, never doing much, except wasting time talking about silly things together. You'll need to imagine your own gremlins because everyone has their own kind.

Cognitive Behavioral Training

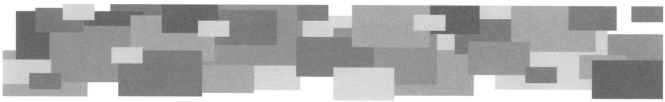

Let's spend some time thinking about them, because before you can control them you have to know exactly what they look like. What are their shoes like? Are they blue or yellow, long and pointy, or dotty, spotty or stripy? What about their socks, their clothes, their hairstyle? Tell me more. Start drawing their faces, and the clothes they wear. Make them large so you can see them really well.

Now we need to find out what makes your gremlins come out to play, and when they like interrupting you. You probably think you don't know this, but you do. There is always a pattern. For some it's when they play at recess or lunch. They become overexcited, and have fights with friends. For others their gremlins wreck their concentration so they find it hard to listen and remember what the teacher said, or to finish their work.

To practice controlling your gremlins, you need to do some serious imagining. Imagine a mean, nasty- looking gremlin-eating germ. Imagine it as your friend, entering your concentrating pathways and slurping up gremlins. Or, why not imagine a starship zapping them with laser beams? What about a super-COOL gremlin who is in charge of all the other gremlins, and when you speak to the super-COOL gremlin he'll make the other gremlins disappear? Whatever you choose, make it powerful. Practicing each day will make it even more powerful.

Case study ☞ **Tim's story**

Tim was eight and always imagined his gremlin as a muscle-bound soldier attacking his concentration, just when he needed it. This was usually in story-writing time. His gremlin wore khaki army trousers, big black boots, a beret, no shirt, and over his chest hung bullets. He carried a machine gun and held a powerful rocket launcher, and wanted to distract Tim from his writing.

In his mind, Tim could see his soldier pull him away from tasks, and felt annoyed because his friends wrote so much more. Tim worked hard with his mother, father and teacher to get rid of his gremlin. In the end Tim won, but he had to be clever because his soldier gremlin was too well armed to be blasted away, no matter how hard he tried.

Tim used his wild creativity to shrink his gremlin.

He shrank his soldier gremlin using a backwards time machine. His battle-hardened muscle-bulging soldier became smaller and smaller, younger and younger. He no longer wore boots, he no longer had bullets, and the machine gun he was holding became a useless water pistol. This once-proud warrior was reduced to wearing a diaper! And then, that was that - he was gone. Tim was free to do what he wanted. Tim and his teacher developed a secret signal at the beginning of writing times. She knew his secret, and to remind Tim he could beat the gremlin soldier she would draw a small mark on his page. This became Tim's writing goal, and mostly he was able to write past it. From time to time Tim's soldier comes back, but now he can make him disappear quite easily.

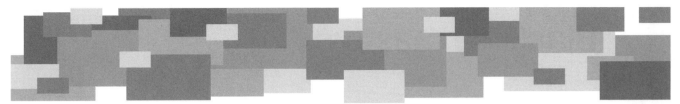

So, send in someone or something that can fight the gremlins. Reassure students that controlling the gremlins is within their power, but they need to think to make it happen. It also helps if they have someone on their side in class to gently insert pre-established reminders.

Dream up a force-field

Teach children to make a force-field. It's so easy and powerful! This technique works well for those creative, visual students and fits nicely into an explanation of personal space. Wrapped in their force-field, children can be taught to feel safe, insulated from noise and separated from distractions. Sometimes when others say mean things, the force-field can be used to block out the mean, hurtful words.

Ask students to sit on their chairs.

Get them to close their eyes and imagine the color of their force-field. For some it's transparent, but for others it may be patterned. Suggest they make it just right for themselves. Each person has their very own. Later, ask them to describe it and draw it. This makes for wonderful design and artwork.

Now the color of their force field has been decided, ask them to begin to explore its shape. Explain that each of our force-fields are about half of an arm's length away from our bodies, just at the end of our fingertips. With their eyes still closed, encourage them to move their arms comfortably above their head, around themselves and all the way to the floor, with their fingers wide apart. Mention they might be able to feel the tingling of the force-field around them in their fingers. That's the edge and shape of their force-field, and it is also the edge and shape of our personal space.

Ask them to imagine they are inside their force-field getting on with their work. Meanwhile, there's some classroom noise which could be distracting, but inside their force-field they hardly notice it! Encourage students to draw how well it can work for them. Suggest they draw their face concentrating on the task at hand.

Continue to use this strategy. Reinforce it in class. Devise individual or class practice times. Craft the approach so the idea becomes a dynamic, usable, day-to-day help. Develop language to support this style of visualization. Say to students: *When the distractions start, switch on your force-field. It will shield you while you get on with your work. Remember your force-field can become stronger as the noise and distractions increase, so make it work for you.* Teach children how to activate their force-fields quickly, and to know it can be powered by their desire to focus on something they need to get done.

Cognitive Behavioral Training

Blackline masters

- How does it make you feel?
- My perceptions
- Similarities and differences
- Islands-of-competence inventory
- Common stresses and useful solutions
- Meltdown cards: A way to cool down
- What I like to do or would like to try
- Make a surprising change!
- Rate your day on the continuum
- Rules for keeping friends
- Rules for meeting people and making friends
- Gremlin buster 1
- Gremlin buster 2
- Gremlin buster 3
- Concentration force-field

How does it make you feel?

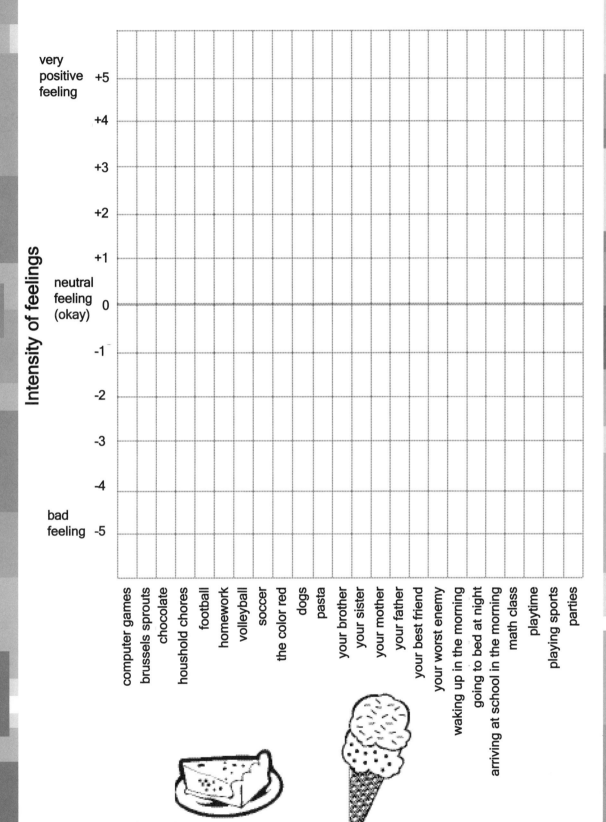

Intensity of feelings

- very positive feeling +5
- +4
- +3
- +2
- +1
- neutral feeling (okay) 0
- -1
- -2
- -3
- -4
- bad feeling -5

computer games
brussels sprouts
chocolate
houshold chores
football
homework
volleyball
soccer
the color red
dogs
pasta
your brother
your sister
your mother
your father
your best friend
your worst enemy
waking up in the morning
going to bed at night
arriving at school in the morning
math class
playtime
playing sports
parties

My perceptions

Put a dot in each column to show how you feel about each thing. Then join the dots to make a graph.

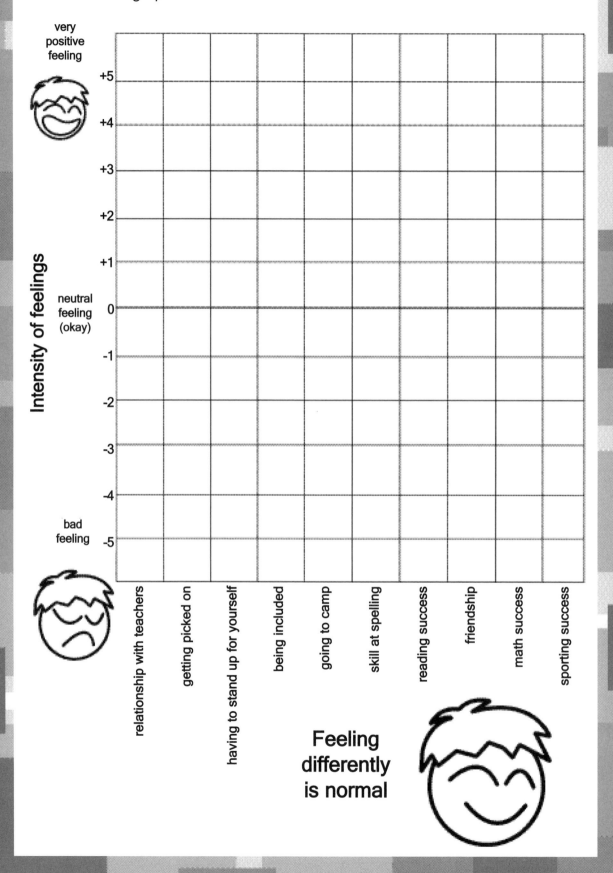

very positive feeling

Intensity of feelings

+5
+4
+3
+2
+1
neutral feeling (okay) 0
-1
-2
-3
-4
bad feeling -5

relationship with teachers
getting picked on
having to stand up for yourself
being included
going to camp
skill at spelling
reading success
friendship
math success
sporting success

Feeling
differently
is normal

Similarities and differences

How old were you when you did each of these things? Mark your age on the graph.

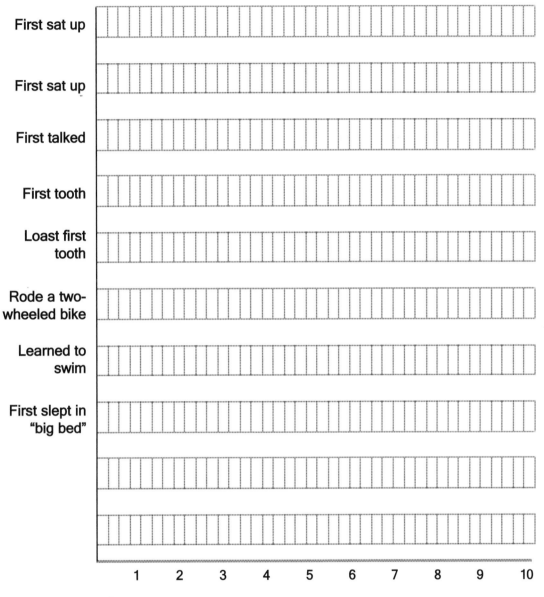

First sat up

First sat up

First talked

First tooth

Loast first tooth

Rode a two-wheeled bike

Learned to swim

First slept in "big bed"

1   2   3   4   5   6   7   8   9   10

Different people develop at different rates. It's normal! Differences are okay; the most important thing is that in the end everybody learns.

Islands-of-competence inventory

Are you involved in sports, clubs, associations or activities outside school? Do you have hidden talents or interests? Where do you go and what do you enjoy? It's time to learn what you do!

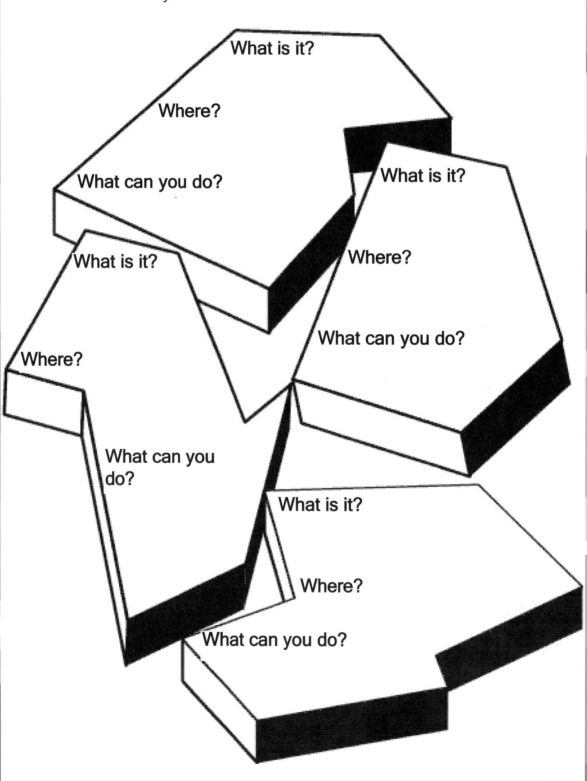

Common stresses and useful solutions

Serious stresses

-
-
-

Solutions to serious stresses

-
-
-

Annoying stresses

-
-
-

Solutions to annoying stresses

-
-

Meltdown cards: A way to cool down

Step in before you lose it! Grab a meltdown card and take time out.

Meltdown card

Places to go to **cool down** are:

- _____
- _____
- _____

See you back here in _____ **minutes** once you're feeling calmer.

Meltdown card

Places to go to **cool down** are:

- _____
- _____
- _____

See you back here in _____ **minutes** once you're feeling calmer.

Meltdown card

Places to go to **cool down** are:

- _____
- _____
- _____

See you back here in _____ **minutes** once you're feeling calmer.

Meltdown card

Places to go to **cool down** are:

- _____
- _____
- _____

See you back here in _____ **minutes** once you're feeling calmer.

What I would like to do or try

Today we brainstormed what we enjoy doing at school and outside school. I shared what I like to do. And I heard great things that others do.

Activities at school

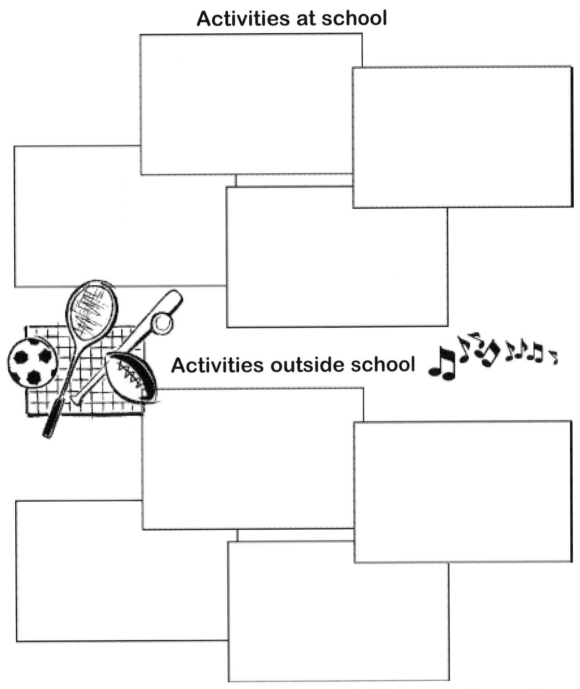

Activities outside school

Take it home and show Mom and Dad. You never know, there might be something here that you can begin to enjoy!

Make a surprising change!

Secretly surprise someone.

Think of someone.

Think of four things you could say or do to pleasantly surprise this person over the next week.

Who?	What could you do?	What could you say?

Rate your day on the continuum

Here's a way to keep track of what happens at school each day. The continuum helps to show the balance between school problems and the enjoyable moments.

Week beginning Monday ___/___/___

Rating: 1 = a terrible day   3 = an average day   5 = a great day

Monday

1	2	3	4	5

Positive comment: _____

Negative comment: _____

Tuesday

1	2	3	4	5

Positive comment: _____

Negative comment: _____

Wednesday

1	2	3	4	5

Positive comment: _____

Negative comment: _____

Thursday

1	2	3	4	5

Positive comment: _____

Negative comment: _____

Friday

1	2	3	4	5

Positive comment: _____

Negative comment: _____

Rules for keeping friends

- Make sure you include them.

- Be nice. Care for their feelings.

- Swap ideas and thoughts.

- Find out their favorite games and play them too.

- Remember that listening as well as speaking is important.

- Do things together outside school, like going to a movie, sleeping over or playing.

- Remember it's okay to say 'No' sometimes, too!

- Spend time talking together.

- Tell them they are your friend.

- Notice how they look – ask, 'What's wrong?' or 'Why are you so happy?'.

- Think before you speak. There are some things that should not be said – you may end up feeling silly.

- Share things.

Rules for meeting people and making friends

1. Approach them.

2. Stand and face them.

3. Look at their eyes.

4. Smile and say hello.

5. Say your name and ask theirs.

6. Ask questions about them.

7. Listen carefully to their answers.

8. Be kind and thoughtful.

9. Think before you speak. There are some things that should not be said.

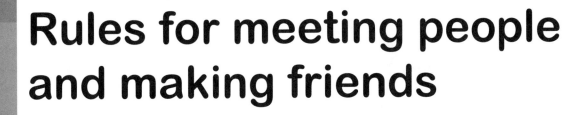

Gremlin buster

Draw your gremlins. Use color and lots of detail so we can really see what they look like!

Gremlin buster

Draw your gremlins.
Use color and lots of
detail so we can really
see what they look like!

Gremlin buster

Draw your gremlins. Use color and lots of detail so we can really see what they look like!

Concentration force-field

Noise and distractions just bounce off the concentration force-field! Draw yourself working well inside the force-field.

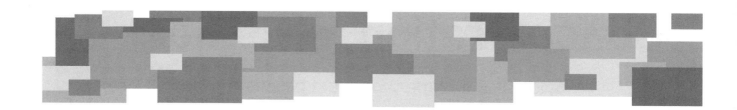

Chapter 5
Reinforcing proactive attitudes

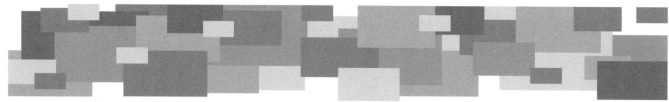

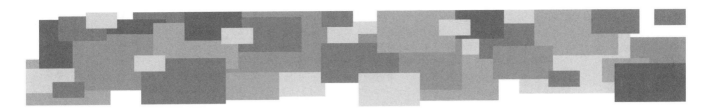

Teaching proactivity

Proactive individuals develop attitudes and behaviors that permit them to influence their destiny. They develop awareness, a keenness to change their lives, secure goals and find success. The opposite are individuals who believe they will end up where life randomly takes them.

Can students learn to be proactive? Of course, but keep in mind this is an osmotic process. It is truly contagious. If we want students to show proactive behaviors then we need to model and teach proactive attitudes and behaviors, and incorporate them in the teaching and learning systems we develop (Rogers 1995). Guiding students to discover their proactivity is a responsibility that begins and remains with us. Yet, many teachers have been on the battle front for a long time. Naturally, they may feel world weary and in need of emotional renewal (Harris 1999). They are ready to come up for air and reflect on why they continue to teach, what they have to offer and what they want from it now. The business of teaching is more than managing children and providing for their learning. W. B. Yeats succinctly reminds us that 'education is not the filling of a bucket, but the lighting of a fire.' To continue to motivate and inspire, teachers need to capitalize on opportunities to gain motivation and inspiration for themselves.

Determining your emotional resilience

To recapture of your first love, teaching, contemplate these reflective questions.

- *Why are you a teacher?*
- *What initially led you into teaching?*
- *What motivates you today?*
- *Do you show kindness to students?*
- *What was your last kind act?*
- *What do students and parents say about you?*
- *How long is it since you took a bag of dried fruit or candy out on playground duty, and shared them with students?*
- *What are your colleagues likely to say about you?*
- *How would you describe your teaching style?*
- *Describe the sort of climate you provide in your classroom.*
- *Is this the climate you want?*
- *Are you aware of your conflict-management style? Would you rate it as competitive, avoiding, accommodative, compromising or collaborative? (Friend & Cook 1996)*
- *What do you say so your students hear that you care about them?*
- *Are you the boss in your classroom, or do you guide?*
- *Do you lead to places that are safe and rich for your students?*
- *Do you know these places?*

Cognitive Behavioral Training

- *Whose learning environment is it?*

- *Do your students see you as safe?*

- *Do you smile, wink, gesture and have fun with students?*

- *How safe does your weakest class member feel?*

- *Who is it? Might there be someone else as well?*

- *Who are the students in your class you would determine as disadvantaged or not empowered?*

- *How do you demonstrate to your students that you enjoy their company?*

- *Each day, week, term or year is there something you consciously give to students? What is it?*

- *Do you link the present to the future for students?*

- *Do you set individual goals for vulnerable students and find ways to help achieve them?*

- *How have you helped a student conquer their own mountain?*

- *Do you communicate with parents (and students) on a regular basis?*

- *Besides scheduled parent interview times, what do you do to initiate contact?*

- *Do you know the greatest worries most parents face as their child is being educated?* (Brock & Shute 2001)

- *Do you address these with parents?*

- *What is it that you value about your students?*

- *What legacy do you want to leave your students with when they remember you?*

- *How important is enjoying rich relationships with your children in the classroom?*

When we question our motivations, the depth of our personal resources and our ambitions, we are likely to find answers that can be healing, renewing and inspirational. They lead us to accept that we are unquestionably part of the problem and the solution. To be fair, unless we know the depth of our personal resilience, the influence we are able to exert in developing proactive pathways for others is likely to be intermittent at best (Wubbles, Levy & Brekeinams 1997). When our thoughts and behaviors are proactive we become more sensitive and perceptive to the needs of our students. Proactive pathways begin with us.

Proactive schools

There are some very obvious features about schools which want to make a difference for students with, and without, difficulties (Corrie & Leitao 1999). Proactive schools promote the development of systems to encourage each student's personal best, whether they're gifted, challenged or different. They believe that best practice is measured by more than academic performance. They know that the depth of pastoral care, the choice of subjects offered and flexibility are pivotal in keeping students connected to learning and opportunity. Proactive schools actively educate their staff, students and parents to understand what best educational practice is and what they should expect from it. They encourage all to contribute their ideas and embrace the changes that striving for inclusivity naturally invites.

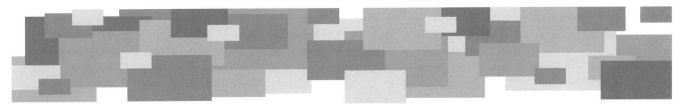

Offer choices

Proactive schools value connecting with students and their families. They realize that a student's skill-development, emotional resilience and resolve to stay engaged is intimately linked to the flexibility, care and innovation offered by their system. According to school principal and highly respected educator Bob Heath, 'The formality of schooling, the social structure of the school and the nature of the curriculum and pedagogy don't necessarily suit the way many kids learn' (Heggen 2003b, p.7). Further to this, because of recent dramatic societal changes, it must be questioned whether school, in its traditional form, remains an appropriate institution to meet the diversity of students' needs. Without responsive, innovative structures, such as models which incorporate a range of community resources, more students are likely to fall victim to the secondary emotional issues of malaise, hostility, anxiety or depression (Booth et al. 2000).

Keep students connected

A powerful means to nourish optimism in students is for them to know that the system intends to keep them connected, or engaged. They need to know it has the scope to offer appropriate subject material, the curriculum delivery will be within their range, that teachers are aware of their special provisions and will implement adjustments. Students also need to know what to do or who to go to when a teacher forgets their entitlements. The elevation of connectedness may be as simple as a principal, home-room teacher, school counselor or adaptive education specialist telling the student, *Together we will make this work. I intend to get you there!*

Adjust curriculum delivery

Adjusting curriculum delivery compensates for the difficulties a student faces. For students with special needs the Individualized Education Plan (IEP) will provide the framework for the accommodations in the classroom. Many of the curriculum adjustments in place for these students will also benefit other students in the classroom. Curriculum adjustment is accepted as good teaching practice for all students when it is deemed necessary. Students who have reading and written language difficulties cannot process the same volume or complexity of text, or may be unable to deliver the same written output as other students. Similarly, students with short concentration spans, hyperactivity or anxiety are not in a position to meet the same demand as their counterparts. By modifying curriculum delivery, outcomes are optimized as the learning playing field is leveled and made fair.

Typical ideas to adjust the delivery of curriculum include:

> **Provide more time and increased flexibility**. The provision of more time in tests, examinations and in other learning situations is appropriate. In situations where it is not practical for students to have extra time, or an abbreviated test, they can be given a mark based on the percentage of items they correctly completed. Other alternatives are take-home tests or open-book tests. These tests still target understanding, but decrease anxiety or reliance on pure memory. If students regularly use a word processor, it is a legitimate accommodation to give them permission to use it in tests and examinations.

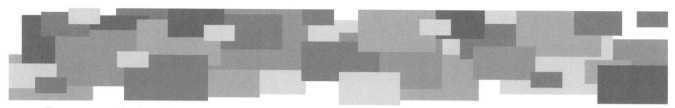

Do away with timed tests for some. 'Timed' situations which present a higher degree of stress (for example timed math tests, mental math, dictation or on-the-spot spelling tests) are likely to lead to poorer performance and unfair results. It is valid practice to negotiate an alternative with students.

Adjust the volume of work. Maintain clarity in your own mind about what is essential curriculum, and what is peripheral. While there is a core curriculum, there is also scope for multiple entry and exit points. Reduce quantity, and instead discuss ways with the student to improve quality.

Use a scribe. With a scribe the student can dictate ideas. Be inventive: use a parent, another child, a tutor, a study buddy, the school-support officer or perhaps cross-age support.

Use a reader. Allow students to listen to text and instructions in tests and examinations. This frees them of their print-related problem.

Suggest students use an audio or video recorder. Teach students to use a dictaphone, tape recorder or video camera to record their knowledge and creative stories. Set up a special place for them to do this.

Short-circuit the writing-to-final-product process. Short-circuiting the process of writing a draft to final product reduces the emotional and physical overload that many students face when confronted by the writing process. Rather than asking students to tackle the entire publishing process each week, extend the time. Or, develop a mechanism for some of their drafts to be typed for them.

Mark work sensitively. Marking work sensitively refers to separating the marks for structure and content from marks for spelling. Many students, especially those with Dyslexia, have genuine difficulties 'cracking the literacy code'. A series of red marks over a page, with copious spelling corrections, will not solve this problem. Work on marking formats that encourage and value their ideas.

Provide material and texts that are easier to read. Students with reading and print processing difficulties benefit from having a lower volume of reading. Allowing the student access to easier reading material with the same content, summary notes, tapes or video support their understanding and reading. Content presented in an abbreviated or shortened form is a sensible accommodation in English and language-rich subjects for print- and attention-challenged students.

Arrange a study or reading buddy at school. Peer tutoring has a strong place in classrooms as students are more positively influenced by peers. A peer who is prepared to answer the student's questions, read the curriculum material and lead by example is the ideal reading buddy. Institute a roster system if necessary.

Give assignments in advance. Having assignments in advance supports students with memory or organizational problems, as it offers opportunity to prepare, read, discuss and plan. For younger students, why not give them their weekly contract on Friday afternoon rather than on Monday?

Offer to review assignments prior to the hand-in date. Reviewing assignments prior to the hand-in date is a proactive practice that continues to gain momentum. Students are guided to present and discuss their assignment draft so they can receive strategic input from teachers prior to the hand-in date. Sometimes the subject teacher chooses to take responsibility for this, although increasingly

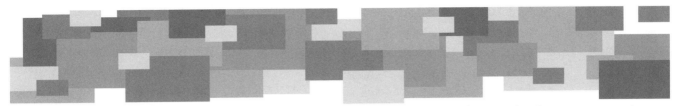

learning-support centers or adaptive-education faculties are developing mechanisms to support students in this way.

Structure tasks. Structured tasks allow students to see the big picture quickly rather than drowning in detail. Work out together what needs to be done, when and how. Document it, and build in reflective times to review and support progress.

Permit students to present work and be assessed in a variety of ways. Develop alternate forms of presentation such as interviews, *PowerPoint* presentations, computer slide shows, the building of models, posters, photographic essays or a practical demonstration.

Expect and demonstrate inclusive practices

From birth right through to the moment of death, everyone has the need to be included. The contemporary view of inclusive education is that schools, and their teachers, are willing to meet the needs of all learners, whether they are gifted, challenged or different. In fact, educational inclusivity is part of a far wider societal commitment to embrace diversity and bring about social justice. Truly inclusive education acknowledges that all children can learn, and respects the differences between students by offering willingness, knowledge, systems and methodologies to meet their various needs (Miles 2002).

Inclusivity defined by a high school student

Lucy attends a school with a large annex for intellectually and physically impaired students. These students are integrated into the mainstream classes as much as possible. During our conversation I asked whether students from the annex ever received a difficult time from mainstream students. 'No way,' she explained, 'anyone who did would get it from teachers, but they'd get it worse from the other kids.' She continued, 'Anyway we've known the annex kids since we started school. They're in our classes. We eat lunch with them. They're friends!'. This school, and its students, teach, model and live inclusivity on a day-to-day basis, and everyone reaps the rewards.

Excluded by 'gross green ketchup'

If anyone in Antone's seventh grade class had visited his home they would have been amazed by his collection of models. These were expensive, intricate models of automobiles, trains, ships and aircraft. They took days to assemble and days to detail. His bedroom was organized meticulously, and all twenty-three models were displayed to perfection. This was Antone's obsession, and, in part, was accounted for by his Asperger Syndrome diagnosis. Building and constructing sophisticated models had become a highly refined skill. Antone was incredibly talented and looking around his bedroom was truly inspiring. At home he was happy living with his mother, father and two older brothers, and regularly helped in his father's floor-covering business to raise money to buy his next model.

However, Antone remained depressed by what he endured at school. He had attended his school since beginning high school and knew his classmates well, but had no friends. It was easy for Antone to miss the point,

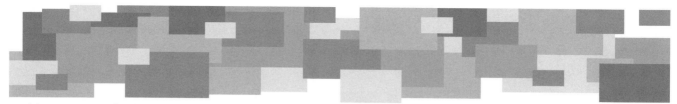

and just as easy for him to become overwhelmed and tearful. When he appeared uncertain, sought clarification from the teacher, or looked tearful, some students would begin to discreetly rub their eyes, mimicking crying. They would deftly point at their nose, or someone would walk past and whisper, 'Going to do some gross green ketchup now?'.

This had stemmed from an incident about two years ago when Antone had become upset in class. He exploded into tears and his nose streamed with green mucus. He was so embarrassed. Since this time he had become the victim of sophisticated taunting from the very peers he had known all of his school life.

Antone did not enjoy good health either, so from time to time he missed school. On his return students would say, 'Hey. Where've you been? At Hungry Jack's getting some more of that gross green ketchup?' Antone also spoke with a strong intonation. It sounded like an accent, and is a notable feature of Asperger Syndrome. When the teacher wasn't around it was considered sport by some to walk near Antone and mimic his speech, exaggerating and demeaning his accent.

Antone continues to persevere with school. His parents continue to ask for help from school staff about the ongoing, highly sophisticated harassment and exclusion their son endures (Prior 2003). His teacher and principal are truly sympathetic, but believe there is little they can do because they never witness it. They try to reassure Antone's parents by drawing their attention to the school's newly updated 'anti-teasing and bullying policy'. Antone's parents, like many, believe that while the adults in schools fail to address students who promote ridicule, harassment and the exclusion of others, they fail to grasp the bigger picture of who really is in charge in the playground and classroom.

Educational and psychological assessments

Students showing learning, behavioral, emotional or self-management difficulties require a comprehensive educational and psychological assessment. A few schools automatically screen new students or, as a matter of course, assess all students at particular year levels. An educational and psychological assessment provides the student, their family and school with maximum information about their learning style, strengths and weaknesses, and sensible management options.

Following an assessment, one exceptional psychologist presents a page to her clients containing a series of linked circles around the border. Within each circle in large, bold type are the student's strengths (for example reasoning, concept formation, comprehension, general knowledge, problem-solving, vocabulary and critical thinking). She explains in everyday language what these mean for the student, and ways they can make more of them. Next, she presents a similar page, but in the middle, in small type, are the student's difficulties (for example working memory, processing speed and phonological skills). She explains what these weaknesses mean, and provides notes for the student, their parents and teachers on what they can do to develop or compensate for these weak spots. For older students, psychologists are often able to capitalize on their strengths, and lead them towards career opportunities worth consideration.

Once a diagnosis has been made, there are critical milestones along the way when reviews are useful. In many cases these provide information to support strategic planning, and in a few cases are imperative for the student's very survival. Ideal times to consider a review are:

- when a student's optimism, learning or behavior suddenly deteriorates
- moving from one school to another
- the transitions between elementary, middle and high school
- when students approach the end of high school.

Depending on their difficulty or disability, a psychologist can enclose a medical report which can be forwarded to the controlling assessment board verifying the need for special provisions to be put in place.

Use 'access cards'

A student access card states the student's difficulty and the type of accommodation to which they are entitled. For students who receive special education services, the access card would include the accommodations and adaptations which are listed in the students IEP. Due to confidentiality, the access card should be approved by the teacher, student and parent.

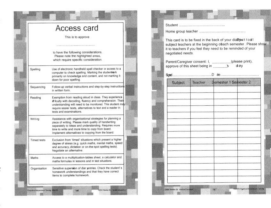

For example, the access card for a student with a learning disability may state that handouts are to be provided in place of copying extensive notes from the board, daily writing is sensitively supervised, extra time is allowed for written tests or that tests may be taken orally. A student also exhibits anger control difficulties, may have an access card which states that when frustrated, the student may go to the Resource Center to cool off or to complete the assignment. It may also provide permission for the student to telephone a parent, talk to a counselor.

Normalize attitudes

Insightful, optimistic teachers deliberately maintain a steadying influence for the student and their parents. They advocate for students by working in obvious and subtle ways to help other students, staff and other parents understand the student's difficulty. This helps to avoid discrimination, isolation and exclusion.

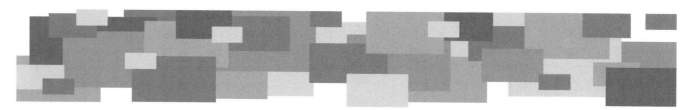

CURRICULUM ADJUSTMENT

This entitles

_____

to the following considerations:

☐   open book during all tests

☐   test read to him/her

☐   extra time during test

☐   fewer questions during test

☐   use of a word processor during test

☐   verbal clarification of tasks

☐   homework clarification/modification/alternatives

☐   test or exercises modified and/or enlarge

☐   laptop/PC may be used for any written work

☐   spell checker or dictionary available during tests

☐   calculator and formulas available during tests

☐   notes photocopied and supplied

☐   special seating arrangements

☐   a negotiated curriculum

☐   test answers to be scribed or taped

☐   management of behavior as specified

☐   other _____

This card is to be carried on your assignment book and shown to subject teachers at the beginning of term. Also show the card to teachers if you feel that they need to be reminded of your needs and circumstances.

Normalizing attitudes

At the beginning of sixth grade life took a wonderful turn for Tobi. His primary school years had been dotted by his emotional, sometimes violent outbursts; outright refusal, running away, arguing with and shouting at teachers and peers, and failure to complete tasks. Tobi was highly intelligent, but his reactiveness could boil over in an instant. He had experienced a succession of teachers who had decided to meet Tobi head on, believing the best approach was to confront him and make him conform. This confrontational strategy had done no more than aggravate and alienate Tobi from the class group. Now, in sixth grade, Tobi was entering a new middle school.

176

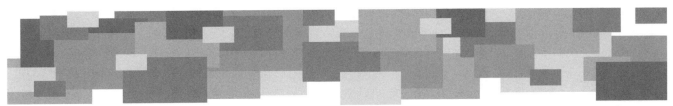

On the first day Tobi's new class teacher spoke to the class about what he called 'public and private difficulties'. Private difficulties, he explained, were the sorts of difficulties most people hold inside. They might include worrying, shyness, sadness, learning difficulties or feelings of not being good enough. Being private meant they are rarely seen by others, but could be as serious as the public difficulties. Public difficulties are the sorts of difficulties that really are obvious to everyone because they happen in front of everyone; loss of temper, impulsivity, shouting or swearing at others, refusal to follow instructions or running away. He explained that public difficulties often leave us with an unfair impression of someone, especially if we choose not to look any further.

What mattered most, according to his view, was to try and understand each other's difficulties. He insisted that each class member must begin to understand each person's behavior as clues to their feelings; they were expected to look deeper than the behavior. The consequence for excluding, alienating or harassing others was to be as serious as it is in the real world. If anyone could not accept another by sensibly working around them or directly supporting their difficulty, public or private, they would need to be counseled, and their parents would also need to be involved to help support their counseling.

Not surprisingly, Tobi took to this new embracing situation just as a duck takes to water. He still had difficulties, but they were no longer anywhere near so public. For the first time, Tobi operated as if he belonged to the group, and wanted to remain a part of it.

Student placement

Transitional times are high-risk times for emotionally vulnerable students, and this doesn't only apply to school. One mother explained that early in the school vacation her son had been decidedly touchy, and it was the small things that bothered him. Once the vacation routines were established, life became easier for all. At school, primary and secondary, consider keeping emotionally at-risk students with the same class teacher, home room teacher and a few pivotal friends over several years rather than changing them to a new homeroom each year. When a winning formula has been achieved, stick with it!

Cultivate significant others

Make it a point to introduce students to individuals and groups who may become significant in their life. These might include a learning specialist, an older peer, a psychologist, an organization or association, or a mentor to encourage the student.

Frank, a tenth grade student, was advised by his homeroom teacher to join the tenth grade football team, as the coach was the school's careers counselor. He would play a leading role in helping Frank with the bewildering subject and vocational choices that awaited him in twelve months or so. Developing a healthy relationship with the careers counselor would work to Frank's advantage.

Cognitive Behavioral Training

Making a proactive start

Borrow from the future

If it helps, try and picture this student twenty years from now. Would you speak to the adult in the same way as you are speaking to the child? Recognizing the young man or woman of the future prompts us to consider the relationship we have with them now.

Ask parents, What do you think will help?

Before the school year begins, write to incoming students and their parents. Let them know about yourself, and set a tone which conveys that you want what they are likely to want. Those teachers who are quick to supply their email address and gather the email addresses of parents do this because they realize this very act reassures parents that their input and communication is welcomed.

Attach a questionnaire that prompts parents to explain their child's strengths and challenges. Ask for ways that have been proven to enhance or compensate for these strengths and weaknesses. Provide the opportunity for relevant history to be explained. Parents have a wealth of knowledge about their children, and it is to our advantage to tap into this. This process helps to fast-track appreciations of the student and devise effective ways to work with the child and family. When parents are included in the planning, we place them in a proactive position where they can provide wonderful backup. After the first four weeks of school insightful teachers prepare a letter to parents outlining how their child has settled in their new classroom or school situation. Contained within the letter are several humorous or positive snippets that illustrate the student's personal, social and academic accomplishments.

Parents are a stunning source of volunteers for supporting children's learning, supplying books and magazines, computers, software, computer expertise, maps, charts, brochures, guest speakers and arranging fascinating locations for excursions. Parents can also be a remarkable resource by virtue of their work, personality or both. Never underestimate the support parents are able to give. Listening and consulting with parents at the beginning of the year is truly an investment.

Get it first-hand

Speak to colleagues to discover what has and has not worked. It is far easier to start on the right footing than to do catch-up. Children react positively if they sense you know something about what they like on the first meeting.

After spending twelve months with a child it is surprising how much vital and incidental information you have to pass on. Make a point to arrange a few moments to sit with the incoming teacher and physically hand over the files of your two or three at-risk students. So much can be passed on in just ten minutes.

Read reports and assessments

Competent professionals build on the judgment and opinions of those who have worked with students previously, in any capacity. Reports, profiles and notes encourage an appreciation of the student's journey. They do not color a competent teacher's judgment. Comments such as 'I don't read the children's files before I start teaching them', 'I like to make up my own mind' or 'I haven't read his file yet, because I want to see what happens first' cannot be interpreted as professional. Competent teachers read children's files and do not feel driven to make snap judgments after reading them. Put simply, the information gathered places the teacher in a far more proactive position.

Connected teachers know the relationship they forge with each student is unique, and central in making a difference for that student. They know the first interaction is the one that counts. It's the one that's remembered as it becomes imprinted on social memory, and because of this, it's likely to be drawn on by the student in difficult times.

Communicate with parents

Staying in touch with parents highlights that teachers think about their pupils after school has ended. To show this some teachers:

- create class newsletters

- send homework samples

- jot an uplifting note in the student's plan book

- make an occasional phone call

- send a journal article that relates to their child

- send home certificates and awards

- offer an extra parent-teacher conference

- send an email

- send home questionnaires for students and parents to fill out together; the feedback helps to keep everybody moving in the same direction

- set up informal occasions where students and parents meet (an afternoon barbecue or breakfast at school).

Promote cognitive-behavioral techniques

There are families who do it tough. Effective strategies and unfaltering moral support can never be overestimated. Encourage parents to establish contact with others (parents with children having similar difficulties, and professionals) and gently feed them information on management techniques that are likely to work. Just as training

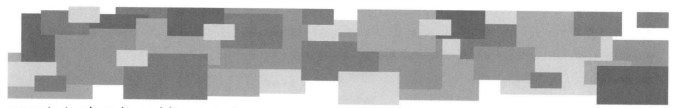

supports teachers in applying strategies, managing behavior and improving their relationships with students, training also supports parents. Direct parents to training courses, or consider running information evenings on the classic parenting hot spots: setting expectations, consequential management, establishing routine, getting ready for school, managing homework, television, tantrums or bedtime are super starters! Reinforce the overwhelming evidence that nurturing environments encourage success. Environments filled with hostility and criticism develop defiance, poor confidence levels and opposition in children.

Start now. The earlier a cognitive behavioral system is started the better, because its effectiveness around the early teenage years can diminish as parental influences decline and peer group influences escalate.

Teaching and learning

Enthusiasm

Deliberately begin each day on a positive note. Think about the way you introduce lessons. Occasionally, grab everyone's attention by doing what students do not expect from you! Be melodramatic, daring, loud or very, very quiet. Plan to be inventive and resourceful. Introduce a new concept or idea with an experiment, a dare, an impromptu play, a video, a guest or something unforgettable that illustrates the point and captures interest. During lessons, be mindful of the difference between saying, 'I told you to keep working at that math' and 'I double dare you to do ten math problems in the next ten minutes.' The choice of phrase and the tone of voice can be enough to tip the balance. Enthusiasm is contagious!

Do what you do best

If there is a topic you enjoy and have developed abundant resources for, arrange to do it in the classes of colleagues as well as your own. In return, ask them to present topics they have expertise in to your class. Invite guest speakers to come in as well; they always set a different tone, adding interest and providing the scope for follow up.

Have a plan. Sort the priorities. Start now.

It's important to know where you want your students to be, especially the challenged and at-risk. In order to do this you will need to create a plan with the student. For students receiving special education services this plan may be made at an IEP meeting or during a periodic review of the IEP. For students who do not receive special education services but are considered at risk a plan is also very important. Take it slowly; ascertain and address top priorities first. Involve the student, their parents and any appropriate school staff and external professional expertise if necessary. The team works together to determine the precise nature of the difficulty, suitable interventions and logical adjustments that will provide support for the student. Once the plans are set up and the goals established, be sure to regularly review the student's progress in obtaining the goals and rewrite them as necessary.

With so much to do, it is too easy for teachers to become overwhelmed. But what a teacher does for a student now makes a difference. Even in the short term, students are able to make changes just by knowing their teacher is participating alongside them. In doing so, teachers put in train a proactive, therapeutic process.

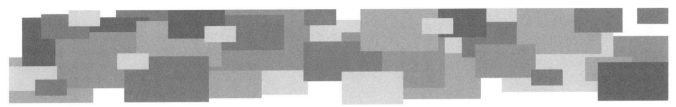

Conceiving a plan is a therapeutic act

Nathan's comment to his parents crystallized the therapeutic value his teacher provided. At seven years old Nathan was experiencing a severe obsession-compulsive episode. He was finding it extraordinarily difficult to enter the classroom at the beginning of the day, and to leave to go home in the afternoon. Nathan, a psychologist and Nathan's teacher Julie had put a series of simple measures in place to help, but more than anything it was Julie's responsiveness that helped. One night while Nathan was having a bath he announced to his mother and father that they didn't need to worry about his problem at school because Julie had said, 'Don't worry Nathan. We'll get through this together.'

When learning and memory are weak

While memory weaknesses are common, it is the inconsistency in recall of rote-learned information that is a prominent feature of students with concentration problems and Specific Learning Difficulties. It does not necessarily mean that the mode of teaching and learning has been unsuccessful. Individuals with memory difficulties often have trouble retrieving information stored in their short-term auditory or visual memory. In contrast, their long-term memories are likely to be sound.

Teach strategies to reinforce memory. Strategies include tricks like mnemonics, illustrations to scaffold ideas and concepts, charts, graphs, cue cards, concept maps, summaries, an indexed book with often-misspelled words, an indexed book of how to do math problems, a catalog of business-size cards with important definitions, acronyms, flash cards, rhymes, silly rhymes, finger tricks (for remembering the nine-times table) and so on. When learning words to read or spell, times tables or math sequences, remember that over-learning is imperative. These students need incentives, structures and support to keep them in constant rehearsal to prevent the information from being lost.

Part of the success recipe for students with poor short-term memory in math includes providing a calculator or a number square when teaching new math operations. Memory difficulties with tables can interfere with the integration of new learning (Chinn 1999). Paradoxically, while students with poor memory may find arithmetic difficult, they may easily grasp conceptually challenging math. Teach students to summarize what they have learnt: key words, definitions, formulas or the sequential steps in a math problem. Either use a special book or develop review files under subject headings using the word processor. Provide students with a disk containing the necessary information. Encourage them to read it and edit it so they are left with key words and key phrases meaningful to them. Students enjoy 'destroying' information and reworking it so it makes sense to them.

Cognitive Behavioral Training

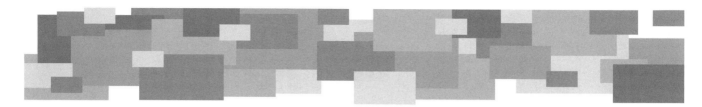

Vary teaching for different learning styles

Students learn best when the task makes sense to them. When the task is meaningful, they are more likely to see it as worthwhile and remain engaged. Teachers who know how to engineer learning experiences to match a student's age level, intellectual ability and learning preferences offer the best possible opportunity for academic and personal success. A teacher's instructional style can play to the student's strengths and minimize their learning weaknesses (Tomlinson 1999). Teachers who understand this are able to choose from the following instructional styles:

Didactic. The teacher tells the facts and students learn them.

Direct instruction. The teacher demonstrates a task and students copy and apply it.

Guided learning. The teacher specifies parameters and students explore the topic within these.

Discovery learning. The teacher sets up a learning environment and students participate to discover core principles.

Creative experimentation. The teacher provides basic resources and with these resources the students create 'unique products'.

Astute educators draw on each of these to create content, process or product. Each approach has the capacity to achieve a particular goal, and when used artfully they can respond to student differences in readiness, interest or learning (Pohl 1998).

Further to this, John Joseph explores the significance of learning styles in his book, *Brainy Parents - Brainy Kids* (2002) and agrees with most educational theorists; that is, no child has just one learning style. Learners may have strength in one style, but most benefit is gained by teachers providing variety and choice in their learning approaches. Teachers who draw on a variety of learning models are most successful in maximizing success for students (Lasley & Matczynski 1997). Examples of learning models include:

• Gardner's theory of multiple intelligences, which provides a varied framework for designing learning experiences (1993)

• Bloom's and Williams' taxonomies, which can be used to categorize levels of thinking and assist critical and creative thinking skills (Bloom 1956, Williams 1970).

• Tony Ryan's Thinker's Keys (1994), which encourage divergent thinking.

Similarly, Edward de Bono's contribution is based around the idea of six thinking hats. This approach trains individuals to be more flexible in exploring solutions (de Bono 1987).

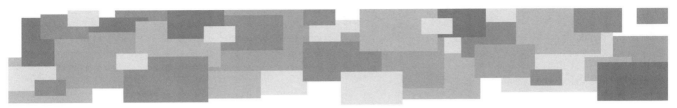

Incidental learning

Respected educator and psychologist Thomas Armstrong believes we should use more 'off task' or incidental learning (Armstrong 1999). He, as many do, accepts that this is the way some students, particularly those diagnosed with impulsivity, concentration, and learning difficulties, do much of their learning. Yet, this style runs counter to what teachers are trained to appreciate. The model teachers have assimilated during their own training to be teachers, is that students should direct their attention to the teacher, appear as though they are listening intently and then proceed with the task. For most students, this is a sound model to work within, but for some their best learning occurs in an incidental or oblique way. Their natural, stronger learning preference is attuned to the manner most of us used in the first few years of our lives. If you have forgotten, organize to spend time with a kindergarten or elementary teacher, as their skill to embrace and capitalize on incidental learning is astonishing!

It's important to cultivate in all students the ability to look, listen and remain attentive during instructional time. It is equally important to provide opportunities for students who do their learning in predominantly 'off task' ways. Begin by watching a student who you believe has a strong incidental learning style. Find ways to make more of what they do incidentally rather than focusing on wanting them to change to exactly what you do. What they do incidentally may become a trigger for something to be pursued more formally.

Draw on a diverse range of products

Above all else, talk with the student often and provide scope for them to express their preference for learning. Be willing to negotiate tasks that match their talents, interests and challenges. Provide hands -on activities and deliberately digress from the chalk-and-talk/book-work pursuits. By encouraging students to absorb information and express what they have learned in a mix of ways, you are likely to witness the emergence of new talents, interests and confidence. Proactive, flexible strategies help students succeed rather than feel powerless within an uncompromising system.

Judy Parker, author of *Effective Teaching and Learning Strategies for All Students* (1999), writes that traditionally a student's capacity to show what they have learned has been restricted to writing in conventional essay-type formats. She suggests that one of the keys to successful student outcomes is to encourage them to draw on 'a diverse range of products':

graphs	news reports	self-reflection
cartoon captions	autobiographies	murals
surveys	debates	craft items
card games	legends	jingles
folk dances	concept maps	simulations
lyrics	experiments	creative dances
conferences	slide shows	sound effects
advertising campaigns	group logos	class meetings
newsletters	story maps	charades
values statements	collages	number patterns
cards	mood music	designs

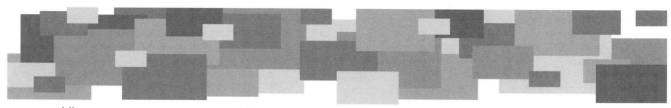

mobiles	sociograms	musical compositions
mimes	sets of instructions	interviews
raps	personal journals	translations
songs	reviews	learning reflections
dramatic performances	oral presentations	videos
opinion polls	reading circles	gestures
justifications	feelings books	predictions
puppet plays	percussion pieces	flow charts
scale drawings	measurement series	sound stories
screen printing	photographic prints	role-plays
harmonies	musical scores	speeches
monologues	joke books	peer tutoring contracts
definition lists	self-portraits	headline summaries
preference lists	codes	strengths lists
constructions	brochures	body language acts
equations	board games	matrices
calligraphy	recipes	tangrams
audio tapes	personal time lines	hymns
cooperative tasks	story illustrations	group games
slogans	poems	

Source: Parker, J. (1999). *Effective teaching and learning strategies for all students.* Melbourne: Hawker Brownlow Education, p.33.

Preparing for transitions

Preparing students in advance for changes to routines is always helpful, and for ADHD and Asperger Syndrome students it is often essential. It is usually the obvious transitions (guest speakers, special assemblies, returning to school after vacation, a term break, or following a long weekend, excursions, camps and so on) which throw them into disarray and attract our attention. Even the apparently basic day-to-day transitions, such as lining up for class, walking across the yard with the class, entering the classroom after recess or lunch, or entering the class of another teacher, can cause turmoil and upset.

One low-key strategy might be to arrange for a buddy to walk with the student when changing classes, working alongside them, offering advice in coping with new situations, assisting them to prepare for the end of the day and supervising the items needed to go home.

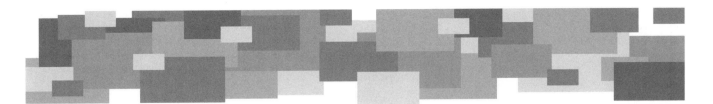

The snapshot

Anticipate who is likely to become overexcited by new situations and assist them to prepare for it internally. School camps, excursions, even breaking routine and having guests in the classroom are tricky times for the quick, busy, impulsive students. As their excitement builds they are less inclined to think about how their behavior might look, how it might impact on others and what they should be doing. Help them know what is going to happen, and what will be expected so they can prepare for it in advance. Teaching the snapshot reinforces success in these situations.

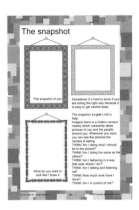

Jane's snapshot plan

Jane was in sixth grade. Everyone liked her because she was fun, energetic and always had interesting things to say. Her teacher thought she was fun too, but also knew Jane had an excitability problem. Jane and her class went on a field trip to the museum. Everyone had worksheets they needed to complete during the excursion. Jane was so talkative, and so excited about being at the museum that it wasn't until Jane's teacher collected the worksheets that she noticed Jane hadn't recorded much at all. When Jane's teacher returned her worksheets the next day she wrote a few comments about Jane's poor performance, and failed her on the first part of the assignment. Jane was really disappointed.

Before Jane and her class returned to the museum the following week, her teacher took her aside and taught Jane how to use the snapshot. She explained:

'Sometimes it's hard for you to know if you are acting the right way. I know it's easy for you to get carried away. The snapshot is a great trick to help you. Imagine there is a hidden camera nearby, and it is constantly taking snaps of you and the others around you. Whenever you want, you can see the pictures the camera is taking. Look at a picture, and think:

Am I doing what I should be in the picture?

Am I doing the same as the others?

Am I behaving in a way that fits where I am?

What can I see? Am I talking, talking, talking or am I listening too?

How much work have I done?

Am I in control of my gremlins or are they controlling me?

Next week, at the museum, I want you to take a few snapshots of yourself.

1. Let's start to think about the field trip now. How do you want to look in the snapshots? Let's talk about it. Fill in the blank photographs and show me two behaviors you want for yourself at the museum. Start preparing your thinking!

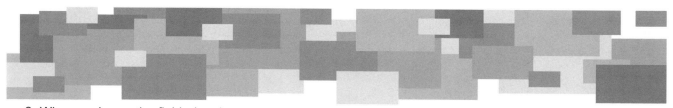

2. When you're on the field trip take a snapshot of what's happening around you every now and then. Set your watch so the alarm beeps every fifteen minutes. When it sounds, think, *Am I doing what I planned to do? Look around: Have I completed about the same amount of questions as the others?*

3. Choose wisely: Team up with a friend who can help you.

4. I'll be taking photographs, Jane. When you see me taking pictures that can also be a reminder for you to think about what you need to be doing.'

Jane's next visit to the museum was better. She is older now, but still knows the best way to get through new and exciting situations is to take snapshots. The more excited she is the more snapshots she knows to take. The snapshot helps children and young teenagers to notice their behavior. When they are acting differently to others, they learn to shift their behavior closer to where it should be.

Proactive classroom structures and attitudes

Classrooms and seating arrangements

The ideal student- and teacher-friendly classroom would be generously proportioned, have perfect temperature and ventilation, display good acoustic properties, offer ample natural lighting and conditions that encourage plants and animals to be cared for. It would boast flexible fixtures that allow learners to make the classroom what they need it to be, making it stimulating and inspiring to work within. The ideal classroom would have enough space to invite students to work alone, in pairs or in groups. Soft pillows, soft furniture and the right size furniture could be maneuvered into positions that suit the varying learning situations.

However, the truth for many is that their classrooms are too small and overcrowded. In fact, over twenty years ago Weinstein commented, 'Nowhere else, but in schools, are large groups of individuals packed so closely together for so many hours, yet expected to perform at peak efficiency on difficult learning tasks and to interact harmoniously.' (Armstrong 1999, p. 8) The reality is that if teachers wish to successfully engage students within the restrictive constraints of the classroom environment, they have to plan seating arrangements, placement of students, room displays and room layout very carefully.

One thing we all know with wonderful certainty is that students perform better when nearer the teacher. Locate students with distractibility issues and low tolerance to frustration closer rather than further away. Circulate among them more often and stand near when giving instructions. Traditionally, best places are at the front of the class close to the teacher's desk (do it in such a way that they really want to be there), to the side of the classroom or at a separate desk. The aim is to reduce the student's visual field, making it easier for them to look, listen and remember what to do. Think about incorporating a low-distraction work area in the classroom. Corrals are excellent barriers to reduce distractions. Introduced in a positive way, they become 'the' place to work! The use of headphones connected to a small portable CD player playing gentle music also helps to eliminate distraction from classroom background sound. So many students frequently are caught up by distractions. Their intermittent attention progressively impacts on their learning, and academic gaps emerge.

A grouped desk configuration, rather than traditional rows, invites socialization, conversation and distraction. One configuration is not necessarily better than another, but each plays a role in setting the classroom tone. Classroom layout dictates patterns of control, social interaction, learning styles and affective climates. Consider deliberately seating the poorly organized, forgetful or easily distracted student with an intuitive and grounded acquaintance. Keep fine-tuning placements when students do not work well together or as friendships shift, but avoid moving children around the classroom by lottery draw simply for the sake of it. This method disadvantages the socially vulnerable.

Seat breaks, tall desks and errand-running

Some students experience difficulty being still and remaining seated. This is a physiological problem and needs to be appreciated in this light. It is too easy to read such behavior as noncompliance, defiance or oppositional behavior. Try to avoid making their fidgeting into too much of an issue. No matter what their age, discuss their difficulty in order to begin to stretch their awareness. Together develop several 'legal places' in the classroom the student may move to providing they deliver a cue before moving. In other words, moving is fine, but the student begins to develop an appreciation of their need and yours.

Part of legalizing movement is to accept that the physically restless child needs to work in a different way. Some teachers arrange for a desk to be modified with tall legs so that students can stand and work. Everything from their arms down may move, yet surprisingly this movement seems to strengthen concentration and work output. Together, set up classroom tasks the student can do to help compensate for their physical restlessness: cleaning the board, organizing a display, collecting or distributing books and so on. Find acceptable ways for students to leave the classroom and 'burn off' energy. Send them on errands, even if it's just taking a note in a sealed envelope explaining to a colleague that you, and the student, need a break. This is so much healthier than both climbing the walls together!

Another arrangement to support physical restlessness is to have a red, green or yellow counter that the student places on the teacher's desk. Each color designates what the student has gone to do. Red indicates a quick drink and toilet stop, green designates a brisk run around the playground and yellow a five-minute wander to a predetermined spot.

A touching reminder

Daniel was an extraordinarily energetic ten-year-old who could easily fall prey to quick emotional overload. In earlier years he developed the habit of slipping out of the classroom and wandering the school. Yet, this practice was not due to defiance. It had more to do with an instinctive response to escape the emotional or physical rigors of being confined to the classroom and having to conform to expectations. As a ten-year-old, he could do the work, but between his restlessness and short concentration span it was difficult for him to complete written tasks.

Daniel and his teacher developed an idea to help him gather together a little more concentration when he needed it. This offered him greater control over his restlessness and improved his work output. She gave him a small soft stress ball at the beginning of the day to keep in his pocket. It was the sort that could be squashed and pinched into different shapes. It remained there as his touch reminder to finish the task he was on, or to stay calm in

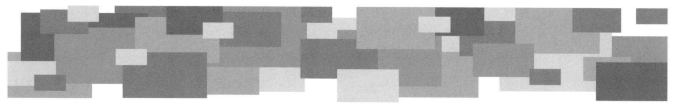

stressful times. Once he had completed a task he was able to quietly slip out the room and visit the resource center, or go to the gymnasium to join in a P.E. activity with any class.

This arrangement meant Daniel's work times were briefer than most, but far more productive than otherwise. The agreement allowed him to negotiate and achieve predetermined goals. As Daniel left the room he would place the stress ball on the teacher's desk, set his watch for fifteen minutes and head off. Occasionally, because of poor performance, Daniel would lose the privilege, but this helped increase the value of the arrangement.

Use a think strip to buy time

Many children face difficulty in controlling their lightning reactions. The 'think strip' and 'wristband' are simple tactile tools to help them think about, and take some control over, their impulsiveness. They serve to memory jog the link between feelings, behavior and outcomes. Think strips can be contacted to school desks, doors, the back of rulers, bulletin boards, or placemats at the dinner table; anywhere to help strengthen the decision-making process. When there is a problem to be resolved, children's spontaneous reactions can be slowed as they run their finger across the strip, helping them to think more reflectively. Wristbands are made by sewing or attaching three or four small, colored beads to fabric worn around the wrist. This highly tactile, dress-savvy application is capable of supporting students of all ages. By training the student to touch their 'wristband' at the pivotal decision-making moment they can buy some time as they move their fingers along the balls. This physical action offers the chance to insert thinking between feeling and reacting.

Legal movement for Jack

Case study

Nine-year-old Jack was diagnosed as a student with learning disabilities and ADHD. He displayed a short attention span, restlessness and experienced difficulties with reading and writing. Jack had been playing a pretend game of motorbikes with friends at recess. When the bell rang he lined up at the end of the line, hands in front still clinging to his imaginary motor bike and revving it at full throttle. As the students walked into the classroom, Jack continued to make loud motorbike noises. Resisting the temptation to disapprove, his teacher asked him to wait for a moment while she got the other students working on a short task. She returned to Jack and asked if he could do something for her. She asked if he could ride his motor bike up to the small oval, (within view of her classroom) and once he got there ride it around the oval as fast and noisily as he could. He could do it ten times if he wanted. Off he went! Out of the corner of her eye she saw a speedy motorcyclist raising dust as he roared around the small oval. He even had the right leather jacket on that day! When Jack returned he was flushed and happy to settle for the lesson.

Concentration enhancers

Purchase one or two fitness balls for the classroom. These are large, inflated, rubberized balls which can be bought in various sizes for around $20. They are ideal for the active, restless students who need to be constantly on the move. They seem to allow them to work longer as they gently move on the ball, almost unconsciously, maintaining

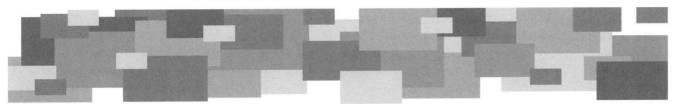

their balance. Also consider products such as Disc'O'Sit or Movin'Sit. These are comfortable, air-filled, rubberized cushions which encourage students to continually seek balance while they are seated. A growing body of opinion believes they help in sustaining perseverance during quiet, focused work times as their need to move is gently catered for.

What about investing in a couple of small stress balls? For some students, holding the ball in one hand while they write is calming. Again, this subtle movement permits students to focus more easily and for longer. One of my colleagues developed an understanding with his students that when he places a stress ball in front of them this is their cue to settle. No words are required. He delivers the stress ball, and the student takes it and understands the message. Similarly, lightweight portable posture desks that sit on the desk providing a sloped surface seem to strengthen the handwriting process and written output for some. Finally, if you can stand it, there are a range of balance boards and rocking see-saws that students with hyperactivity and attention issues do well on while listening to instructions or stories. This constant, gentle movement helps keep them engaged for longer.

Self-monitoring techniques

Self-monitoring is an easy method to establish and monitor the frequency of particular behaviors (Reid & Harris 1993; Rankin & Reid 1995; Reid 1996). Researchers have determined that the very act of self-monitoring has a positive effect on a variety of behaviors within and outside the classroom (Kanfer 1988, 1991). The process of assessing and recording their behavior acts as a cue and helps individuals make a stronger link between their behavior and what is happening around them. The advantages of self-monitoring are the immediacy of feedback, the scope for students to select the target behavior, the motivation it delivers and the promotion of communication about behavior.

A simple self-monitoring plan

Give the student this recording form and ask them to record each time a specified behavior occurs (calling out, crying, rocking on their chair, talking in quiet times, getting angry, forgetting, being last, being first and so on) The very act of recording and keeping track of one specified behavior will often, without any other intervention, reduce how often the behavior occurs (Graham, Harris & Reid 1992). You may wish to consider attaching incentives for recording, monitoring and discussing the behavior.

 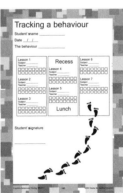

Self-monitoring Jamie's compliance

Jamie, a ten-year-old diagnosed with Asperger Syndrome, Learning Disabilities and ADHD, agreed to fill in a tracking behavior form each time he needed to stop an activity and move to another. His teacher wanted to improve his compliance during transition periods. At these times he, just like the other students, was expected to stop the activity, pack up and move to another activity. Under the new plan his teacher would ask the class to pack up, and at this time Jamie colored a square in green and was expected to pack up. In the past he usually chose to continue what he was doing, and it took half a dozen prompts over ten minutes to get him to pack up and move to the new

Cognitive Behavioral Training

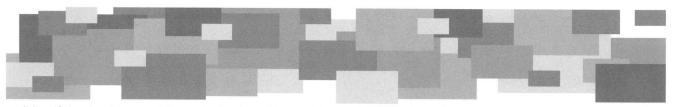

activity. If Jamie chose not to make the transition within an agreed minute he would color the next square on the form in red. By recess, lunch, or at the end of the day, he had a running record of red and green colored boxes making his level of transition success unmistakable. Reinforcement was not offered as the aim was to simply allow Jamie to keep track of how many times in a day he was able to do it as well as expected. This program ran for half a term and was successful in establishing new habits and raising Jamie's awareness.

Self-monitoring trips to the restroom

An idea to reduce the frequency of bathroom breaks is to issue the more dependent students with three, four or five bathroom tickets per week. They need to hand over a ticket each time they decide to go. Knowing they have to ration their visits motivates students to think just how necessary a visit to the bathroom is, and is an incentive to fit breaks into recess and lunch periods. One clever teacher attached a token value to each ticket remaining. Friday afternoon they could be cashed in for a predetermined item.

Tracking behavior with Happy-faces

Discuss with a student, a group of students or the entire class a particular behavior you want to see more of. Explain that each time you see it, you'll stamp their blank Happy-face card with a Happy-face stamp. Contact the card to their desk. Once the Happy-face card is filled, and they have a Happy-face family, it's time for the student to, collect a prize or select a story or a game as positive reinforcement. Ideas like this are simple and astoundingly effective. They let students know the teacher is on their side, and can stay on their side as they help get rid of old habits not working for them.

Case study ☞

Tracking behavior with 'thumbs-up, thumbs-down'

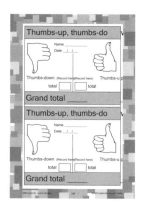

'Recently I've made some progress with three boys in my class who have had a habit of calling out without raising their hands. They find it so hard to wait to be asked. I wanted something that would immediately remind them they had not followed this basic classroom rule. I wanted something each child could see and monitor themselves; something simple, immediate and less intrusive.

The three boys were each given a score card which was contacted to their desk. We discussed why I needed to use this and how it would work. The score cards have a thumbs-up side (positive) and a thumbs-down side (negative) and if they impulsively called out I'd give whoever called out a thumbs-down sign. This meant they recorded a stroke on the thumbs-down side of their score card. When they put up a hand and made a positive contribution I'd give the thumbs-up sign and a stroke would be registered on the thumbs-up side of their score card. In this way they achieved immediate reinforcement for their behavior with a minimum of interruption to the lesson.

All three boys responded well to the thumbs-up, thumbs-down score cards. An unexpected incentive to do well came in the form of a small element of competition which emerged between the boys. At the end of each day I'd

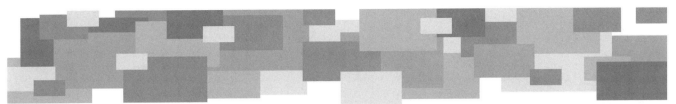

check their scores. Negatives cancelled out positives, so whatever they were left with was added as bonus points to class teams. We used the thumbs-up, thumbs-down score cards consistently for four weeks and stopped about a term ago. The effect has been lasting as all three continue to try to put their hands up and contribute positively. The score card system was worth the extra time I spent each day monitoring it, and now that it's been used and accepted we could always return to it if the old behaviors re-emerged, or a new challenge emerged.' (Jeremy, Waldorf School, Mt Barker)

A variation to thumbs-up, thumbs-down

 Case study

After collecting baseline thumbs-up, thumbs-down data for a week John's teacher, Margo, arranged for John to earn a reward when more thumbs-up were achieved than thumbs-down. John, a quick-witted third grade student, had long been a victim of failing to get on with his work and interrupting in class. Despite being very bright, his ever-present distractible behaviors undermined his performance. John's parents and Margo proposed the purchase of a new computer game as a reward if John achieved specific targets. Prior to commencing, his father took him to the store and bought the computer game. He photographed John with his new purchase. The photograph was photocopied, enlarged and cut into twenty jigsaw pieces. These were handed to his teacher. Margo rewarded John with one jigsaw piece each day for the first two weeks when he achieved more thumbs-up than thumbs-down.

Over the next two weeks they decided the reward would only be available on three weekdays, but John would not be told which days these were. He was shown the sealed envelope where his teacher had recorded the reward days, ready to be revealed at the end of the week. She told John each day whether he had been successful or not, but did not disclose final outcomes until the fateful Friday afternoon. In the final two weeks only two days a week were nominated and placed in the envelope. Also assisting John's motivation was the knowledge that his computer program would not be available through any other means; not for his birthday or for Christmas. This was the only way he could achieve it, and how soon he held it was dependent on John stretching his self-management.

Tracking behavior with a student-monitoring system

This monitoring system is a helpful tool for parents, teachers and students alike. It provides a quick, systematic way to monitor how a student with attention issues, learning difficulties or behavioral problems is progressing each week at school. The system provides feedback on:

- how well the identified difficulties are being managed

- the student's behavioral, social and emotional functioning

- the student's weekly academic and work-output performance

- times when adjustments to treatments and interventions need to be considered.

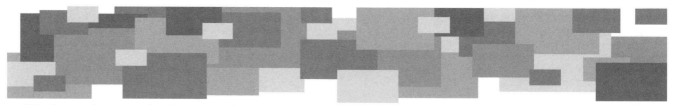

We know that the development of students is always enhanced when we regularly monitor their school performance and offer them more frequent levels of feedback.

This style of program usually works best with primary students who have a single teacher. However, it is useful for middle- and senior-school students when someone is willing to take a particular interest in the student and coordinate information provided by other determined staff. Completing the form only takes five minutes or so, and sharing it with the student on a regular weekly basis aids in reflective discussion, reinforces motivation, provides insights and allows new initiatives to be forged. The information collected through this system is designed to provide everyone involved with accurate baseline data, rather than being dependent on opinion, which can sometimes plummet when a hiccup occurs. The data helps everyone to make informed decisions about the effectiveness of management.

Using a reflective plan

The program begins with the student, teacher and parents selecting several behaviors worthy of reshaping. This plan is effective in changing many types of behaviors as the student receives feedback from their teacher about the behaviors they have agreed to target. The intention is to normalize behavior without the exercise becoming tedious or time-consuming. Success is reliant on engaging the student to see value in expanding their awareness, so maintaining a lightweight approach is best.

Jordan's reflective plan

Case study

Jordan had moved a long way from the emotionally charged behaviors he displayed in earlier years. Consistently well managed at home and school, he remained in touch with his promising intellectual abilities. Now, at thirteen, Jordan was aware of how far he had come, and the distance remaining. These days he was better able to control his low frustration point, volatile temper, excitability and hurtful comments. As Jordan moved into seventh grade he was influenced by his new teacher, Ms. Rita, to fine tune a few more behavioral changes. He knew this last year was a chance, in a familiar and supportive environment, to step up his self-management. Jordan, his parents and Ms. Rita independently identified several behaviors worth targeting.

His parents identified

- Starting and finishing. Jordan would start assignments, activities and chores, but often lost interest and did not complete them.
- Thinking more carefully about what he had to do. To think, 'Does this piece of work have to be done to the best of my ability?'.

His teacher identified

- Thinking before speaking. Jordan's frustration could make him look and sound rude, and this did not help him maintain friendship.
- Stopping to listen, look around and think. When Jordan got an idea it was full speed ahead, sometimes in the wrong direction! He needed to be more aware.

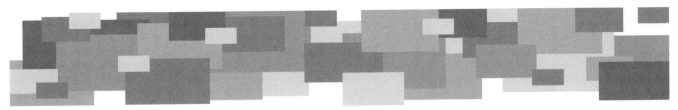

Jordan identified

- Using class work time more productively. 'I need to know that I'm not talking or wasting time when I should be working.'
- Keeping friends. 'I say dumb things that annoy them.'

Ms. Rita shared everyone's goals with Jordan. They discussed them and agreed to target four behaviors:

- maintaining friendships
- starting and finishing work more regularly
- catching more cues by noticing what others are doing
- using class time more effectively.

The program ran for ten weeks. It suited Jordan and Ms. Rita to meet on Tuesday and Thursday afternoons in the first five weeks. If all went well, conferencing would be reduced to once a week in the last five weeks. Conferencing was brief, ranging between one and five minutes, and beyond the act of scoring, conferencing provided a forum for Jordan to engage in dialogue to help sharpen his self-management. Ms. Rita printed the behaviors to be targeted on each of the weekly sheets.

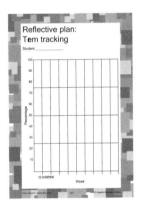

The scoring criteria used for each category was to compare Jordan's behavior to that of his peers. He could achieve 25/25 for behaving the same as most others in his class most of the time. Ms. Rita converted Jordan's results to a percentage and updated the graph at each conference. In this way there was something tangible to measure and compare progress.

Jordan and his teacher devised several cueing ideas to act as reminders.

- The teacher's hand on his shoulder as she walked past would mean, 'You look as though you need to settle.'
- Quietly saying, 'Go for it, Jordan' meant, 'You have been doing well, stick with it a little longer.'
- When Ms. Rita placed a yellow counter discreetly in Jordan's hand or on his desk, it signaled, 'Things are sliding. Do what you need to, but take action now.'
- A red counter meant, 'Get up and leave the classroom immediately. Come back when you can fix what's going wrong.'

As an incentive Jordan and his parents decided to purchase a new model car to build. They were expensive and he usually had to wait for his birthday or Christmas. Jordan went shopping with his parents and purchased a model of his choice. They negotiated that if by the tenth week he scored 75% or better the model car was his!

A reflective plan for Tony to reinvent himself

Case study

Tony blurted out his school worries. 'I want to leave my school. No-one listens to me. I get harassed. I get called fat. I get teased. They never stop. The more they tease, the more I hit back. The more I hit back, the more they tease. It's hopeless.'

Tony was seen by his peers as unpredictable and reactive. In earlier years he would barge into groups of children, disrupting their play. Once checked or criticized he would explode. He found it difficult to be patient, to accept the opinions of others and take turns. For a long time he needed to be guided by teachers in play situations. In the classroom his behaviors lurched between work-avoidance and attention-seeking, pushing, poking or knocking children and their work as he moved about. Increasingly, Tony felt distressed and isolated by his learning difficulty in combination with his highly active, boisterous, egocentric nature. Undeniably, Tony had been high-maintenance for teachers and students over the past six years. In addition to his behaviors, staff had weathered a barrage of complaints from the parents of other students about his demanding behaviors. The school had done well, but despite improvements, years of difficult behaviors had left teachers, classmates and parents exhausted. The teaching staff was now more inclined to speak in negative terms, and students tended to exclude him and employ sophisticated niggling forms of harassment to wind Tony up.

The tide had to be turned. Tony's reputation had gathered momentum and now impeded further progress. Finding success in this environment would be difficult. Tony and his parents were sensibly counseled and assisted by the Principal to find another school. In hindsight it was a wise decision. Tony realized his part in this. He knew that to make school work for himself in a new situation he needed to make changes.

Following is an excerpt of a letter and checklist sent to Tony.

Dear Tony,

I enjoyed our sessions. Here's the checklist we worked out together to reinvent yourself at your new school. Remember, it's just a reminder to keep you on track. It's easy to do, and should only take a few moments to fill out on Monday and Wednesday afternoons for the first three weeks of school. Score yourself out of ten. Ten would show you are doing really well, but a score of four or five might show some warning signs. If you are rating yourself at four or five I want you to talk to Mom or Dad, to your teacher or call me right away. This should give you a chance to think about how things are going. And there will be other success signs too. Like when friends ask you to join in. When that begins to happen, you know it is working.

You are right. It is up to you to get off on the right foot, and it is up to you to get the relationship with your teacher right. Think about what is important to her and what she wants from you. What you do over the first three weeks will set you up for the rest of the year. Work yourself into a groove early and you are likely to stay that way.

I have included a spare checklist you might like to give to your new teacher. She can fill out hers and compare her thoughts with yours!

I think you will do okay because you have been through some tough times at your old school and understand that your old behaviors caused a lot of the trouble. The time is right to reinvent yourself. Added to this, you know that I've spoken to your teacher, and she's happy to support you.

From your friend,

Mark

Techniques to improve schoolyard success

Structuring lunchtime troubles away

A useful idea is to structure part of lunchtime play, especially the last fifteen minutes. This is when the easily overloaded and overexcited children unravel. Structure can take many forms, and most prized are the low-maintenance schemes. Structures which are easy to implement and run are more likely to remain a permanent support. Include the student in building the strategy and share the reason for developing this mechanism. Begin generating ideas together and establishing guidelines. What do you think they could do? What would they like to do? Might it be wise to include a stabilizing friend? Where might this happen? It may be as easy as permanently reserving the computer at this time, or scheduling them to help in the office or to water the indoor plants throughout the school. The possibilities are endless. The critical concept is to provide the student with a purposeful direction away from the turmoil of free play as their emotional tolerance begins to wane.

A playground reminder

Case study

Stephanie talked a lot, but at recess and lunchtime when she became excited her talking exploded and drove her domineering behavior to excessive heights. Stephanie was good natured, and from her viewpoint wanted the games to go well. But over-excitability resulted in endless disagreements with her second grade friends. The friends were reaching a point where they were starting to tire of her company. It was Stephanie who chose the games, ran them, told others what to do, made the rules and determined who was in and out. Often tears and resentment were the fruit of lunchtime play.

Her principal came up with a novel idea to help stretch Stephanie's awareness. She spent time talking with Stephanie about her playtime problems. Stephanie adored Mr. Hallett, everyone did, and even though Stephanie was young she was able to understand her play problem. Pat implemented a system where, for several weeks, each time Stephanie went to lunch play she would visit him. He would staple a play message to Stephanie's shirt. She would attach it under her jumper or on the inside of her pocket so no-one could see it. Together they constructed a few messages that might help Stephanie. He encouraged Stephanie to secretly rub her fingers over the piece of paper during playtime. Rubbing her fingers over the note reminded Stephanie of the 'daily play message'. Stephanie knew the goal was to make playtimes happier for everyone.

Cognitive Behavioral Training

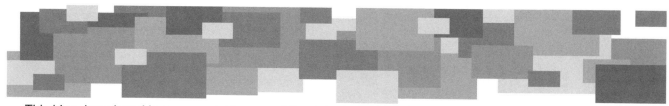

This idea, introduced in an acceptable way, at the right time, helped to reshape Stephanie's playtime behavior. It didn't turn Stephanie into a perfect playmate because she had a natural, tricky exuberance to contain. However, the plan provided Stephanie with an opportunity to make distinct small changes.

Frank's playground monitoring card

Frank was a tall, blonde, well-built sixth grade student. His friendly nature was acknowledged by many, but students often reported difficulties when playing with him: bullying and sudden angry outbursts regularly spoiled playtimes. Frank's home life was exacting, as his father, also tall and powerfully built, hadn't worked for two years following a work injury. Dad's focus had closed in on the family, and although well intentioned, he was controlling and domineering. He expected each member of the household to perform, and had set up routines and expectations that mirrored his regimented attitude. Frank's teachers believed his difficulties were exaggerated by the immense pressure he was under at home, as over the past year or so Frank had become a louder, more dominant figure in the schoolyard. As much as Frank's friends were upset by his behavior, so was Frank. His teacher decided to intervene, and set up, in consultation with Frank and the yard duty teachers, a system to help him monitor his yard behavior more closely.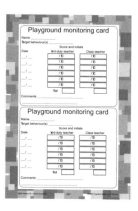

His teacher took these proactive steps:

- He and Frank discussed the repeated lunchtime difficulties. Frank acknowledged they were persistent, although he believed it wasn't always his fault. His teacher accepted this, but explained that Frank was mostly at the center of things. They discussed and recorded the sorts of behaviors that had to stop.

- His teacher introduced the idea of a behavior monitoring card. During lunchtime the on-duty teacher would keep an eye on Frank as he tried to make changes to the way he played and reacted.

- At the end of lunch he would bring his card to the on-duty teacher, receive a score out of ten and brief verbal feedback. On returning to class, Frank deposited his card on his teacher's desk, and she would score him later in the afternoon based on complaints, lack of complaints or feedback received from others.

- At the end of the week the scores were added, and when Frank's score leveled or exceeded the previous week's tally, he was entitled to a treat from the vending machine. Frank chose ice-cream, no matter what the weather!

- His teacher suggested he wear a red shoelace in one of his shoes as a reminder to think before blurting out his first reaction at play. Frank liked the idea as he thought the one red shoelace looked good.

At the end of two terms, Frank's principal created a graduation certificate, congratulating Frank for overcoming his schoolyard problems. Frank's home pressures continued; however, this example illustrates how rules and expectations for school can, on occasions, work independently from home difficulties.

Peer mediation and peer counseling

Peer mediation is another way of solving conflicts between students that occur at recess break and lunch. The peer mediation program promotes the idea that conflicts can be managed by talking and negotiating. All peer mediators are involved in a training program to learn how to promote:

- win-win conflict resolution skills

- decision and choice-making skills

- leadership skills

- listening and speaking skills

- the skill to present a fair argument

- the culture of resolution rather than punishment.

Peer mediation actively discourages victim and aggressor behavior. At playtimes students choose to ask a mediator for help. The trained mediator will ask students in conflict to agree to the responsibilities of negotiating: no put downs, be honest and to think of solutions to the conflict. While peer mediation is an excellent vehicle for students to offer community service to their school, it is also extraordinarily useful to involve students known to have their own social and conflict resolution difficulties. The very act of supporting others and consistently following the principles of the program helps to reinforce and reinforce their own thinking.

Thinking benches and spaces

Whether it is a specially colored bench in the playground, or a place in the classroom, a number of schools are picking up on the idea of having thinking seats or spaces. These spaces give students the opportunity to calm down and think about what is likely to happen if their current behaviors continue. Students are trained to use them proactively, or when directed by a teacher to take some time out, rather than finding themselves in trouble because they behaved unthinkingly.

Improving schoolyard cooperation

Repeatedly, one of the most effective ways to positively influence schoolyard behavior is to increase the presence of teachers engaging and having fun with students: a teacher or two to kick the football, to play basketball or to umpire or score a match, or a teacher who walks the yard giving sweets away to students engaged in positive communication. These extraordinarily simple approaches have a profound effect on the playground atmosphere. The presence of the teachers acts as an external reminder to students about what is expected, and sets up opportunities to develop special rapport with students who especially need it.

Blackline masters

- Access card
- Fact finding
- School update
- The snapshot
- Think strip
- Tracking a behavior 1
- Tracking a behavior 2
- Tracking a behavior 3
- Happy-face family
- Thumbs-up, thumbs-down
- Universal student-monitoring system
- Self-awareness strengthening
- Reflective plan: Term tracking
- Checkpoints for a successful start
- Checkpoints for a successful start (blank)
- Playground reminders
- Playground monitoring card

Access card

This is to approve

....

to have the following considerations.
Please note the highlighted areas,
which require specific consideration.

Spelling	Use of electronic handheld spell checker or access to a computer to check spelling. Marking the student's work primarily on knowledge and content, and not marking it down for poor spelling.
Sequencing	Follow-up verbal instructions and step-by-step instructions in written form.
Reading	Exemption from reading aloud in class. They experience difficulty with decoding, fluency and comprehension. Their understanding will need to be monitored. This student may require easier texts, alternatives to text and a reader in tests and examinations.
Writing	Assistance with organizational strategies for planning a piece of writing. Please mark quality of handwriting separately from ideas and understanding. Requires more time to write and more time to copy from board. Implement alternatives to copying from the board.
Timed tests	Exclusion from 'timed' situations which present a higher degree of stress (e.g. timed math quizzes, mental math, speed and accuracy, dictation or on-the-spot spelling tests). Negotiate an alternative.
Math	Access to a multiplication-tables sheet, a calculator and math formulas in lessons and in test situations.
Organization	Sensitive supervision of Assignment book. Check for student's understanding and be sure that they have correct items to complete homework.

Student ....

Home group teacher ....

This card is to be placed in the back of your assignment book. Show it to all subject teachers at the beginning of each semester. Please show it to teachers if you feel they need to be reminded of your negotiated needs.

Parent/Caregiver consent: I, _____ (please print), approve of this sheet being in _____'s assignment book.

Signed ....   Date ....

Subject	Teacher	Semester 1	Semester 2

Fact-finding

Your child's name

....

This is the beginning of my relationship with your family so I'm excited to find out about your child. I hope you will be able to spend a few minutes filling in these questions. This will help me to get to know your child more quickly.

1. Tell me about your child's strengths.

2. What are the challenging areas facing your child?

3. Does your child have a learning difficulty, a concentration problem or behavioral issues?

4. What challenges does your child believe they have?

5. What assessments have been done (if any)?

6. What prompted these?

7. What were the outcomes?

Fact-finding (cont.)

8. Are these on file here at school?

9. What supports, interventions and resources have helped in the past at school?

10. What supports, interventions and resources have helped in the past outside school?

11. Does your child take any medications I should be aware of? Can you explain why?

12. What do you do at home to support your child's learning?

13. What can I do in the classroom to best help your child? Be as specific as you wish.

14. What priorities you would like me to work on?

15. What interests does your child have outside school?

Fact-finding (cont.)

16. What would they say are the 'best things' about school for them?

17. Who are their trusted friends at school?

18. Do they enjoy stable, generally happy friendships?

19. Who are the children they worry about at school?

20. Have there been problems with teasing, bullying or harassment in the past?

21. Tell me about your child's achievements, successes or highlights in life.

22. What kind of support are you able to offer at school or within the classroom?

   - Listening to reading.
   - Learning assistance for children with learning needs.
   - Mentoring.
   - Providing resources such as paper, art and craft materials.
   - Are you in a position to be a guest speaker at school, or to help arrange an excursion to your workplace?

School update

Name _____

During the week, find a few minutes to spend with Mom or Dad to fill out this update. It's a chance for you to think about how school is working out for you. Your answers will help me to understand what makes you happy and alert me to things that could be worrying you. Together, we should be able to improve your time at school because everyone learns best when they are feeling happy.

• Are you happy working in the classroom?

• Do you usually have someone to play with at recess and lunchtime?

• What do you usually do at recess and lunchtime?

• Who have been your best friends this term?

• Are you happy about coming to school most days?

• What are the sorts of things you have enjoyed over the last term?

• What things have you not liked, or have upset you during the term?

• Is the classroom, or school, a safe place for you to be?

School update (cont.)

- Are you having problems at home, like getting your homework done or getting ready for school in the morning?

- Is there a special lesson or activity you would like to see at school?

- You know I want the classroom to be a great place. Do I smile enough and give the right signals that I feel happy about being here?

- Are you bullied at school?

- Is there anyone at school you worry about more than you should?

- Is there anyone in the room who interferes with your belongings?

- Give me one piece of advice that would help you feel even better at school next term.

- Each of us works best when we've got some personal goals. What are your goals at school at the moment?

- Do you have a personal goal you're aiming for at home?

The snapshot

The snapshot of you

Sometimes it's hard to know if you are acting the right way because it is easy to get carried away.

The snapshot is a great trick to help. Imagine there is a hidden camera nearby which constantly takes pictures of you and the people around you. Whenever you want, you can see the pictures the camera is taking.

THINK: 'Am I doing what I should be in the picture?'

THINK: 'Am I doing the same as the others?'

THINK: 'Am I behaving in a way that suits where I am?'

THINK: 'Am I talking and listening too?'

THINK: 'How much work have I done?

THINK: 'Am I in control of me?'

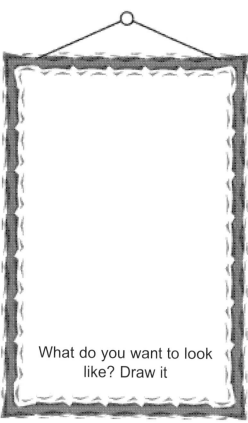

What do you want to look like? Draw it

Think strip

A THINK STRIP: How to think about it

| **I've got the feeling ...** it may be sad, angry, upset, mean, or excited | **1** Count | **2** Count | **3** Count | **4** Count | **5** Think ... whatever choice I make now will have a consequence |

A THINK STRIP: How to think about it

| **I've got the feeling ...** it may be sad, angry, upset, mean, or excited | **1** Count | **2** Count | **3** Count | **4** Count | **5** Think ... whatever choice I make now will have a consequence |

A THINK STRIP: How to think about it

| **I've got the feeling ...** it may be sad, angry, upset, mean, or excited | **1** Count | **2** Count | **3** Count | **4** Count | **5** Think ... whatever choice I make now will have a consequence |

A THINK STRIP: How to think about it

| **I've got the feeling ...** it may be sad, angry, upset, mean, or excited | **1** Count | **2** Count | **3** Count | **4** Count | **5** Think ... whatever choice I make now will have a consequence |

Tracking a behavior

Student's name _____

Date _____/_____/_____

The behavior _____

Lesson 1

Subject _____ Teacher _____

☐☐☐☐☐☐☐☐☐☐☐☐☐☐

Lesson 2

Subject _____ Teacher _____

☐☐☐☐☐☐☐☐☐☐☐☐☐☐

Lesson 3

Subject _____ Teacher _____

☐☐☐☐☐☐☐☐☐☐☐☐☐☐

Lesson 4

Subject _____ Teacher _____

☐☐☐☐☐☐☐☐☐☐☐☐☐☐

Lesson 5

Subject _____ Teacher _____

☐☐☐☐☐☐☐☐☐☐☐☐☐☐

Lesson 6

Subject _____ Teacher _____

☐☐☐☐☐☐☐☐☐☐☐☐☐☐

Lesson 7

Subject _____ Teacher _____

☐☐☐☐☐☐☐☐☐☐☐☐☐☐

Student's signature: _____

Tracking a behavior

Student's name _____

Date ____/____/____

The behavior _____

Lesson 1
Subject _____
Teacher _____

☐☐☐☐☐☐☐☐
☐☐☐☐☐☐☐☐

Lesson 2
Subject _____
Teacher _____

☐☐☐☐☐☐☐☐
☐☐☐☐☐☐☐☐

Lesson 3
Subject _____
Teacher _____

☐☐☐☐☐☐☐☐
☐☐☐☐☐☐☐☐

Recess

Lesson 4
Subject _____
Teacher _____

☐☐☐☐☐☐☐☐
☐☐☐☐☐☐☐☐

Lesson 5
Subject _____
Teacher _____

☐☐☐☐☐☐☐☐
☐☐☐☐☐☐☐☐

Lunch

Lesson 6
Subject _____
Teacher _____

☐☐☐☐☐☐☐☐
☐☐☐☐☐☐☐☐

Lesson 7
Subject _____
Teacher _____

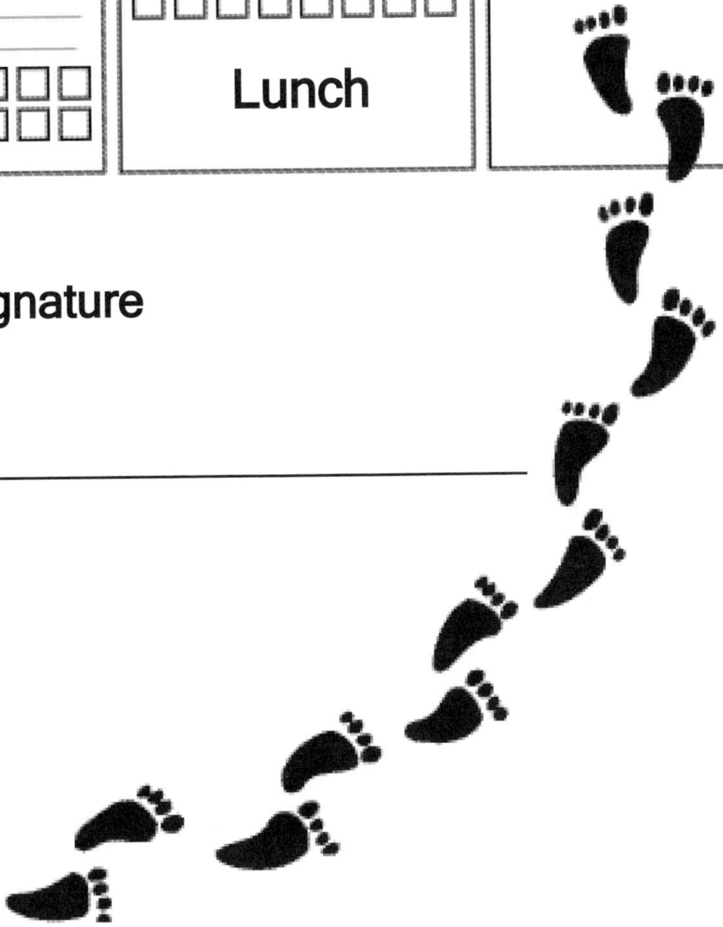

☐☐☐☐☐☐☐☐
☐☐☐☐☐☐☐☐

Student's signature

_____

Tracking a behavior

Student's name _____

Date _____/_____/_____

The behavior _____

Mon ____	Tue ____	Wed ____	Thurs ____	Fri ____

Tally ____   Tally ____   Tally ____   Tally ____   Tally ____

Happy-face family

The behavior I am looking for is _____

Fill the card up with the Happy-face family. Each time I see the new behavior I'll add a Happy face to your chart. Once the chart is full you can, collect a prize or choose a story or a game.

Thumbs-up, thumbs-down

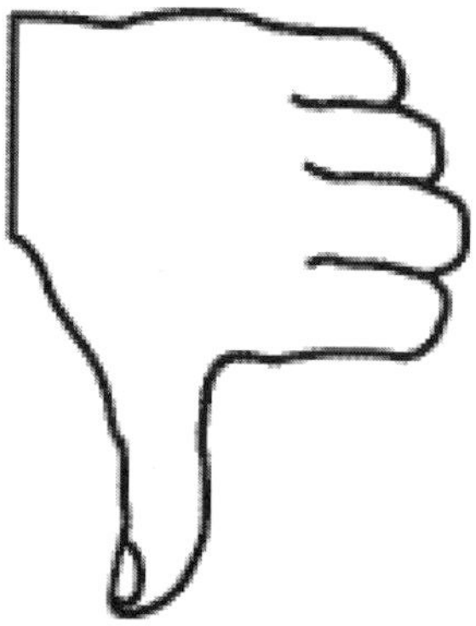

Name _____

Date _____/_____/_____

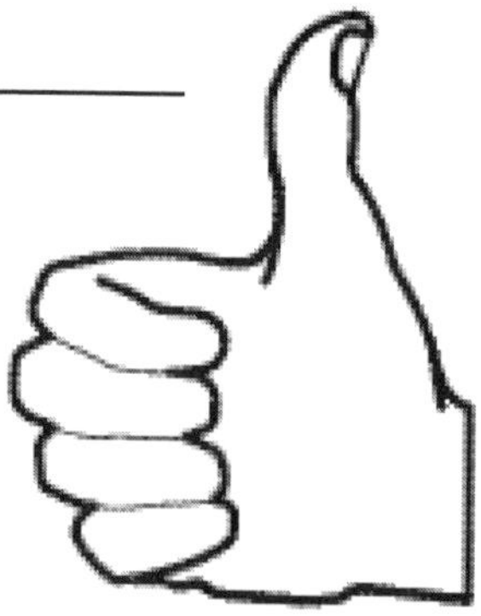

Thumbs-down (Record here)

(Record here) **Thumbs-up**

total [ ]

[ ] total

Grand total _____

Thumbs-up, thumbs-down

Name _____

Date _____/_____/_____

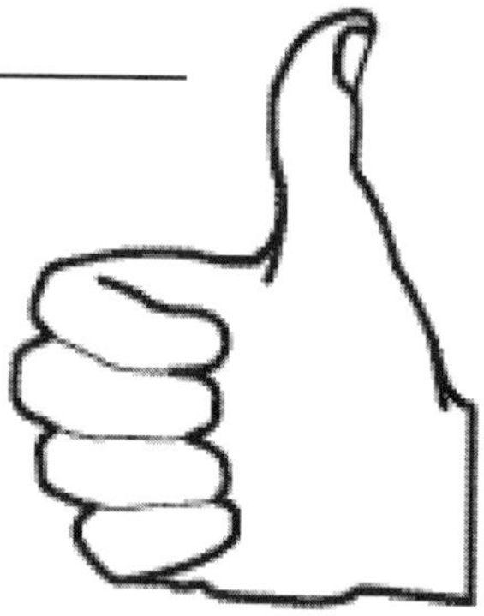

Thumbs-down (Record here)

(Record here) **Thumbs-up**

total [ ]

[ ] total

Grand total _____

Universal student-montoring system

Student _____

Date _____/_____/_____

Teacher _____

Please answer the items below based on your observations of this student or feedback you have received during the past week.

	Not at all	A little	Pretty much	Very much
Fidgets or squirms in seat	0	1	2	3
Has difficulty remaining seated	0	1	2	3
Is disrespectful to teacher	0	1	2	3
Talks too much	0	1	2	3
Interrupts	0	1	2	3
Is argumentative/talks back	0	1	2	3
Is easily distracted	0	1	2	3
Fails to finish work	0	1	2	3
Has trouble maintaining attention	0	1	2	3
Presents careless/messy work	0	1	2	3
Does not seem to listen when spoken to	0	1	2	3
Has difficulty following directions	0	1	2	3

Universal student-montoring system (cont.)

Note: For the next 3 items, higher scores indicate better functioning by the student.

	Not at all	A little	Pretty much	Very much
Follows class rules	0	1	2	3
Gets along with peers	0	1	2	3
Seems happy and in good mood	0	1	2	3

Is the student better in the morning or the afternoon?   Which one? _____

Place an 'X' on the line below to indicate the percentage of work the student completed in class during the past week:

0   10   20   30   40   50   60   70   80   90   100

The quality of work completed by the student this week was: _____

very poor   poor   satisfactory   good   very good

If the quality of work varied significantly between subjects, please indicate:

Did this student hand in all assigned work? This <u>includes homework</u> requirements. Specify the assignments that were missing:

Please include any other comments or observations you believe are important:

Based on the information collected, do you believe we should be considering further adjustments or interventions?

Self-awareness strengthening

A reflective plan

Structuring a reflective approach helps students to think about the elements in their day-to-day life that they find elusive.

Student: _____

Year level: _____

Program commencement date: _____/_____/_____

Proposed end of program: _____/_____/_____

Conference times: _____

Behaviors to be targeted, week _____

	Tuesday	Thursday
	/25	/25
	/25	/25
	/25	/25
	/25	/25

Total score achieved: /100 /100

Average achieved for week # _____ [____] %

Student's comment: _____
_____

Teacher's comment: _____
_____

Reflective plan: Term tracking

Student _____

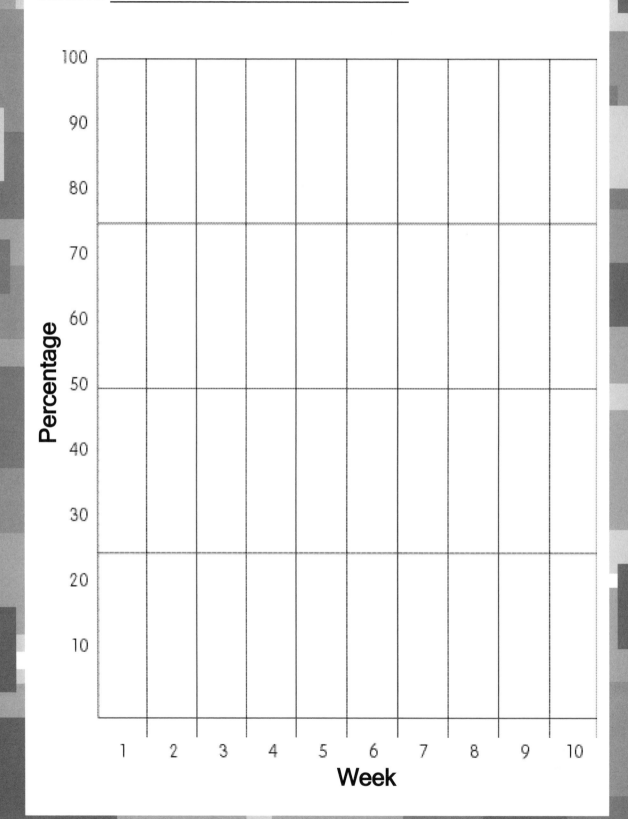

Checkpoints for a successful start

How well are you doing? Rate yourself by circling a number between 1 and 10: 1 = not at all, 10 = 100% of the time.

1. Making **friends** and fitting in to a group.

Wednesday
1 2 3 4 5 6 7 8 9 10
Friday
1 2 3 4 5 6 7 8 9 10

2. Making friends with your teacher. **Think**, what is it you are doing?

Wednesday
1 2 3 4 5 6 7 8 9 10
Friday
1 2 3 4 5 6 7 8 9 10

3. When it's time to **listen** in class, are you are listening? Remember to fold your arms and keep eye contact.

Wednesday
1 2 3 4 5 6 7 8 9 10
Friday
1 2 3 4 5 6 7 8 9 10

4. Finishing your **homework**. It doesn't need to be perfect, it just needs to be done!

Wednesday
1 2 3 4 5 6 7 8 9 10
Friday
1 2 3 4 5 6 7 8 9 10

5. Are you keeping a **balance** between how much you speak and listen?

Wednesday
1 2 3 4 5 6 7 8 9 10
Friday
1 2 3 4 5 6 7 8 9 10

6. Is your teacher speaking to you about your **behavior** no more than he/she does to most others?

Wednesday
1 2 3 4 5 6 7 8 9 10
Friday
1 2 3 4 5 6 7 8 9 10

Checkpoints for a successful start

How well are you doing? Rate yourself by circling a number between 1 and 10: 1 = not at all, 10 = 100% of the time.

1. _____
   _____
   _____

Wednesday
  1 2 3 4 5 6 7 8 9 10
Friday
  1 2 3 4 5 6 7 8 9 10

2. _____
   _____
   _____

Wednesday
  1 2 3 4 5 6 7 8 9 10
Friday
  1 2 3 4 5 6 7 8 9 10

3. _____
   _____
   _____

Wednesday
  1 2 3 4 5 6 7 8 9 10
Friday
  1 2 3 4 5 6 7 8 9 10

4. _____
   _____
   _____

Wednesday
  1 2 3 4 5 6 7 8 9 10
Friday
  1 2 3 4 5 6 7 8 9 10

5. _____
   _____
   _____

Wednesday
  1 2 3 4 5 6 7 8 9 10
Friday
  1 2 3 4 5 6 7 8 9 10

6. _____
   _____
   _____

Wednesday
  1 2 3 4 5 6 7 8 9 10
Friday
  1 2 3 4 5 6 7 8 9 10

Playground reminders

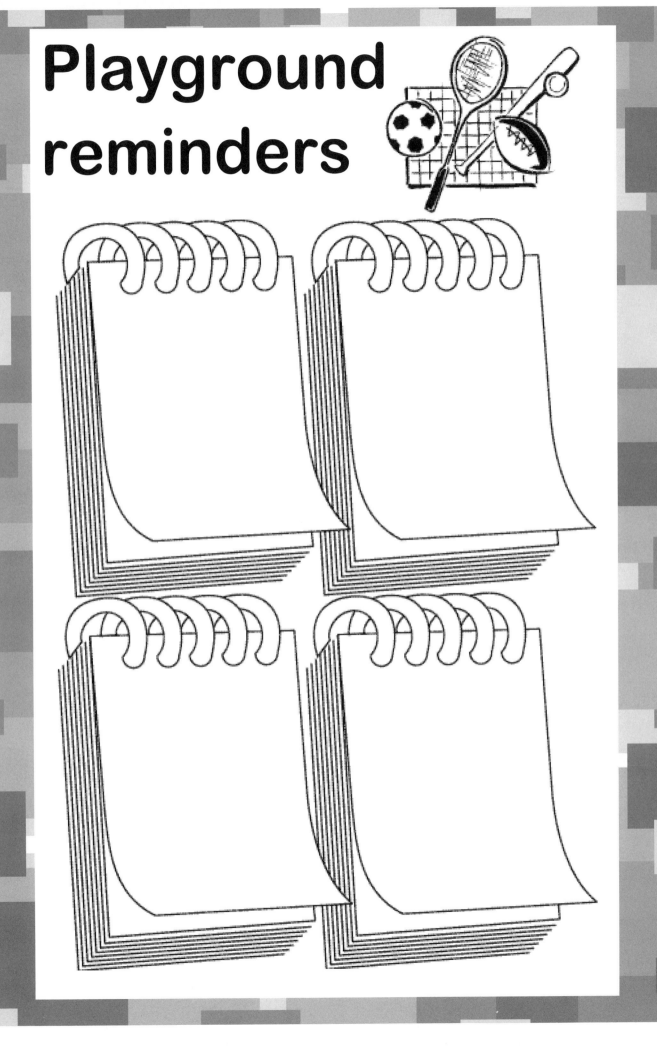

Playground monitoring card

Name _____

Target behavior(s) _____

Score and initials

Date	On-duty teacher	Class teacher
____ / ____	/10	/10
____ / ____	/10	/10
____ / ____	/10	/10
____ / ____	/10	/10
____ / ____	/10	/10
	/10	/10
	Total	

Comments _____

_____

Playground monitoring card

Name _____

Target behavior(s) _____

Score and initials

Date	On-duty teacher	Class teacher
____ / ____	/10	/10
____ / ____	/10	/10
____ / ____	/10	/10
____ / ____	/10	/10
____ / ____	/10	/10
	/10	/10
	Total	

Comments _____

_____

Chapter 6
Developing organization

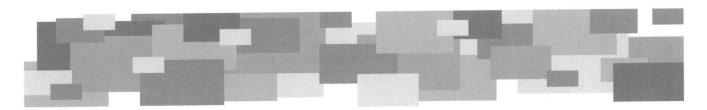

Can organizational ability be developed?

One of the prerequisites for success at school, at home, in fact anywhere, is an individual's capacity to be organized. How often do parents and teachers say 'He can't get organized to save himself', 'She's got a memory like a sieve', 'He loses everything!'.

Occasionally, adults become so frustrated with a child's poor memory that they create situations, sometimes unwittingly, which set them up to fail. In one case, a father would regularly ask his twelve-year-old son, with diagnosed significant memory difficulties, to go to the local shopping center to buy four or five items without taking a list. Predictably, his son usually forgot an item. On his return this young teenager became the victim of teasing, and was reminded how unreliable he was at remembering or being organized.

Then, there was the tactic of a well-meaning, but inexperienced teacher. In a bid to upgrade the organizational capacities and readiness of his students, he grouped his class into five teams and created competitive situations where points were awarded to the fastest organized team. Not surprisingly, one of the teams consistently came in last due to the persistent failings of a particular student. This student had a documented history of severe attention and working memory difficulties. Invariably, when under pressure, his remembering and organizational skills further deteriorated. Increasingly, he felt embarrassed and decided to withdraw from this game that he had to lose. His embarrassment was not seen by his teacher, but instead interpreted as noncompliance. The boy was dutifully reprimanded.

This was not a poor teacher, nor was the previous example an illustration of a poor parent; more to the point, they are vivid reminders that it is remarkably easy to overlook, or not really grasp, the root cause of organizational difficulties. These children, and numerous others with organizational problems, display forgetfulness, distractibility, confusion, negative learning attitudes, avoidance and time-wasting. They lose belongings (especially schoolwork and homework) and have a poor sense of time, planning and sequencing. They lack the individual building blocks responsible for higher-order organizational skills. Of course without these primary components, they cannot look, feel or be well organized. So often their disorganized appearance reflects their genuinely disorganized thinking.

Why is this? For some, it is in part their style, the evolution of poor habits and the absence of arresting interventions. For others, their memory inconsistency is associated to a specific learning difficulty (such as Dyslexia), attention difficulty (such as ADD or ADHD) or chronic illness. Memory weakness also features in students with developmental immaturity, low motivation, auditory processing weaknesses, poor listening skills, depression and anxiety. For others, disorganization is the product of underlying pervasive personality issues (such as Asperger Syndrome or Autism) as they find it remarkably difficult to grasp what is expected in varying situations.

As parents and teachers, we have a clear choice. We can ignore the basis of their difficulty, which will ensure they continue to trip over and fail our imposed organizational expectations. Or, we can accept that independent organization is a higher-order skill, being complex and many faceted. If we wish to be a positive, progressive force in a child's life, we need to embrace methodologies, many of them ever so simple, to strengthen their independent organizational repertoire (Custer et al. 1990).

Cognitive Behavioral Training

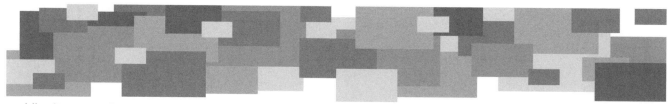

Like it or not, these students have little choice but to remain dependent, in varying degrees, on our influence, whether we use:

- routines
- habits
- accountability and natural consequences
- post-it stickers with reminders
- key words
- countdowns
- charts
- pictures
- a look
- a smile
- checklists
- calendars
- daily or weekly timetables
- the same repetitive reminding joke again
- a sound
- a touch
- a gesture
- notes
- cue cards.

Anything that helps to keep the distractible, difficult to engage or easily overloaded mind to sort priorities and stay with the task (Williams 2003). Their delayed internal organizational skills can be expanded providing we keep them in constant rehearsal. We are required to set up expectations and systems that nudge change.

Student organization begins with ours

Building group cohesion with class rules

It's important to create a class identity. At the beginning of the year, as relationships are being formed, contrive a class identity. It might be as ordinary as 'Room 4M', but it's an identity everybody in that room shares. While there are variations on this approach, a popular idea is to arrange a photo of the class and yourself, and position it on the classroom door with the class name alongside it. These are the members of 'Room 4M'.

Next, provide a large robust scrapbook. Take lots of photographs and encourage students to add drawings and comments day-by-day, week-by-week, to help reinforce class connections. The electronic version of this is to create a class webpage, and

continue to build to it throughout the year. Keep in mind that class projects also help to unite students. Consider developing a class garden, fundraising, running class plays, establishing a class link with another school, sponsoring a child, regularly visiting a retirement home, or preparing for a class barbecue, excursion or camp.

Develop rules and expectations with students at the start of the school year. This is also an investment in constructing optimal learning conditions and social harmony. Student involvement in this process helps to secure their understanding, ownership and compliance. Begin by giving students general information about classroom goals, and lead them to establish rules, guidelines and procedures. Precise positive statements are best, for example, *One person speaks at a time in group discussions.* Other rules can be blanket rules, such as, *Always follow the teacher's directions immediately.* Too many rules weaken their impact.

Next determine ways to positively reinforce them, and ask the group to work out negative reinforcers (consequences) to be attached to rules that are not followed. A popular idea is to create a large poster linking the agreed rules to positive and negative reinforcers. Have each member of the class sign off on the poster showing their acceptance of the rules.

In addition, a small booklet displaying the rules can be produced for each child. Start it with an attractive cover titled *Our Class Rules* and provide spaces for the student's name, their photograph or hand-drawn picture, class identification and teacher's name ready to be filled in. Each page presents a class rule, positively framed, with a bordered area for the student to complete a picture that complements the rule.

Frequently discuss and review the rules in order to make them live and become an integral social part of the classroom. Children are reassured by knowing what to expect for keeping and breaking rules. This scaffolding is important for students who have difficulty with concentration and self-control. These students are especially dependent on prompts, reminders and clear rules. Always check behavior that breaks class rules, but work primarily in the context of using positive reinforcement. As obvious as it is, it is important to appear calm and in control when managing consequences for noncompliance or difficult behavior. This reassures those who are feeling out of control that someone knows what they are doing! It is fine to state an opinion; keep it brief though, as spending too long on a negative event gives it far more power than it deserves.

A badge to reinforce class rules

'Once our class rules are decided we select the three most valuable rules. They might be: put your hand up when you want to speak, be kind to others and care for people's belongings. During our first few art lessons, the children create designs that will eventually become three badges to wear. Each design depicts one of the rules. The badge-making machine easily transforms the designs to vibrant, ready-to-go badges. Over the next three weeks, as a way to focus attention on expectations, one of the badges is worn each week. After three weeks the children wear all three badges for a week to show they understand these rules. It is not fail-proof, but does support the students who rely on external structures and reminders to guide their behavior. Often we wear the badges for the first few days when returning from holidays.'

Cognitive Behavioral Training

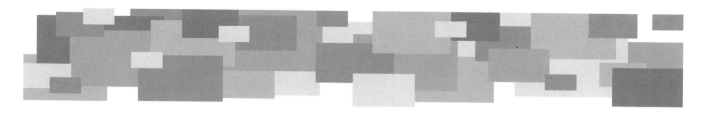

Expectations make a difference

'Like most teachers, at the beginning of the year I set class rules in partnership with the children. Our first rule is: *When you get to school, hang up your backpack on your hook. Take out your belongings and organize what you need. Then you can play.*

This simple expectation makes a world of difference. I find children running out to play in the morning saying, "Have you taken your books out your backpack?" They actively monitor each other. To begin with, during the first days of school, I give them a second chance. As soon as we are together I remind them of the rule, close my eyes, and give one minute for them to organize themselves. After the first few days there is a consequence for not remembering, and not listening to the advice of others.' (Bronnie, year-two teacher)

Teaching how to put your hand up

'When Laura got an idea she'd call out, and Laura was never short of an idea! As a way to curb her calling out, and forgetting to raise her hand, we traced our hands onto paper. Then we painted them, cut them out, and glued them back to back on a 30-centimeter piece of dowelling. Using heavy-duty tape each child made small pouches on the sides of their desks in which their multicolored hands could be kept.

Over the next few weeks, multicolored hands waved in the air whenever there was a question, an answer or a contribution to be made. This novel exaggeration of "raising your hand" set the tone and helped Laura follow the lead of others. After a week or so the children used their own hands again, but when somebody forgets and calls out, I take their decorated hand from the side of their desk and place it in their hands as a silent reminder.' (Mandy, fourth grade teacher)

You've got the Talking stick, so talk!

'I am not sure where this idea originated, but I've used it for a long time. At the beginning of each year we buy a large lightweight piece of timber, about 3 feet tall and approximately 3 inches in diameter (soft pine is great). I make quite a production about the significance of the talking stick, explaining that it will symbolize our class unity. Usually, we are able to get the timber carved by someone with a lathe. Then, we use permanent markers or a soldering iron to burn individual motifs and the names of each class member on to it. In any sort of group discussion, only the person holding the talking stick speaks. We tend not to use it in general lesson time, but reserve it for discussion, class meetings or when the children become excited about presenting their point of view. The talking stick is a physical reminder to wait.' (David, sixth grade teacher)

Introduce structures and routine

The first few weeks of school each year is a critical time to build the framework of class routine, systems and expectations. Structure means arranging conditions (the play and classroom environments) to give students the

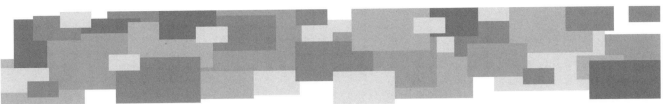

best opportunity to function predictably and successfully. Obvious, easy-to-follow systems allow students to operate proactively rather than reacting to what seems like a series of endless surprises.

Set up places where things belong, and encourage students to put their belongings in the same place every day:

- hats on the hat hook
- backpacks on the bag hook
- books in lockers
- library books in the class return box
- pencil cases on desks
- lunch orders in the lunch tray
- assignment books in the return box
- sports equipment in the sports bag.

Having a place for assignments and homework to be handed in is much better than assignments being placed on the teacher's desk.

Establish systems to manage the natural chaos, which, unaddressed, easily occurs within the hectic classroom environment. An ordered, clean and tidy room encourages a sense of calm and confidence for students and parents alike. Structuring should be seen as a basic survival technique. It sets the scene to tackle curriculum less encumbered by basic procedural issues. Develop extensive class-monitor systems and rotate them regularly so students are thoroughly connected to the systems and to one another.

Integrate timetabling and programming

Many poorly organized students struggle to retain and sequence information. They depend on prompts to jog their memory about when lessons occur, the materials required and what comes next. These organizationally vulnerable students rely on us, the adults, having a consistent routine.

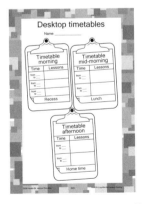

Organize a small morning, daily or weekly timetable that students can stick to their desk so they have a better idea about what is happening. Each morning, set up a routine so students expect to see a morning timetable with a list of basic requirements for each lesson. Take it a step further, and help students make their own timetables for after school in an effort to avoid the ugly 'homework blues'.

Cognitive Behavioral Training

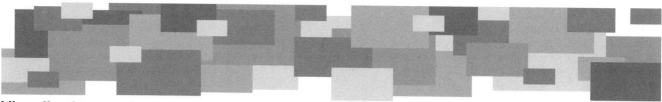

Visualize how a class activity will look

We know that high-performance sporting stars and athletes are trained to visualize a successful outcome moments before putting it into action. This rehearsal, no matter how brief, maximizes success. Similarly, moments spent beyond gathering and organizing physical resources for a lesson are value-added moments in preparation. How often do you visualize yourself beginning the lesson? How will you tune the class in? Where will you position students? What will you use to show how this new information integrates with what has already been covered? Do you imagine how you want the students to respond and how you want the lesson to progress? Does your mind's eye visualize how you will conclude the lesson? These essential preliminary steps can be overlooked in the bustle of school life.

The next crucial step is to help students visualize what they want for themselves in a lesson, from a particular topic or even from a homework session (Newton 2003). A starting point for students is to allow them to discuss and describe what they need to do, to explain when and where they intend to do it, and how they will need to look in order to achieve it.

Handing out new assignments

Reflect on how you present assignments to students. Is the assignment accompanied by a written task sheet? A task sheet ensures students have the opportunity to read and re-read to ascertain instructions. It also assists parents to understand the task, rather than having to rely on unreliable student recall. Consciously design the layout of the task sheet. Keep it uncluttered. Simplify the visual impact by limiting the content. It is common to see students overwhelmed by too much information and unnecessary educational jargon. The task sheet needs to contain:

- the topic

- the due date

- one or two interim review dates which allow the monitoring of progress. This also alerts parents that they will need to help plan their child's time.

- clear instructions about specific areas to be covered

- desired format

- expected length

- resources required (specific references and specific websites) and how they should be used.

As the assignment is handed to the class, insist each student write their name on the task sheet and supervise the gluing of these into a book or filing into the designated folder. At the same time, provide students with a checklist to help them keep track of what they need to do, and a review sheet they will fill out later when the project is handed up.

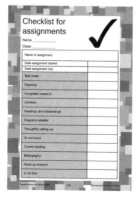
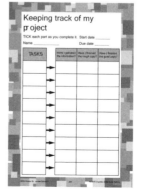
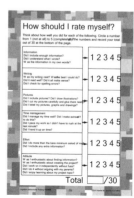

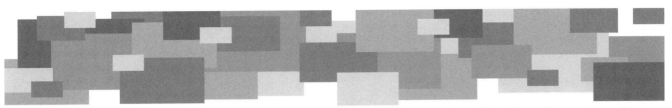

Having the review sheet early draws their attention to the types of skills and qualities they will need to achieve a successful outcome.

A light-hearted approach is to give the student three additional copies of the task sheet and organize them to place one in a 'spare' folder at the bottom of their drawer, one in a zip compartment in their school bag and give another to a friend for safe keeping! Finally, spend time discussing the new assignment and allow plenty of time for answering questions. Allow students to start the assignment midway through the lesson. This provides the opportunity to check in with those two or three students who need additional talk time to consolidate the organization of their thoughts. It helps them to know what they are doing.

Continuous assessment

Continuous assessment or mini-tests, have long been acknowledged as the best form of assessment for students with concentration, organizational and memory difficulties. Assess topics continuously, every few days or weekly. The more often students are exposed to short, low-stress test situations to review topics, the more confident they become in dealing with test preparation and their performance in test situations. Continuous assessment, used frequently, sustains student organization, planning and perseverance as small parcels of work are constantly reviewed and evaluated. Vary the approach between multiple-choice, short-answer, open-book, cloze-style, matching question and answer, take-home tests, essay-response and so on.

Well-structured continuous assessment allows students with memory-retrieval, processing, concentration and/or anxiety difficulties to:

- have more time in tests

- write on the test that more time was needed so the test may be scored differently

- complete mini-tests a day or two before a larger test to help over-structure the review process

- discreetly complete their unfinished test later in the day or the next day

- be presented with tests written in large, clear, easy-to-read fonts

You can also help them by having a test format that is logical to follow, and only examines work that has been covered - resist surprises! Concentrate on the basic core material first, so that if the core section is completed relatively well a pass can be achieved without needing to attempt extension questions.

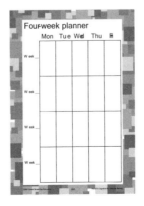
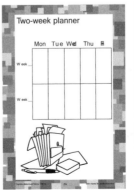

The four-week planner

Prepare a section of the class board so it is permanently designed as a 'four-week planner'. Write in dates for assignments, excursions, arranged visitors, class

Cognitive Behavioral Training

activities, special school days and plans for the future. Discuss changes as they occur and make alterations with the class participating. This constantly underscores the usefulness of this organizational device. As a bonus why not assist students to convert essential information from the 'four-week planner' into their daily planner?

There's more to it than issuing a personal planner or assignment book

For most students a personal planner or assignment book barely functions as a reminder for homework requirements. Yet these tools have the potential to be an exceptional reminding, planning and communication tool. More often, it is the anguish around the loss of a student's planner, or their inability or unwillingness to fill it in, that makes it so memorable for students, parents and teachers. The truth is, we are quick to issue planners to students and expect the rest to follow, and for some it does. For others we turn a blind eye. We know from the outset that these students will not use these without explicit intervention. We surreptitiously choose to overlook the possibilities of explicit instruction, the establishment of an organized school routine to promote a diary habit, instituting closer parent liaison and even parent education. This applies as much to the primary and middle school students as it does to secondary students. Start today. Make it a rule that the two or three disorganized students check in with you before they go home. Ensure they have the right books and are able to explain the homework. This adds to their understanding.

In a few instances this system will not work for students. Their forgetfulness and disorganization is so profound that the system itself keeps tripping them up. When you sense this is the case, invent other communication and remembering systems: faxing, emailing, mailing, texting, telephoning and leaving messages on answering machines are all helpful, easy systems to put in place.

The planning buddy

Allocating a planning buddy is easy, non-invasive and proactive! Select a more accomplished student to oversee or help fill out their classmate's planner each afternoon. Instruct the buddy to maintain the same method each day: filling in the planner, clearing the desk, returning items used throughout the day, gathering belongings needed for homework and delivering them to their backpacks. Try the system for a term using two or three buddies, so they're not overused. Then allow the student to become a buddy to someone else. The result of this role-reversal may pleasantly surprise you. If it does not, the option of returning to the original plan remains. This system provides sound peer modeling, and does away with higher-level teacher input where the student can interpret adult intervention as irritating nagging.

Case study ➡ **Homework books and planners**

'Changing the way I ask children to write their homework entries into their planners has helped the forgetful and disorganized to be more successful. In the past, as the day drew to a close and I felt pressure to get things finished, I used to bark out the homework and expect students to make notes in their planners. Even though I taught seventh grade, and it worked for the majority of them, there were always several who failed to record accurately or at all, or forgot to take the right books home. This set up a negative homework cycle.

230

Organizationally, I have changed my approach. Now we stop work twenty minutes before dismissal. I write brief assignments onto the white board, which is permanently ruled as an assignment page. As students copy it into their planners and take out appropriate books to take home, I circulate between the two or three children who tend to forget. This process takes about ten minutes. Students are dismissed from their desks with planner and books in their arms. I'm convinced that this approach adds integrity to the homework process. It also adds order to a part of the day that can easily degenerate into chaos.' (Margie, sixth grade teacher)

Watch and mimic routines of others

An eighth grade student who had a reputation for losing belongings, forgetting and being dreadfully disorganized stumbled on a simple solution because he was fed up with his disorganization. Charlie's solution was to start copying the routines and habits of one of his closest friends, Claire. Claire felt comfortable about this as she had been in most of Charlie's classes over the past eight years. Charlie began to stack his locker the same way as Claire stacked hers. He took the same books to lessons as Claire took. He mimicked what Claire did in the classroom as well, from note-taking and organizing his folder to filling out his planner at the end of lessons and making sure he bagged the same homework books.

It wasn't a cure-all, but for the first time ever, Charlie was working at a functional level, and it felt so good! Engaging students to watch others with a view to imitating their organizational routines can be useful, even inspirational, providing students see an advantage in it for themselves.

Generate organizational ideas at class meetings

Surprisingly, inspirational and workable suggestions often come from students themselves. Use class meetings to raise worrying classroom and organizational issues, and seek suggestions to resolve these. Teachers who consistently put class problems back to their students to solve deliver a 'vote of confidence' message to their students. Their premeditated stepping back says they believe students are capable of solving problems. Avoiding over-involvement and over-availability generates an atmosphere which promotes student self-reliance, as opposed to management that encourages dependency.

Auditory cueing systems

Different students respond to different remembering cues and instructions. Determine whether an individual responds best to the spoken instruction (auditory cueing) or written instruction (visual cueing). We need to discover which cues work best. Usually, most preferable is a combination of auditory and visual cueing.

Teach the 'how-to-listen' steps

It is impossible for students to know what careful listening is if they have never experienced it. Equally, it is unrealistic to expect all children to listen and remember effectively without explicit training. Begin by teaching the basic listening steps. Display them on a checklist.

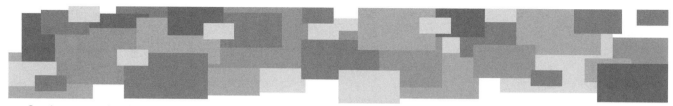

Students need to know the difference between hearing and listening. Even our youngest students are up to this. Hearing provides no more than a rough guide to what is happening, but listening steps them up to a new level. Listening means they are ready to take-in the information, create ways to remember it, follow directions and act independently.

Listen with SLANT

It has long been said that accurate listening cannot happen unless we SLANT.

Sit up
Lean forward
Act interested
Nod
Track the teacher.

Another approach, particularly for younger students, is to develop the five Ls. Impress upon them that what they do with their bodies is a prerequisite for good listening. It is not possible to listen and remember unless they place their body in a position where it is able to hear and see all the information and cues. The five Ls are: legs crossed, hands in laps, eyes looking forward, ears listening and lips closed. One minor adjustment to this is to allow the physically restless students to fidget with something that has been predetermined. This seems to fill a need to dissipate some energy, allowing them to listen and attend longer.

Use a minimum of words

Simplify instructions and choices. Be concise.

Touch, look and lock on

One or two students in most classes require that little extra to elevate their engagement. Work out with them a touch cue, so they know when you touch them on the arm it really is time to listen. Teach them to maintain regular eye contact while the instruction is being given. The additional benefit to this is the development of intimacy between teacher and student. Ultimately, a look is worth a thousand words.

Say it and see it

Always use visual information to supplement verbal instruction or directions. Hold the book up so students can see the illustration as the explanation is given, use task cards providing written information about the task, or write keywords, dot points or draw pictures on the white board to serve as memory joggers. Understand that auditory memory difficulties are insidious problems that undermine student's self-confidence and ability to learn independently.

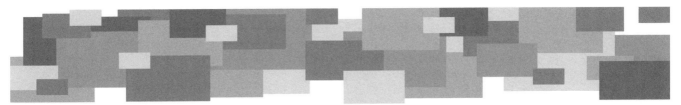

Group your instructions

Deliver verbal instructions in pairs, so that students automatically expect two instructions. For example, *Grab your pencil case and put it on your desk* or *Take this note to the library and return this to the sports room.* Build it out, and consistently group instructions in threes. *I want you to remember three things. It's as easy as one, two, three. One, clear your desk. Two, put your belongings in your schoolbag. Three, return to me and expect a surprise.* (The surprise may be a very pleasant smile).

Remember the vital question!

State the instruction, then say, *Tell me what you need to do. Have the student repeat it.*

'What does your partner think?'

Having students work in pairs can be an effective strategy to reinforce listening and memory. Once the instruction is delivered ask students to spend a few moments with a partner for confirmation. Make it a legitimate strategy for the easily disorganized student to consult a friend when in doubt about what to do. Build this pattern of seeking clarification into your classroom routine.

Select a student to retell

Give the instruction or explanation and then choose one or two students to reiterate the main points to the class. This works well for students who may not have maintained attention initially, and for those with memory weaknesses.

Never automatically repeat yourself

Once the instruction or explanation has been delivered try not to impulsively restate it. Otherwise, there is no incentive for a student to listen when it really matters. Explain this to students.

Accept signals from the student

When a student has not caught on to the instruction, teach them to use a subtle, private signal to alert you that they need to be reinstructed. Once again, this expands the level of nonverbal communication between student and teacher, and promotes the student's capacity to develop their self-awareness.

'I'm not available for ten minutes!'

Make it a rule. Once the instructions supporting the task have been given, and you know you have catered for the students' auditory and visual memories, put on something special - a hat, a coat, a jacket, plastic glasses, a scarf or gloves - which indicates you are not available to speak to anyone for ten minutes. This reminds students that when

Cognitive Behavioral Training

commencing any activity they need to work on proactive ways to determine what to do rather than repeatedly requesting advice because they did not listen in the first place.

Tomlinson (1999) explains the four-step RICE method to assist children in developing independent listening skills. Training students to use RICE gives them a valuable life skill.

Recall. Try to remember what was just said.

Imagine. If recalling does not work, use logic. Imagine the instructions most likely given.

Check. If recalling and imagining do not help, check with a friend.

Expert for the day. If the friend doesn't know, try the 'Expert for the day'.

Experts for the day are students, selected on a rotational basis, who wish to help out. Arrange for them to wear an Expert-for-the-day badge. When the RICE procedure is unsuccessful, and the teacher becomes available for help, students may of course ask the teacher.

Pre-teaching

Pre-teaching new information or new vocabulary for the following day, one-to-one or in group situations enhances student understanding. This also offers them the advantage of processing new concepts and language overnight so they can follow the upcoming events in the classroom more easily.

Visual cueing systems

Teach the 'how-to-look' steps

Even though there are obvious benefits attached to looking more carefully, students with impulsive and distractible traits do not have a natural disposition to do so. They must be taught the instrumental steps to look, so they can really see what is happening, what is expected and what they need to do. Encourage students to think about and brainstorm behaviors that are indicative of careful looking. Develop a 'how-to-look-carefully' checklist similar to the one on the right.

Catch the eye and grab the attention

When an important instruction is delivered hold up a bright or visually impressive object. This is an effective method to cue students into knowing that NOW is a critical time to listen. It may be a large, brightly colored ball, smaller juggling balls or an impressive replica staff. Once held, this bold visual cue reminds students to look, listen and remember. Teachers who use this to perfection tend not to overplay it. Other successful attention-grabbing measures include the teacher saying, *Look at my left shoulder. Now listen.* Or a teacher saying, *Watch the cards.*

They're counting down from eight. When zero comes up I want you in your seat and looking at me. Alternatively, tapping sticks or playing a burst of 'Simple Simon says' can provide firm visual and auditory cueing. These techniques help to engage students so they are ready to listen.

Write on the hand

Get students to jot the reminder on their hand using a pen or marker. It works well because it is within their vision at all times. If there is more than one thing to remember, then use a pen to write a key word on each finger. It's a novel idea and it works!

Highlighters benefit visual strengths

A highlighter can make a difference to a student's remembering, understanding and organization. The use of highlighters appeals to visual learners, and is frequently reported to be helpful for students with ADD and ADHD. Teach students from quite young ages to scan text for key information, and to highlight key words or important sections. Good places to practice are highlighting information in newsletters, prioritizing tasks, proofreading work and detailing relevant research information. It provides a chance for students to slow down and sift through information while using their busy fingers. Try modifying reading comprehension tasks by allowing students to answer some of the questions by highlighting relevant parts in the text.

Make and use lists

Lists are probably the most widely used visual reminder tool employed by adults. Many adults live and die by their lists, yet we can overlook teaching this effective remembering strategy.

Whatever needs remembering can be added to a list. Crazy-looking or personalized lists can be made on the computer or bought from stationery retailers, or the list can be as simple as a blank pad. Suggest to students that they attach their list to the wardrobe, a bulletin board, the back of the toilet door, the fridge or where they eat their meals. The golden rule is to keep it in the same place and make sure it can be seen daily. In this way it becomes a part of the daily routine. It helps to attach a pencil!

Lists can also be helpful to prompt students to stop an undesirable behavior or encourage them to do something differently. Enjoy discussing these with a student and devise ways the list might become useful.

Make and use checklists

Checklists are invaluable for home and school. They don't take long to devise, print and

Cognitive Behavioral Training

contact to a student's desk, inside their locker or to a book. They can be attached anywhere that captures attention and triggers memory. Checklists help sequence the smaller steps:

- getting ready for school in the morning
- what to bring to school
- the routine upon arrival at school
- setting up the student's desk
- remembering a special task
- how to pack up at the end of the day
- homework tasks and what to take home.

Never underestimate the power of checklists when used in a climate of structure, routine and uniform expectations (Barkley 1990). Students also benefit when they see their teacher working from a checklist!

An organizational contract

Checklists can support secondary students who have difficulty organizing and managing tasks. They double as a contract, or understanding, that the student and teacher have forged without unnecessary formality.

Electronic organizers

A small hand-held organizer is an asset to students with memory problems, especially for those in middle and high school where organizational requirements become more important. They are easy to use and can be set to beep as reminders, flash reminders on screen and display lists of jobs to be done. Homework can be typed in, notes, reminders, phone numbers and so on. These electronic supports deliver best results when students are explicitly taught how to use them. They are far superior to having scribbled notes and pieces of paper scattered between school and home.

Stickies

Stickies are messages that can be easily placed on Macintosh computer screens. Once the computer has booted up, the message is on the screen facing the user. Stickies can be used as a reminder to complete tasks, to provide simple instructions on how to tackle a task or as a reminder about homework, phone numbers or websites that need to be remembered. They are powerful little memory joggers and take only a moment to construct!

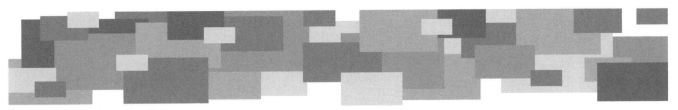

Organizing the desk

Work-space ethic concerns how students organize their desk and utilize their belongings. Start by making posters which show students precisely what is permitted on their desks. Desk organization needs to be specifically taught and constantly reinforced. They need to know the rules to stop the growth of mess.

Another option is to attach pieces of contact to the desk, and use markers to create outlines showing where the pencil case, ruler, pencils, pens and books go. Fill in each outline with a picture or the name of the item for this location. When teaching students how to organize their desk encourage them to watch others who do it well, but accept the physical organization of belongings is truly tricky for the poorly organized student. A few students are destined to rely on our organizational systems for a long time. When the desk becomes out of control, and past the point of no return, develop an understanding with the student and parents. Gently and privately slide everything off the desk into the student's bag to be sorted out at home, ready for a restart tomorrow. A simple checklist like the one on the right can help as a strategy for keeping a desk neat.

Computer planners

Computer programs such as to *Inspiration* and *Kidspiration* are wonderful planning tools for the visual thinker. They allow the student to flexibly organize ideas on the screen with the use of color and shape at the click of a mouse. The ideas can be moved around, grouped and categorized, making assignments and essay planning far more visible. It helps students to see the relationships between ideas, to brainstorm outlines for assignments, to keep track of what's happening in the novel, or to review a chapter of geography or science. This information can then be converted into notes for a speech or become the basis of a PowerPoint presentation. For information on Inspiration try <http://www.inspiration.com>.

A visual reminder to slow down

Eight-year-old Nikki had just completed a six-month sensory-integration 'Alert Program'. She enjoyed the occupational therapist and the association had nourished her motivation to learn and adopt new strategies. Nikki began therapy because her natural tendency was to run at one speed - fast. She had repeatedly been described as hyperactive, although her saving grace was her willingness to positively direct this surplus energy. Her voice was usually loud, and when she became excited she spat out words like a machine gun, making it difficult for anyone else to have a say. Nikki's father designed, built and drove cars as a hobby, so she knew all about cars, and felt obliged to tell everyone about them. The occupational therapist compared how cars needed to travel at certain speeds in certain places, and how Nikki needed to match her speed to the places she worked and played.

Fast moving cars, for example, need lots of space around them, and it wasn't a good idea to have them running fast indoors. Nikki began to see that she was a 'high-revving girl', and when she arrived from sport or play, she naturally continued running at 'high revs' in the classroom. Nikki and the therapist worked with her teacher to

introduce a system to remind Nikki to run at the right speed. They made three small cards that Nikki could hold in the palm of her hand. Each card had a picture of a car; one running fast, one at a medium speed and one running slow. When Nikki's teacher thought she needed a reminder to slow down she would slide a slower car into her hand. No-one saw the action and no words were needed. Nikki knew it wasn't a threat, but aimed at assisting her awareness about the speed she needed to run in the classroom. Never underestimate the power of easy-to-use visual reminders.

Establishing routines and habits

Go for a daily piggyback

Piggybacking is an appealing and logical strategy for putting together something students avoid or forget with something that is part of their usual routine. Piggybacking can work for different things, both at home and school.

Case study → ***Piggyback with your undies***

Jamie kept forgetting his locker key, which caused inconvenience and anguish for himself and others. One morning he announced, yet again, 'I can't find my locker key!'. His teacher quipped, 'So are you wearing your undies?'. Everyone laughed, including Jamie who blushed a little. She continued, 'From now on when you put your undies on, put your key in your pocket. Work them together. Your undies and your locker key!'.

Things progressed well for longer than usual, but a few days later Jamie apologized as he had left his locker key at home. His teacher responded, 'So you're not wearing your undies today?'.

Immediately Jamie reached for his pocket and found his key deep inside. A year or so later Jamie's forgetfulness was strengthened by a student trend to wear exclusive surf brand-name key chains and belt clips.

Color-code books and folders

Instead of students having a batch of exercise books in their book tray or locker, try paring them to a bare minimum. Color-code the covers and have two subjects per book, one subject beginning at the front, and the other starting from the back. The combination of having fewer books to sort through and knowing the red-covered book is for math, and graphs makes locating books a lot easier. It's less confusing and there are fewer books to lose themselves! Keep spare books in a separate cupboard and replace them as needed. This does away with the problem of students having to straddle between three different math books within a week.

Keep a folder for work in progress

Rather than losing bits and pieces in the school bag, somewhere in the bedroom, at school or - even worse - somewhere in between, encourage students to use a plastic folder to keep assignments that are currently in

progress. Once they are handed in, marked and returned they can be filed elsewhere. It's a simple system, allowing students to keep the bits and pieces of current work in one place.

Use cell phones as memory aids

Increasingly, more and more young students carry cell phones. Parents, schools and teachers continue, in all manner of ways, to respond to the inevitable distractions they cause. However, this technology is here to stay. Teach students to take advantage of the organizing systems many phones now have built into them. These include calculators, reminder notes where a short message will appear when the alarm sounds, a built in alarm clock, a stopwatch and a count-down timer. It is a bonus for students to know how to effectively use these functions because their cell phones rarely leave their sides.

Develop computer competence

Some students benefit by mastering word-processing and keyboarding skills sooner rather than later. Not only does their presentation look so much better, but the computer has the capacity to check grammar and spelling, save work and store it in folders. So much easier than physically handling and misplacing loose pieces of paper! If you do not have time to do this, arrange for someone to teach students the essential computer competencies. Begin with how to:

- touch type
- create and begin writing a document
- undo mistakes
- change font, size and style of print
- use the spelling and grammar check
- access the thesaurus
- check the word count
- cut and paste
- access drawing documents
- save and retrieve the same document
- save as
- save onto a floppy disk or memory stick
- retrieve from a floppy disk or memory stick
- create and label folders for storing files
- send emails.

Encourage students and parents to take advantage of the proliferation of touch-typing CD-ROMs offering sequential tutorial lessons. These are inexpensive and can be purchased from most software outlets. Increasingly, a number of schools now offer structured, formal keyboarding classes during lessons and after school. Encourage students to take advantage of these. Students are almost never too young to begin to type.

Cognitive Behavioral Training

Keep school bags tidy

While it is challenging for poorly organized students to keep desks, classroom drawers and bedrooms tidy, keeping the confines of their school bags in order is far more demanding. Do not allow this to become an issue of consequence.

Instead, arrange that once a week parents go through the school bag with their child. This supports parents in discovering or rediscovering notes, newsletters, library books, lunch bags and belongings that have worked their way to the bottom of the bag.

Organize the pencil case

Ensure your students use a pencil case. It is invaluable for containing the small items: pencils, colored pencils, pencil sharpener, pens, eraser, glue, ruler, small scissors, protractor, highlighters, even the school planner. Have you ever noticed the pencil cases of students with ADHD? They are either lost or bulging with all sorts of incidentals collected since kindergarten. To alleviate problems, send the pencil case home every night and ask the parents and child to reorganize and restock it with the basic requirements listed above. The organization of the schoolbag and the pencil case has to be adult-driven. Rather than criticizing the student for the pencil case not being restocked or the school bag being in disarray, take it up directly with the child's parents.

Lost belongings

All of us lose belongings. However, the problem can be minimized if items are named and we keep the difficulty in perspective. Kenneth Shore, in *Special Kids Problem Solver* (1998), has two ideas worth considering. First, when a student loses or forgets to bring a necessary belonging into class, and has to borrow from the teacher, they must offer something in return. At the time of arranging the loan it is wise to insist that if the item is not returned at an agreed time then the consequence will be an after-school detention or something equally inconvenient. Once the loaned item is returned, so is the collateral. His second suggestion relates to students who constantly lose their pencil. Shore suggests putting a piece of velcro on the student's desk as well as on the pencil to keep it contained.

Case study → *Keeping Jack's drawer tidy*

It was too hard for Jack to keep his desk tidy. Try as he might, by the end of day it was always full of crumpled papers, overdue library books, pencils and bits of various collections brought in from home. This made finding things near impossible, and propelled his disorganization.

In response his teacher set up an arrangement with Jack and his mother. At the end of each they would visit the classroom after everybody had left. Together they, placed the contents on the floor, cleaned and reorganized. Within minutes it was repacked, ready to begin a new day. Even though Jack was ten years old, he was genuinely overwhelmed by the task. His teacher recognized this, and accepted his willingness to participate in this alternative way as demonstrating his responsibility.

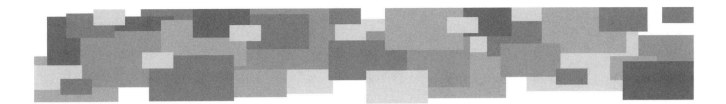

'I've lost my pencil' – again

Case study

Phillip's teacher found him really annoying. It seemed every time the class started a writing activity Phillip couldn't find his pencil. At eleven years old he was the only student in class who habitually lost his pencil. No amount of praise or discipline seemed to improve this. Phillip never intended to lose his pencil, it was more that his organizational skills (keeping track of his belongings) were delayed. He just could not do it, and criticism would not improve it.

Finally, impelled by frustration, his teacher resorted to handing him another pencil whenever he needed it. Sometimes it was new and at other times it was little more than a barely functioning relic, but the result was amazing! Phillip got to his work earlier, the level of tension over the issue decreased and Philip asked for far fewer pencils than his teacher had anticipated. Interestingly, the pencils did not disappear into a black hole, but reappeared when half-a-dozen were found in the bottom of his desk or the bottom of his school bag every so often.

Managing time

ADHD interferes with the ability to sense and use time. Informed educators now accept Professor Russell Barkley's *Theory of ADHD: Inhibitions, Self-Control and Time*, which assumes ADHD students suffer from time blindness, an attention deficit that involves the executive functions (Barkley 2001).

Executive functions control task completion, organization, time management, persistence and impulsivity. Barkley has determined, from long-term research, that ADHD students have a 30 to 40 per cent delay in their executive functions. Consequently, a fourteen-year-old with ADHD is very likely to perform at the age level we usually expect from a ten-year-old, even though they function well intellectually. This is the way it is. In terms of parenting and educating students with ADHD this understanding is profound. This information alerts us that managing time is a genuine deficit, or impairment. ADHD interferes with the ability of these students to sense and use time. It is a temporal disability where the gauging of time and how long tasks will take are distorted. This makes the management of time tantalizingly tricky for these students, despite their sound intellectual capacities. From a teaching point of view, this does not necessarily mean reducing intellectual content, but reducing the demands on their attention and organizational skills. It is imperative that we modify and accommodate for their inconsistency and lack of persistence, as they do not have the capacity to do this themselves (Jenks 2003).

Procrastination and time blindness

Time management and organizational skills remain elusive for a significant group of students, who may or may not have ADHD. These are our poorly organized students. They find large projects and independent research challenging: the thought of deciding where to begin, discovering where to find the research, defining what is important and processing the information is overwhelming. This is then followed by the physical marathon of writing up the information in their own words. What strategies are available to support students with procrastination and time blindness difficulties? These modifications and accommodations provide a start:

Cognitive Behavioral Training

- Set up a checklist to remind students what needs to be done: compile contents page, label diagrams, insert main headings and subheadings, compile bibliography, check spelling, do a word count and so on. They can check each item off as they do it.

- Provide the student with a jump-start by organizing an older student, another staff member or a parent to spend two or three sessions one-on-one, early on. This is the time to teach students how to use 'AutoSummarize' effectively (http://www.microsoft.com). This innovative technology, found in the latest version of *Microsoft Word*, can identify the key points in electronically downloaded articles and reports. Although the automatic summary is not foolproof, it is easy to use, and brings into concise focus the key points of the article without the student having to note-take as they wade through pages of readings.

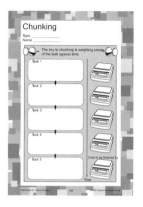

- Maintain momentum.

- Frequently check in by creating pivotal catch-up and review times together. Short-circuit any anticipated problems. To be candid, work out a solution to head off the difficulties you instinctively know will arise.

- At each review meeting break down the remaining tasks into smaller, more easily managed pieces. Chunk precisely what needs to be done in the time remaining until the next review meeting, and ensure the student knows what to do and how to do it. Drip-feeding the poorly organized student small pieces of work, guarantees they can arrive at the end point at the same time as their peers.

- Physically map out time allotments. Use the chunking forms to draw and record what needs to be done and when it is to be done. Create time in their day where they can attend to what needs to be done. These can be blocks of time either at school or at home, and often require direct adult supervision or support.

- Make the task achievable. This is an ideal time to modify work. Step back and make a distinction about what is core curriculum and what is more peripheral in nature. It is the tedious 'busy work' or extension work that often overloads these children. As a colleague once lamented, 'Why do we insist these kids jump through the same hoop a dozen times to demonstrate they have learned a skill, when three or four clean jumps tells us the same thing without the suffering?'.

- Home help is vital, so cultivate it by teaching parents how to support their child's developing independence, rather than doing the project for them. What really counts for students is that they feel as though the time management process has worked for them.

Whether teaching third or ninth grade, before setting fully-fledged independent research-based work (projects), introduce and model key individual skills required, and have students try these. Work alongside students, giving them the opportunity to watch, listen and discuss various ways to read, research, chunk and present information. Sometimes the poor mastery of basic skills adds new layers of complexity to time blindness difficulties. Students with attention difficulties who are consistently coached gain a better sense of how to plan within time constraints. Gradually, by providing appropriate structures, students develop independence. They learn to conquer time management, plan, ask for help and know how to stay in control.

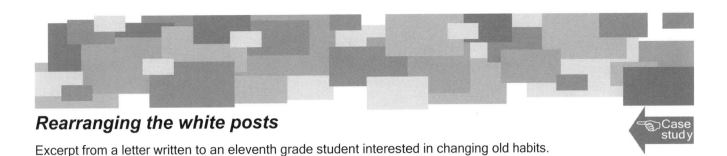

Rearranging the white posts

Excerpt from a letter written to an eleventh grade student interested in changing old habits.

'Let Mom and Dad know what we discussed today. Remember to tell them how pleased you were to find out that many other students (and adults) struggle with the sort of organizational difficulty you have. It's even common enough to have a name! It's called time blindness. It disrupts the ability to efficiently sense and use time, but take heart – you're in good company, and there are ways around it.

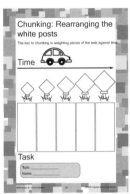

Do you remember the analogy I used of driving along a country highway with the white posts flicking by either side of you? At the end of the highway is the due date for the assignment and you felt that it wasn't until you had reached the end, and the assignment was due, that you would really look seriously at it. You recalled your usual pattern. You receive your assignment and complete the bulk of research fairly early, at the first few white posts. Then there is a lapse in what you do. Time progresses and the white posts continue to flick by, but the task doesn't. Suddenly, as the last white post comes up (the night before the assignment is due), you realize the assignment must be done. We agreed this is your motivation, and it too has a name – PANIC!

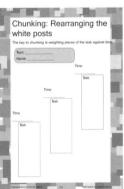

Ideally, it would be best to progress through your assignment, bit by bit, as each of the white posts flashed past. In this way the volume of work could weigh nicely against available time. Realistically, it doesn't work as smoothly as this for most of us. So to improve it is best to work on winning small changes. Instead of relying on the last white post to set off panic motivation, why not aim, at least as a start, at the second to last white post? Then you have one additional day up your sleeve!

You might like to follow up on this idea by saying to someone you trust, perhaps your mom, 'Mom, I've got an assignment due on Friday, November 25, and have two weeks to do it. I want you to write these three dates in your planner and ask which white post I'm up to. It will help remind me that I need to be at a certain point with my assignment'. This is called external reminding, and assists in managing time more effectively. It isn't about Mom making you do things. In fact, Mom doesn't need to know what you have or haven't done.'

Keep a time journal

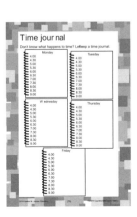

Work with students to determine how they spend their time. How is their time spent from school dismissal to nine in the evening each school night? Do they know? Can they account for those five hours per day, or twenty hours per week? Surprising as it sounds, they may not be able to. Ask them, or ask their parents to go undercover, and keep a time journal for two weeks. It is often very revealing, and sets the stage to create times in their day where they can attend to what they need to do. These can be blocks of time either at school or at home.

Cognitive Behavioral Training

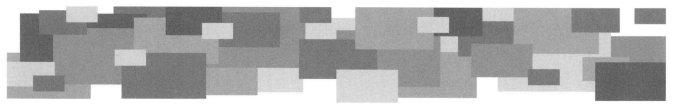

Get involved with time

Teach how long two minutes, five minutes, ten minutes, half an hour and so on really is. Time-blind students need this practice. Allocate them as timekeepers for class activities or sporting events to help them gain time appreciations. Locate a three-minute timer, a ten-minute timer, a stopwatch or a large wall-clock and use them to develop an awareness about how much work students can finish in a nominated time. Timers provide a continual visual reminder of time progressing. Knowing that the ten-minute timer only runs for ten minutes helps the student persist, rather than feel as though the work is never ending. Teach parents how to apply this concept to tackling homework more productively, completing a household chore more efficiently, or sharing computer or television time more easily.

Consequences for forgetfulness and disorganization

Deciding on consequences for persistent forgetfulness and disorganization embodies walking a very fine line. On one hand we have an appreciation that many students find organization genuinely difficult, and we accept that it may even be part of a disability. Yet, if we continually allow students to forget and ignore sensible organizational structures and routines they have helped to put in place, they have no incentive to improve and to get it right. So, providing intelligent structures are in place, when a student forgets to hand up their homework, asking them to do it the next day at the most inconvenient time for them is an appropriate consequence. Similarly, when a student forgets to bring their permission slip after working through a series of reminders and checks, it is right for them to miss out on the excursion. For most individuals, disorganized or otherwise, personal inconvenience usually increases the desire to maintain a system and keeps them thinking.

Blackline masters

- Class identities
- Our class rules 1
  - ★ Classroom contract
  - ★ Classroom rules 1–6
- Our classroom rules 2
  - ★ Rules 1–3
- Desktop timetables
- Weekly school timetable
- After-school homework planner
- Homework timetable
- Visualize what you'll need to look like!
- Checklist for assignments
- Keeping track of my project
- How should I rate myself?
- Four-week planner
- Two-week planner
- Term planner
- The how-to-listen steps
- If you're not sure, try RICE
- The how-to-look steps
- Must-do list 1
- Must-do list 2
- Things I should ...
- Checklist
- My checklist
- Checklist: HEY! What do you need to do?
- How to organize my desk
- How to organize my desk (blank)
- Cue cards
- Keep an eye on the time!
- Chunking 1
- Chunking 2
- Chunking 3
- Chunking 4
- Time journal

Class identities

- My name is … _____
- I enjoy … _____
- One day I want to be … _____ _____
- My favorite … _____
- It's best when … _____
- My favorite movie is … _____ _____
- My best food is … _____ _____

- My name is … _____
- I enjoy … _____
- One day I want to be … _____ _____
- My favorite … _____
- It's best when … _____
- My favorite movie is … _____ _____
- My best food is … _____ _____

Name _____

Class _____

Year level _____

Classroom contract

I have helped develop these rules for our class. We have discussed them, and I think they are fair. I understand they are about keeping everyone in our class safe and helping all of us to learn as well as we can.

I agree that I have to take responsibility for remembering and following the rules. Making positive choices about my behavior is always up to me.

Signed _____

Date ____/____/____

Parent's signature _____

Teacher's signature _____

Classroom rule no. 1

_____

_____

_____

Draw a picture and put yourself in it to show this class rule.

Classroom rule no. 2

_____

_____

_____

Draw a picture and put yourself in it to show this class rule.

Classroom rule no. 3

_____

_____

_____

Draw a picture and put yourself in it to show this class rule.

Classroom rule no. 4

_____

_____

_____

Draw a picture and put yourself in it to show this class rule.

Classroom rule no. 5

_____

_____

_____

Draw a picture and put yourself in it to show this class rule.

Classroom rule no. 6

_____

_____

_____

Draw a picture and put yourself in it to show this class rule.

Our class rules

Name _____

Class _____

School _____

Rule no. 1

Rule no. 2

Rule no. 3

_____

_____

_____

Desktop timetables

Name _____

Timetable morning

Time	Lessons
from _____ to _____	
from _____ to _____	
from _____ to _____	
Recess	

Timetable mid-morning

Time	Lessons
from _____ to _____	
from _____ to _____	
Lunch	

Timetable afternoon

Time	Lessons
from _____ to _____	
from _____ to _____	
Home time	

Weekly school timetable

Time lesson	Mon	Tues	Wed	Thu	Fri
Morning lessons					
Break					
Mid-morning lessons					
Lunch					
Afternoon lessons					

After-school homework planner

Time	Mon	Tue	Wed	Thu
3.30–4.00				
4.00–4.30				
4.30–5.00				
5.00–5.30				
5.30–6.00				
6.00–6.30				
6.30–7.00				
7.00–7.30				
7.30–8.00				
8.00–8.30				
8.30–9.00				

Homework timetable

Time	Mon	Tue	Wed	Thu	Fri	Weekend
4.00–4.30						
4.30–5.00						
5.00–5.30						
5.30–6.00						
6.00–6.30						
6.30–7.00						
7.00–7.30						
7.30–8.00						
8.00–8.30						
8.30–9.00						

Visualize what you'll need to look like!

To get what you want, try imagining yourself doing it before you start. Sporting stars are trained to imagine themselves being successful moments before they do something amazing. It increases their chances of success!

Draw what you need to be doing to get this task done successfully.

The task _____

Checklist for assignments

Name _____

Class _____

Name of assignment	
Date assignment started	
Date assignment due	
Task sheet	
Planning	
Completed research	
Contents	
Headings and subheadings	
Diagrams labelled	
Thoughtful setting out	
Word count	
Correct spelling	
Bibliography	
Hand up research	
In on time	

Keeping track of my project

Check each part as you complete it.

Start date _____

Name _____ Due date _____

TASKS		Have I gathered the information?	Have I finished the rough copy?	Have I finished the good copy?
	→			
	→			
	→			
	→			
	→			
	→			
	→			
	→			
	→			

How should I rate myself?

Information Did I include enough information? Did I understand what I wrote? Was the information in my own words?	→ 1 2 3 4 5
Writing Was my writing neat? Was it the best I could do? Did it read well? Did it all make sense? Did I check for spelling errors?	→ 1 2 3 4 5
Pictures Did I include pictures? Did I draw illustrations? Did I cut my pictures carefully and glue them neatly? Did I label my pictures, graphs and drawings?	→ 1 2 3 4 5
Time management Did I manage my time well? Did I make extra effort to do this? Did I pace my work so I didn't have to rush at the last minute? Did I hand it up on time?	→ 1 2 3 4 5
Effort Did I do more than the bare minimum asked of me? Did I include any extra information?	→ 1 2 3 4 5
Attitude Was I enthusiastic about finding information? Was I enthusiastic about creating the project? Did I work on it independently? Did I do it without arguing with my parents? Did I enjoy learning about my project topic?	→ 1 2 3 4 5

Think about how well you did for each of the following.
Circle a number from 1 (not at all) to 5 (completely). Tally the numbers and record your total out of 30 at the bottom of the page.

Total [   ] /30

Four-week planner

	Mon	Tue	Wed	Thu	Fri
Week ___					
Week ___					
Week ___					
Week ___					

Two-week planner

	Mon	Tue	Wed	Thu	Fri
Week ____					
Week ____					

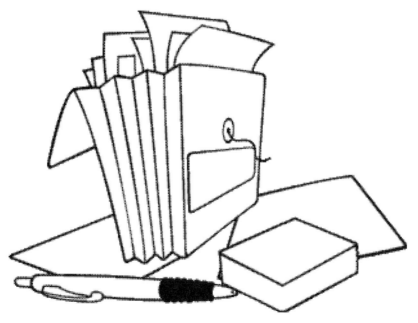

Term planner

Subjects	Week 1 Mon / /	Week 2 Mon / /	Week 3 Mon / /	Week 4 Mon / /	Week 5 Mon / /	Week 6 Mon / /	Week 7 Mon / /	Week 8 Mon / /	Week 9 Mon / /	Week 10 Mon / /

The how-to-listen steps

⊕ **When someone is talking to you, stop.**

STOP moving, talking, writing or daydreaming.

⊕ **Find a place where you can look at the person who is speaking.**

THINK about what they are saying.

THINK, Why are they saying this?

THINK, What do they want me to do?

⊕ **Once the information has been given, don't rush off unless you know what to do.**

LOOK AROUND. Check what others have heard and are doing.

⊕ **ASK if you don't understand.**

If you're not sure try RICE!

Recall. Try to remember what was said.

Imagine. What instruction was most likely given?

Check with a friend.

Experts. If your friend doesn't know, try the 'expert for the day'.

Independent learners use RICE

The how-to-look steps

✛ **STOP**

✛ **Sit down at your desk and put your hands by the work.**

✛ **Face your head and body towards what you need to look at.**

✛ **Say to yourself:**

   This is all I need to think about.

   What am I looking at?

   What do I have to do with this task?

✛ **Read it.**

   Look for hints, keywords or helpful pictures.

✛ **Try the task.**

✛ **Ask for help if needed.**

Must-do list

Need help to remember?

- Make a list.
- Put it where it gets your attention.

Lists trigger memory!

Must-do list

Need help to remember?

- Make a list.
- Put it where it gets your attention.

Lists trigger memory!

Things I should say every day

_____
_____
_____
_____
_____

Things I must stop saying

_____
_____
_____
_____

Things I should ...

Need help to remember? Make a list!

Put it where it gets your attention.

Lists trigger memory!

Things I want people to notice about me

_____
_____
_____
_____
_____

Things I should never do again

_____
_____
_____
_____
_____

Check ✔ List

Name _____

✺ _____

✺ _____

✺ _____

✺ _____

✺ _____

✺ _____

✺ _____

✺ _____

✺ _____

My checklist

Name _____

CHECK!

✸ _____

✸ _____

✸ _____

✸ _____

✸ _____

✸ _____

✸ _____

✸ _____

✸ _____

Check  List

Name _____

Hey! What do you need to do?

- ☐ Put on your watch, to help you be on time
- ☐ Pick up your pencil case, subject text, workbook and diary
- ☐ Grab your homework
- ☐ Sit where agreed
- ☐ Contribute to class discussion
- ☐ Make notes of things to ask the teacher after class
- ☐ Show teacher your notes
- ☐ Record homework in your diary

How to organize my desk

Name _____

CHECK!

☐ **Organize pencil case**
Take out ruler, pencil, blue pen and red pen –
put at top center of desk.

☐ **Check next lessons**
Check the timetable to see what the next
three lessons are.

☐ **Organize books**
Stack books for the next three lessons at the
top left-hand corner of desk.

☐ **Make sure there is nothing else on desk**
Store other things in tray or bag.

How to organize my desk

Name _____

CHECK!

☐ **Organize pencil case**

_____

_____

☐ **Check next lessons**

_____

_____

☐ **Organize books**

_____

_____

☐ **Make sure there is nothing else on desk**

_____

_____

Cue cards

SLOW

JUST RIGHT!

FAST

Keep an eye on the time!

Topic _____

Week 1 (Date started ____/____/____)

Monday	Tuesday	Wednesday **Review day**	Thursday	Friday **Review day**

Week 2

Monday	Tuesday	Wednesday **Review day**	Thursday	Friday

Week 3

Monday **Review day**	Tuesday	Wednesday	Thursday **Review day**	Friday

Week 4

Monday **Review day**	Tuesday	Wednesday **Review day**	Thursday	Friday **Due today!**

Display in classroom. Each day, discuss progress and color in a square so that students with time-management difficulties gain a visual connection with the progression of time and what needs to be done. Insert **review days** to review work and set new goals.

Chunking

Topic _____

Name _____

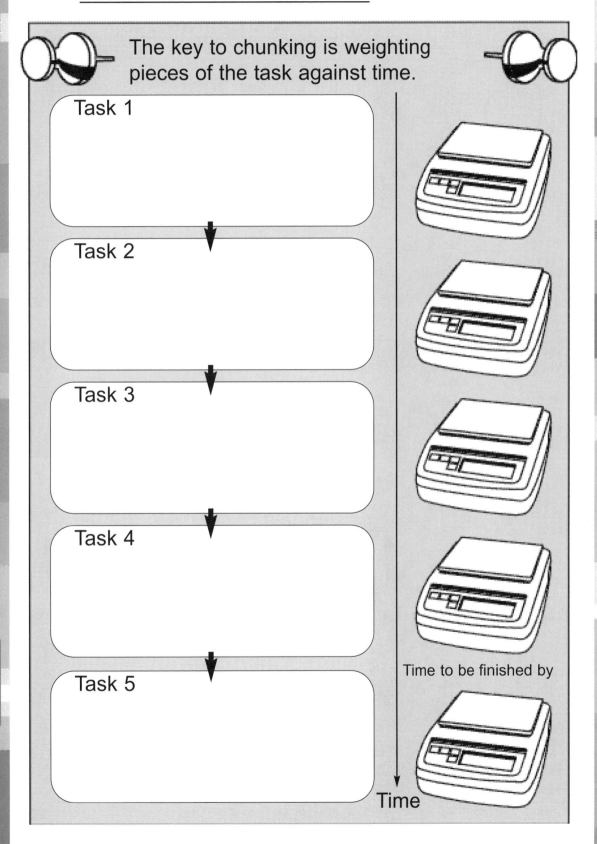

The key to chunking is weighting pieces of the task against time.

Task 1

Task 2

Task 3

Task 4

Time to be finished by

Task 5

Time

Time

Task

_____

_____

_____

_____

_____

Chunking

The key to chunking is weighting pieces of the task against time.

Topic
_____

Name
_____

Chunking: Rearranging the white posts

The key to chunking is weighting pieces of the task against time.

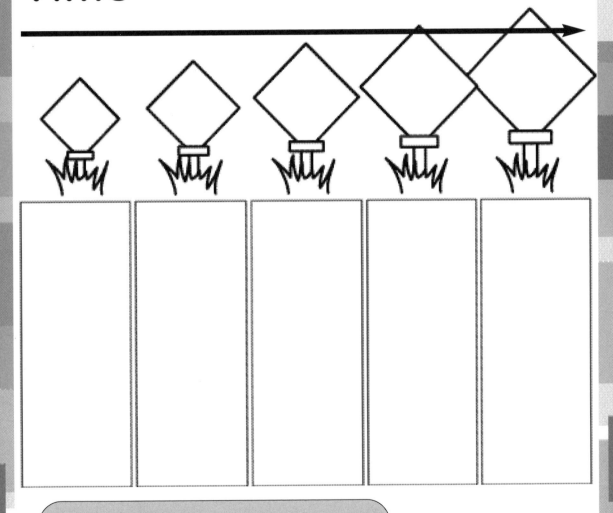

Time

Task

Topic
_____

Name
_____

Chunking: Rearranging the white posts

The key to chunking is weighting pieces of the task against time.

Topic
_____

Name
_____

Time_____

Task

Time_____

Task

Time_____

Task

Time journal

Don't know what happens to time? Let's keep a time journal.

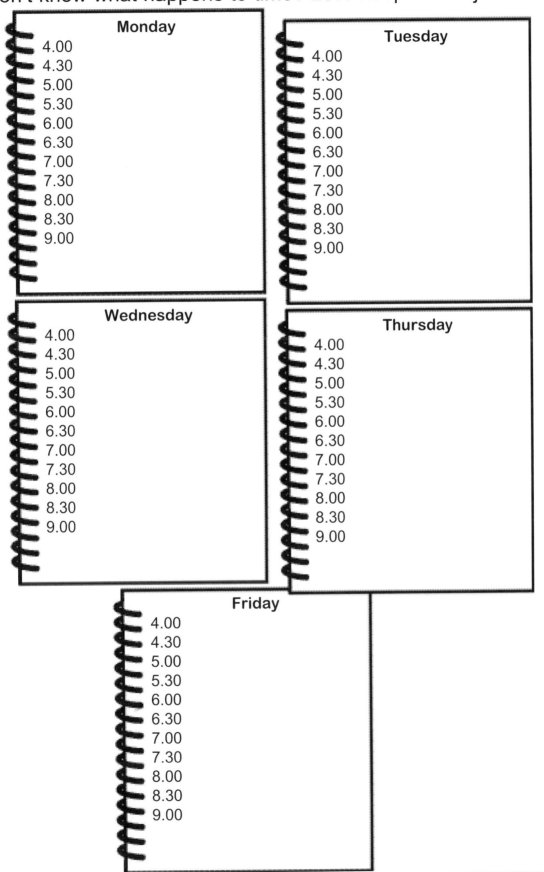

Monday
4.00
4.30
5.00
5.30
6.00
6.30
7.00
7.30
8.00
8.30
9.00

Tuesday
4.00
4.30
5.00
5.30
6.00
6.30
7.00
7.30
8.00
8.30
9.00

Wednesday
4.00
4.30
5.00
5.30
6.00
6.30
7.00
7.30
8.00
8.30
9.00

Thursday
4.00
4.30
5.00
5.30
6.00
6.30
7.00
7.30
8.00
8.30
9.00

Friday
4.00
4.30
5.00
5.30
6.00
6.30
7.00
7.30
8.00
8.30
9.00

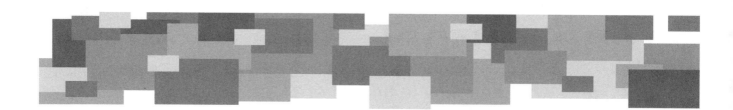

288

Chapter 7
Optimizing perseverance and motivation

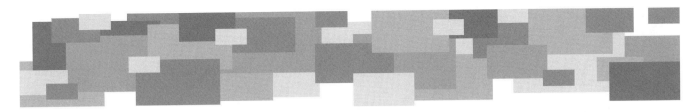

Perseverance and motivation: Fickle companions

Motivation and persistence are usually interpreted as 'stickability', willpower and tenacity. They are revered personal ingredients which are thought to fire individuals with resilience to pursue their goals despite personal difficulties, unfortunate circumstances or unfair setbacks. These highly sought qualities are believed to underwrite sustainability, the capacity to bear up, tolerate and endure. They radiate an attitude which says, 'I'm not giving up', 'I can fail, but I'm not a failure', 'I learn from my mistakes', 'I like to prove I can' and 'Let me try again.'

Yet motivation and perseverance are not constant qualities. Little wonder, as these processes are highly complex involving physiological, cognitive and cultural factors. Frequently they are decidedly fickle companions, waxing and waning from one setting to the next. Circumstances that galvanize the motivational forces in one individual can just as easily deter another. A student may not be eager when it comes to mathematics, but is responsive, committed and absorbed during art or design lessons. Similarly, how many adults demonstrate disinterest when it comes to persevering with something mechanical? However, their stickability in another circumstance or their ability to excel at another task may be exemplary. Some of the classic barriers to perseverance and motivation are:

- perfectionism
- fear of failure
- negative responses to pressure
- inability to relate to the task because of its lack of meaning
- sensitivity to past failures
- peer influence
- home influence
- anxiousness
- sadness
- depression
- learning difficulties
- relationship issues
- learned helplessness.

The truth is that most students, most individuals, at some point are bound to feel unmotivated. The key for educators is to unravel what motivates and demotivates students. They can then progressively engage their students in discovering when this is likely to occur, why it happens and how to make adjustments to move past it.

In a perfect world we would wish for individuals to have a well-tuned internal set of perseverance and motivational assets. After all, successful individuals look as though they possess these attributes. Is it possible for a young, developing student who does not posses adequate internal levels of perseverance and motivation to be positively influenced by external forces? In reality, if a student is not internally motivated, then beyond magic cures, all we are left with are strategies that optimize determination and motivation. There is no other way. Progressive

Cognitive Behavioral Training

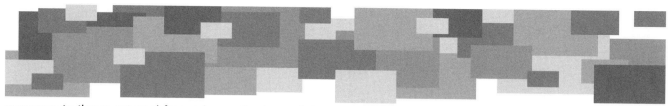

exposure to these external forces buoys the immediate success of students, and supports the gradual emergence of their internal perseverance and motivation attributes.

Sparking motivation

Where does the lack of motivation occur?

Assess whether a student's motivational difficulties are global, or relate more specifically to school or to a particular subject. Commonly, perseverance difficulties are confined mainly to school. 'I'm not motivated by schoolwork', 'It doesn't do anything for me', 'I want to be successful, but can't see the point in what I'm doing.' Reassure them that they are not disordered, peculiar or sick. Many fine human beings have had low motivation about school, schoolwork and homework. They may, at the moment, find it difficult to embrace its relevancy, and while this is not helpful, it is quite normal. A critical step is to normalize their attitude. Figure out what they enjoy and what they are good at. Work to create balance and rekindle interests, talents and areas that arouse success feelings.

Together, determine an initial, easy-to-implement idea that might gain them a foothold to success in an area they are struggling with. Ask, *What could we do that would take the smallest amount of effort to make a change?* As the relationship and small successes build, gradually insert more supports. Once a little momentum is built the rippling of change can be startling.

What might help?

On an individual basis and at class meetings, ask students for suggestions: *What do you think will help your motivation?* Be daring; offer engaging and attractive ideas for discussion. Sometimes it is not the idea that tips the balance. It's the act of asking, suggesting and participating with students which makes the greatest difference (Dempster & Raff 1992). Would they like the class to be run differently? Would they like to take a more active role in planning and delivering lessons? Could we cut homework back to three afternoons per week? What could we do to reinvigorate ourselves when we hit the occasional flat spot in class? Do we need a project of some sort to strive for? Would each student like to deliver a lesson based on an interest they have? Would students like to choose afternoon activities one day a week?

Use visual triggers for motivation

Ask students to collect pictures that will remind them why it is worth persisting over the term or year. An older student in his last year of school was eager to become a nurse, an ambulance officer or a paramedic. When he spoke about these occupations his eyes lit up, yet he knew his school performance, which often suffered from poor motivation, would be critical in determining this choice. His selection did not depict a student solemnly studying, but rather dynamic pictures of what he wanted to be involved in next year. He placed one picture in his wallet, another in his school planner, contacted one to his desk at home, and found several for his pin-up board. He knew they would not make him work, but they reminded him that persevering with the tediousness of study was central to achieving his goal.

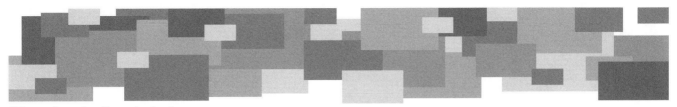

Share inspirational stories

Tell stories, have students find stories, read biographies and autobiographies, and watch movies about people who have persevered in the face of adversity. Develop lists of people, pictures, magazine articles, novels and movies that show this. Maintain the momentum and adapt it as a unit of study.

Sayings of the week

Reinforce the desire of students to do well by introducing an inspirational saying each week and briefly discussing it. There are a multitude of these, like:

- *Don't wait for your ship to come in, row out and meet it.*

- *A diamond is a piece of coal that has stuck to the job.*

- *If you can't have what you like, like what you have!*

It's surprising how some students seize hold of a saying and use it as an aid. These sayings can be influential, and the best sources for these are inexpensive, inspiring books often found at the local bookstore.

A perseverance study

Encourage students to write scripts, create plays or make a video. Use the theme 'Perseverance'. Select cartoon characters and sitcom characters, and discuss:

- *Who demonstrates perseverance?*

- *Who demonstrates perseverance in the face of difficulty?*

- *Select events which demonstrate perseverance.*

- *Identify characters from these programs who do not demonstrate perseverance.*

- *How can you tell whether they do or do not? What are the qualities?*

- *How do you think they see themselves?*

- *How do you think others see them?*

A reflective study

Have students share their own stories about times when they have or have not persevered, and what the outcomes have been. Arrange for students to keep journals focusing on tasks or activities they know require their perseverance. Set up mechanisms for students to self-monitor their behavior and attitudes when enjoying an activity compared to their behaviors and attitudes when being challenged by an activity. Occasionally, seize the moment when students reach an impasse. Guide them to reach into their developing 'tool box' of perseverance strategies, and find a way to deal with the problem at hand (Raskind et al. 2002).

Cognitive Behavioral Training

The inner critic and perfectionism

A surprising number of students need permission to worry less about how their work looks. Start by giving them permission to do the task just well enough to get by. Many students have a persuasive perfectionist inner critic and need to be taught the art of self-bargaining and compromise. Explain that most people have inner critics, which are really the worrying, unconfident part of themselves. Your inner critic suggests almost irresistible negative thoughts simply because you feel uncertain. Our inner critic taunts each of us ... *Don't ask that question - the others will laugh. It's not worth starting. It's too hard. Do it later. It's stupid anyway. It should look better than this! Everyone else's will be better. It's meant to be more complicated than that! That was too easy; it must be wrong.*

When we listen to our inner critic's messages we feed it with too much power, and this saps our motivation. Teach students how to combat this controllable human trait by using positive self-talk. Program Achieve refers to the inner critic as the 'Head Hassler'. This program asks the question, *Who decides whether the Mind Master or the Head Hassler is in charge?* Students are led to see they can think constructive thoughts versus negative irrational thoughts. They are reassured that the Mind Master and themselves can make a great team. The more they practice together, the more likely that the Head Hassler - who they don't want to know - will be out of a job!

Self-talk and the inner critic

Negative self-talk switches thinking off. Unchecked, it invites procrastination, frustration and failure. Insidiously, negative thoughts triggered by negative self-talk can also end up attracting negative people and negative events. On the other hand, conscious, positive self-talk (metacognitive instruction) switches thinking on, feeds creativity and opens the mind. Positive self-talkers are more inclined to take healthy risks, to set new goals and to attract positive people and be involved in positive events.

Quiz students about their self-talk. Randal Clinch calls it the 'chaps in the top paddock'; the little voice inside our head that has an opinion on everything (Clinch 2000). Find out what sort of self-talk students hear. When is it positive, and when is it negative? What does their self-talk say? What do they feel and do? Teach them, individually or as a class, to collect positive speaking prompts to combat the chaps in the top paddock. Ask students to talk through how they approach a task. This sets up a framework for all students to talk themselves through an activity using their positive prompts.

To change self-talk takes a while, but it can be done. Old, negative self-talk habits are converted into a new, positive language. Respected researchers propose self-talk procedures as an effective way to steer students through a task (Parker 1999; Westwood 1999). As students actively talk to themselves they are thinking about how to proceed through the learning process. Studies reveal that self-talk training results in an increase in task persistence and helps to positively self-regulate learning behavior (Thomas & Pashley 1982).

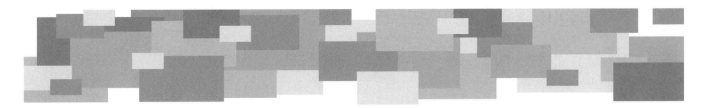

Steps in making self-talk changes

Help students recognize their inner critic's negative self-talk. Assist them to explore their inner critic's secret language, and discover how to translate worrying and negative thoughts into positive thoughts, words and actions!

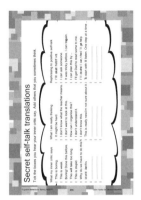

- Identify situations where negative self-talk occurs.

- Teach students to say 'STOP' in their minds when they hear it. Remember, it's a trick that worry is playing.

- Reinterpret the message. Say, *Sure, I might feel uncertain, but my thinking tells me I can do it.*

- Replace the negative self-talk with a new, more powerful positive version.

- Always do this. The more it is practiced, the stronger positive self-talk becomes.

Never underestimate the power of positive self-talk

Yanni's letter to himself was found by his mother shortly after he returned to school. It was tucked away in his drawer. Eleven-year-old Yanni had experienced consistent difficulties with friendships and teacher expectations.

To my dear self,

Yanni you are great! You are reading this because you want to remind yourself about THE TIPS you got before school starts.

THE TIPS are:

1. Write a bit more neatly, so Ms. Carlson doesn't go mad.

2. Think before you speak. Remember when you talk blah, blah, blah, talk, shout, chat, chat, chat ... whatever you say gets a reaction from the others. They will either hate you or like you.

3. Remember the three baskets Mark said about. Don't just take the stuff you say from the angry basket.

4. Be yourself because you are okay.

Signed, Yanni.

Yanni had one consult. We hadn't moved mountains, but his letter to himself reminds us never to underestimate the power of sowing seeds.

Suggest to students they write a few tips to themselves. It may not mean these tips will be directly transferred into action, but it does help them to begin to intellectualize their challenges, and strengthen their metacognitive journey.

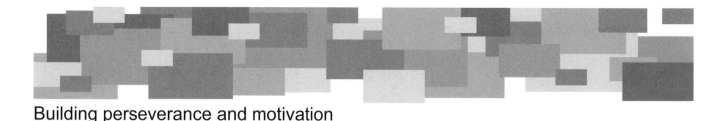

Building perseverance and motivation

How much attention did you pay?

Here is a practical way to help students improve their listening perseverance. Prior to an activity requiring attending skills (for example listening to a story, receiving instructions or listening to peers speak) let them know that once it is completed you will ask them to record how well they were paying attention. Ask students to mark on the continuum how well they used their attending skills. Attending skills include good eye-contact (meeting the teacher's eyes and subtly nodding their head as they listen), body directed towards the teacher, feet on the floor, hands still, listening instead of speaking and knowing what has been said. Praise students for their good audience or attending skills and remind them how they looked and what they did to persevere and pay attention. This explicit approach keeps in rehearsal how individuals need to look to effectively attend.

Starting and finishing

For 'on-the-go' impulsive students, staying on one topic is not part of their natural repertoire. Their urge is to constantly lane swap, and it works against them even though they might want to see things though to a conclusion (Thompson & Sears 2000). Help students stay with tasks:

- know and monitor what they are doing

- ensure that topics requiring perseverance are shortened and made manageable

- negotiate points along the way to stop, take stock and take a break

- devise ways to help them listen to a story from start to finish, and progressively build on the skill

- steer them to pack up the activity they have been engaged in once they have finished, or the time is up

- lead them to organize their belongings before the next lesson or before the next task

- encourage students to finish work at a negotiated point before the end of the lesson.

Regularly ask students questions that reflect what they are doing is invaluable for those who forget, lose the thread and suddenly find themselves engaged in something else. They can be delivered unemotionally and require little effort: *Jane, do you know you are out of your seat? Rob, is that what you've started to do? How do you plan to finish the task if you're doing that? Have you made a choice to do something else now? Do you know why you're doing that? Are you following the agreement we made together?*

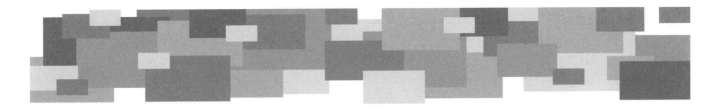

Giving responsibility before they earn it

Case study

Sammi was far from one of the best-behaved students in assembly. She was always noticed disrupting others. But by the time she was in fourth grade, Sammi's teachers had learned to capitalize on her electronic and sound production expertise. Whenever there was a television program to be video taped or the sound system to be set up for assemblies, it was Sammi who was relied on. She no longer sat in assembly flicking chewed up bits of paper, making noises and playing with the hair of students alongside her. Instead she was engaged in setting up microphones, checking sound levels, cords and connections, and making sure that everything ran smoothly.

The right place (with the right people) at the right time

Optimistic, encouraging cultures are truly infectious. The choice of school, teachers and friends, and the buoyancy of home life influence an individual's motivation. This is more so for students who do not have deep internal resources. Students in environments that are structured and have routine, and have people who model appropriate behaviors, are far more likely to be swept along in productive directions. Never underestimate the influence of these connections. They can be inspirational or severely limiting. Be instrumental in leading students to surround themselves with proactive people and positive situations. Sometimes the best that can be done for students is to ensure that this happens at school.

What will success be for you?

How successful does the student need to be? It is wise to determine exactly what constitutes success. It must be different for different individuals. Write it down, so you both have a physical record.

Punctuality and rhythm

Expect students to be at school on time. Nothing is more debilitating to a student's rhythm than consistently arriving ten, twenty, or thirty minutes late, and missing essential structural information and the before-school social interaction. Address the problem early and determine whether the problem falls within the domain of parent or student. Students who experience planning and organizational difficulties with the morning routine are surprisingly common.

Assist them and their parents to identify the problem, appreciating that it may be a combination of several issues. Then together set up new ideas, routines and reinforcers to help their mornings flow more smoothly. If, despite everyone's best efforts, the student persists in being late, then apply the two (or three or four) for one consequence. That is, for every minute they are late, you retain the choice of inconveniencing them for two minutes during any part of the day. The choice is yours, and it may be at recess, at lunch, during a favorite lesson or at dismissal. Students bright enough to consistently think through delaying morning tactics are bright enough to realize that getting to school on time is the best option.

Cognitive Behavioral Training

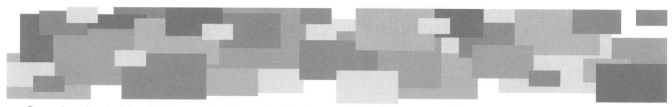

Occasionally, habitual lateness is determined to be exclusively a parental issue. They can remain resistant to change despite empathetic communication and thoughtful interventions. In these circumstances, follow the lead given by theatres during live performances. The parent and the student will need to wait in the administration waiting area until there is a logical break, either between your lessons, at recess or lunch. This puts the inconvenience squarely back with the parent.

Mini-milestones and celebrations

The outcome most students want from their school year is to realize success: academically, socially, even behaviorally. Yet many view the year as a compulsory marathon, feeling overwhelmed by the catalog of tiresome tasks awaiting them. It is possible to help students to think their way around this mind-set by guiding them to reframe their thinking.

Instead of seeing the year in its entirety, break it up into manageable pieces. Together, decide what is manageable: a day, a week, half a term or a term. Guide them so their thinking is logical. In other words, if they are able to put one assignment together, maintain compliant behavior or complete homework tasks during one week then they can be successful in doing the same next week. Build an understanding that small units of success add up to a successful term or year. Decide on a celebration to mark the end of each term or each milestone. These occasions also present opportunities to review progress.

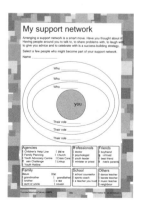

A tutor might be just the thing!

Help students battling motivation and organizational problems by finding a tutor to visit their home and work with them each week. Their tutor can offer moral support, provide impetus to plan and write assignments, suggest routines to help meet deadlines, and be there to listen. Initially, some students feel this is too invasive, too personal and too confronting. Later, with the benefit of hindsight and a little success, these same students discover they actually enjoy their tutor's company and input. The relationship didn't arouse the expected feelings of inadequacy or ineptness, and the tutor was not an overbearing authoritarian. Instead the association became powerful and complementary. When it works, it works very well. Suggest a four-week trial to see how it goes.

Develop a support team

A 'support team' to buoy the emotional resilience and safety of children and young adolescents is routinely employed by a number of programs (for example Program Achieve and the Resourceful Adolescent Program).

A similar approach, aimed at gathering external sources of support and inspiration, buoys the internal motivation of students. While the approach is often used to more successfully tackle the last year or two of secondary school, it can also benefit young

children. Encourage students to think widely and consider their essential needs. Ask them to record their ideal support team. The team may include mother, father, tutor, teachers, relatives or a friend. Select individuals who students trust and know can deliver whatever is asked in a way that is acceptable. Next to each team member's name, assign their role or roles.

What Carly wanted from her team

Myself

- To pay attention, stay on top of things and to keep up. Not to let things slip.

- Less responsibility during term time for taking care of the kids at home, but to take on responsibility for that during the holidays, because I like it.

Mom

- To feed me

- Keep me healthy

- Monitor my sleep

- Help keep channels of communication open so we can make changes if we have to.

Dad

- To remind me to keep the Sunday afternoon homework routine going so I complete homework before watching the Sunday-night movie. I need to start homework or study by 5.30 p.m. Dad, you can nag!

Tutor

- To start with, the usual once a week arrangement.

- Keep it about planning and organizing assignments.

Special Education Teacher

- Make sure that we keep talking about how I feel I'm going, and if I need help to ask for it.

- If any of my teachers forget, or don't understand my learning needs, to get my special education teacher to sort it out.

Rewards for persistence and perseverance

Rewarding for perseverance is a very different concept to rewarding for performance. For some the satisfaction of an internal reward is enough, but for others an external reward strengthens resolve. Realistically sustainable systems, deals and bargains, monetary or otherwise, that drip-feed effort and attitude are healthy. Aim at achieving small goals which gradually combine towards larger achievements. Rewards need to be mutually negotiated so that the chance of success is high. A restart without the loss of dignity remains a palatable fall-back position. When they experience success, students have the wonderful 'feeling of success' imprinted onto their memory, aiding motivation and persistence in the future.

Cognitive Behavioral Training

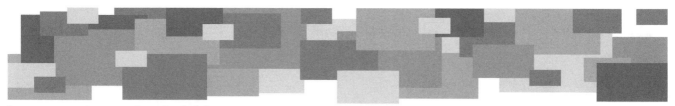

Lesson notes and note-taking

Note-taking techniques require explicit 'how-to-do-it' teaching. These techniques are difficult to master, and all the more so for students with concentration, working memory, visual and handwriting difficulties. Poor visual memory means students take longer to copy from the board. Then, as fatigue sets in, spelling difficulties and deteriorating handwriting make the end product difficult for the student to make sense of. Alternatives always benefit these students. Consider:

- Providing typed notes so they can listen and highlight relevant points during the lesson.

- Supplying lesson notes which also have key words at the top, and asking students to insert them in the blank spaces during lessons that are mainly lecture-based.

- Developing note-taking skills which includes structured headings: name, topic, date, main points arising from this lesson, key words and concepts, what I learned and what I'm not sure about.

- Using peer assistance in note-taking. Encourage students to copy their buddy's notes when they feel they must.

- Encouraging the use of diagrams, pictures and flow charts. These help make sense of the information presented, and function as visual triggers optimizing storage in memory.

- Urging secondary students to write notes to themselves to remind them of questions they should ask. To accommodate for this, over-structure the lesson to allow question time at the end. This helps students to cement concepts in place.

You could also consider using new technology from Mimio. On what appears to be a standard whiteboard the teacher can make notes, sketch out plans and develop lists and diagrams, knowing that every idea can be saved for later review or be immediately printed out for students to take away. This provides students with an instant record of the instruction or explanation, allowing them to concentrate on the content, rather than the process of recording it (for detailed information try <http://www.mimio.com>).

Embracing technology

Schools embracing the use of adaptive equipment offer students an additional route to success. Students in schools that either oppose, or are slow to accept, accommodating technologies soon feel self-conscious as they are constantly quizzed as to why they need to use a laptop, a computer or the less expensive *QuickPAD* and *AlphaSmart* word-processors. As a result, they feel as though they are odd and cheating. Soon they begin to hesitate to use the very tools that could help them learn more effectively. (See 'Using computers' in the Further reading and useful websites section for more information about these products.)

Technologies to compensate for difficulties

Have students research, discuss and trial technology that will be helpful in compensating for their difficulties. Classically, students identified with Learning Disabilities, ADHD and Asperger Syndrome demonstrate poor recall for word and number patterns, display poor handwriting and deliver reduced written output. Sustained practice to

alleviate these problems is often not helpful. However, the integration of appropriate support technologies improves efficiency and is uplifting to students (Minton 2002). These technologies include:

- word processors
- electronic spell-checkers
- calculators
- predictive word-processing packages such as *Co:Writer*, *Read & Write* and *Penfriend*
- software to convert text to speech. ScanSoft manufacture and market *RealSpeak* allowing speech from text to be played back through the media player. This is a wonderful application for Dyslexic students and the visually impaired.
- software to convert speech to text. *Dragon NaturallySpeaking for Windows* is useful for students who have handwriting problems, have spelling difficulties, cannot type or just don't like typing. It allows students to say what they are thinking and obtain a written result. Training the program takes several weeks, and younger students (upper primary level) require explicit teaching and a planned training program initially. Usually, students begin to see an improvement in speed and voice recognition within a few days, and this is inspiring! (See 'Using computers' in the Further reading and useful websites section for more information.)

Don't let reading and spelling difficulties demotivate students

It is all too common to see students with reading difficulties lose heart and give up on interesting or required texts. Many classics and popular books can now be obtained on tape or CD so students can listen. They can be purchased, or located in school libraries, local libraries. It is worthwhile exploring multimedia software similar to the *Britannica 2002* expanded DVD and CD-ROM editions. *Britannica 2002*, for example, contains hours of video, audio and animations, and thousands of photos, illustrations and maps. A real bonus is its capacity to read text to the user. It is a far more effective research tool than leaving students to wander the Internet for hours, often without finding what they need.

Spectronics (http://www.spectronicsinoz.com) have developed *Windows*-based software called *textHELP Read & Write Gold*. This is a word-processing program intended for use alongside an existing word-processing program such as *Microsoft Word*. It is well-recognized as a leading assistive technology program supporting users with literacy and learning difficulties. *Read & Write Gold* incorporates functions such as reading out words as they are typed, reading back text, spell-checking with the spoken word using an advanced phonetic spell-checker, automatic correction of frequently made errors previously programmed into the computer, discriminating between homophones and predicting frequently used words, phrases and sentences. Its capacity to read back the text on screen enables students to listen to what they have written and note the inconsistencies, which can then be corrected. In a more rudimentary form, Macintosh computer users can take advantage of *SimpleText*. It is a standard application allowing the user to select a voice and have it read the text aloud. This is useful for editing and proofreading work.

Cognitive Behavioral Training

What about videos and DVDs?

Videos and DVDs are powerful teaching resources. Ever noticed the difference in class attention and interest when students are processing information from video or DVD compared to the way in which they attend to their teacher explaining the same information? Seize on opportunities to boost knowledge, interest and motivation through these means. They have become a flexible, instant, easy-to-use resource, and there is an array of superb productions available through well-developed catalog systems.

Developing big picture understanding

Guide students to think ahead, and to imagine themselves in their final years of high school. By years ninth and tenth grade progressive dialogue with students can firm up where they want to head and what they need to get there.

This sets the scene to make educational adjustments, rather than watching students become overwhelmed and lost within an inflexible system. It may be advantageous to replace a foreign-language lesson with a more needs-based activity, especially if the foreign-language lesson presents additional difficulties for the student. This leaves more time for targeted remediation and catch-up work. Astute educators remain mindful of the big picture, and are prepared to pare away superfluous subjects and curriculum detail to get students to a position where they can embark on career and life objectives.

Vocational Education and Training courses

Vocational education courses are often offered to students at the secondary level. The courses often address the needs of students who may not want pursue a four-year college or university program. Many vocational schools have programs which are appropriate for secondary students and often these programs are offered to students as an alternative for meeting the requirements for graduation. This option allows students the opportunity to explore various educational options. Some of the options include child-care, nursing assistants and graphic design courses. For students who prefer to work in the trades often carpentry, electrical, or mechanic coursework is available. For many students this is a viable option to course work presented at the secondary level. It has the advantage of building vocational skill and training in areas that often not offered at the secondary level.

Lifting the mood

Try new things

The best advice is to be creative! Be spontaneous. Be unpredictable and have fun with what you do. Introduce novelty and new ideas to secure the engagement of students.

Clever, engaging voices

Teaching relies on voice. A teacher's voice has the potential to become a splendid tool. Deliberately altering voice tone, pitch, pace, volume, intonation and accent is an admired and valuable skill. There is an art to knowing when to

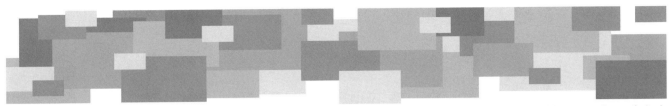

speak so softly that students actually strain and hang on each word; many adults hold vivid memories of their teacher's voice suddenly becoming lower and knowing it was their cue to listen. Honing this skill bolsters the engagement of students and is likely to prevent a teacher's voice becoming raised or pinched toward the end of the day.

Play 'speed ball'

This game is quick (McGrath 2000). Use it to reinvigorate students. Have them stand next to their seats. Throw a beanbag or foam ball throw towards a student. Once the student has caught the ball they engage eye contact with someone new, call their name, and throw it directly to them at chest height. Each person needs to catch and throw the ball within three or four seconds. Students leave the game by sitting in their chairs when they fail to catch the ball, throw poorly or take too long to throw. The last five students standing win.

Red-hot ticket giveaway!

Giving away tickets that can be collected in return for prizes is a way to motivate young students (Thompson & Sears 2000). When executed with finesse it works beautifully with much older students too! Negotiate how many tickets they will need to earn particular rewards. Display the Red-hot ticket giveaway menu when you are ready to start. Tickets are won for right answers, demonstrating requested behaviors, the most beautiful smile, the quickest, silliest or funniest answer. The possibilities are limitless! This sparkling approach lifts the mood of the class, and is especially helpful when they may be facing a challenge of some sort.

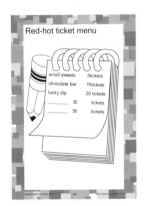

Parent may also want to participate. At home, surprise children with the news that right now is Red-hot ticket giveaway time! Tickets are dispensed when tasks are completed on request - getting ready for school on time, when home chores are finished, saying 'yes' instead of 'no', getting into pajamas without help, getting ready to go to the shops, remembering to brush teeth, anything at all. Give away plenty of tickets and make sure that many tickets need to be collected to win the more desirable rewards. The Red-hot ticket giveaway only lasts for one hour, every so often.

Another variation for the classroom is to offer students raffle tickets to reinforce effort. At the end of a week the raffle ticket is drawn. First, second and third prizes are awarded. This practice is not only fun, but also visibly acknowledges effort, helping to buoy persistence.

The influence of exercise

Individuals who exercise regularly improve the blood supply to their brain, which in turn optimizes functioning. Improved blood supply increases the availability of serotonin to the brain, and an imbalance of serotonin is thought to be a key contributor to impulsive and hyperactive behaviors. Teachers often report that the restless, hyperactive children are able to settle longer, sustain attention and are more compliant following vigorous exercise. Prioritize fifteen to twenty minutes of aerobic physical activity each day, knowing it especially benefits the restless and

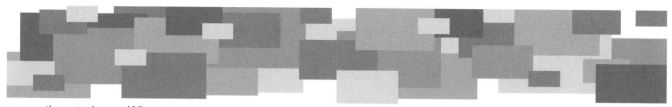

overactive students. Why not arrange a regular swap with a colleague so that your very restless student or two complete an additional physical activity lesson with another class a little later in the day?

Children thoroughly enjoy sports lessons, physical education and exercise times, so consider using these as incentives for the class to sustain their attention or complete manageable tasks. One well-used idea is to write one letter of the word SPORT on the board each time students demonstrate focus or a requested set of behaviors over a set period of time. Set the timer for five or ten minutes and if the class is successful they achieve the next letter in the word SPORT. When all of the letters are earned, they earn an additional sport session. A variation to this is to set a timer for somewhere between three and twelve minutes. When it rings, if the class is settled and working as you have requested, they gain one of their letters for SPORT (Taylor-Neumann 2002).

Disc-swapping

Disc-swapping can be undertaken with individuals or an entire class. It's an ideal method to reinforce behavioral expectations, and may be used alongside a way-to-change plan (see Chapter 3). The idea can also be adapted to support students developing yard behaviors at playtimes. Students begin the day with a green disc, worth 5 points. When the teacher catches them showing perseverance or cooperative behaviors they exchange the student's green disc for a yellow disc (10 points). Similarly, yellow discs can be upgraded to red discs (20 points).

The teacher reserves the right to take back a disc for off-task or uncooperative behaviors when students are not able to self-correct following a warning or helpful suggestion. It is possible, although undesirable, for students to end up with zero points for the day. The accumulated points are used to achieve a predetermined reinforcer.

Case study ☞ → *A board game got Josh off to a faster start*

Making an efficient start on written work poses a problem for a few students. The pattern is common: a pen, or the writing book itself, is misplaced; perhaps the instruction is forgotten; or there seems to be writer's block (despite thorough scaffolding and good visual cueing) when beginning the task. Over time, if left unaddressed and unmanaged, persistent avoidance results in patterns of behavior which erode attention, confidence and output.

Josh, a fifth grade student, had experienced this problem forever. It was the private variety. His poor written performance became apparent by the end of lessons as he only produced about half the quantity of his peers. As he was a quiet, likeable student, little had been said by his teachers. After several weeks in his new class, Josh's teacher decided to tackle the problem. He explained to Josh that he'd noticed it took him a long time to begin written work, often fiddling with things, attempting to find belongings, or just staring at his page. He asked Josh if he knew he did this.

Josh was aware of his difficulty, and explained that writing 'make-believe stories' was hard. He felt more confident with factual writing and genres which offered structure. Josh also shared that finding the right word and getting the spelling right was hard. Often he had

304

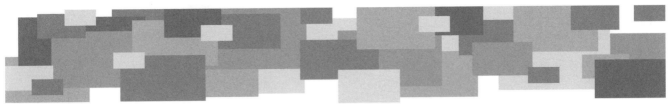

to replace the word he thought he wanted with a simpler one he could spell. This of course made his written expression look immature and poorly constructed. His teacher promised Josh that by working together they could improve this, and devised a board game as a vehicle to structure a collaborative approach.

Josh's teacher promised that from now on if Josh couldn't find what he needed his teacher would supply it, and if he couldn't think of an idea to write about, he could copy the ideas on the board. They devised a simple cue to help Josh get off to a good start. When his teacher noticed that Josh was drifting or procrastinating he would walk past and gently place his hand on Josh's shoulder. Another touch on the shoulder would mean 'Come on Josh, you need to keep writing'. They decided to color up to four squares on the board if Josh had worked well. At worst Josh could always earn one square for staying positive. Josh and his teacher used the board game about twice a week and delighted in reconfiguring it to include bonuses and dares!

Brain snack time

'Food is a powerful drug. You can use it to help mood and cognitive ability or you can unknowingly make things worse'. (Sears 1999)

Listen to the observations of countless teachers. They can tell which students have not had breakfast, or have had a soft drink and a chocolate bar for recess. Their subsequent erratic behavior and poor concentration tells it all. The effect of sugar, preservatives and food colorings on some individuals is now well documented. So too is our understanding that the behavior of some of these individuals is remarkably susceptible to when they eat, and what they eat. It is well documented that, breakfast remains the most important meal of the day. A good breakfast helps prevent children from eating snacks (which are often high in sugar and fat) during the day (Heggen 2003a). Little wonder a growing number of schools now offer breakfast on a regular basis to help place students in the right frame of mind for learning.

Naturally some foods are better than others. Protein foods are considered to be the main source of amino acids, which are thought to produce dopamine and norepinephrine. These important neurochemicals are involved in learning, socializing and decision-making (Joseph 2002). Ideal sources of breakfast protein include milk, cheese, yoghurt, baked beans, soy products, white meat and eggs. It is vital for teachers, parents and students alike to understand which foods play a role in altering mind and mood. Make a start by discussing this with students. Draw up lists or collect pictures of helpful foods compared to those considered unhelpful. Even the youngest of students are ready for this.

A growing number of schools are promoting 'brain snack time' or 'smart brain time.' By organizing snack time prior to morning play, and linking its value to sustaining healthy brain function, playtime does not overshadow this vital replenishment opportunity. Brain snack time becomes an entity within itself and focuses on what is consumed, and how it is likely to affect students.

Similarly, the regular intake of water is vital in maintaining optimal brain function. The consumption (depending on body weight, age, intellectual demands and climate), is around 2 liters a day. Drinking water regularly throughout the day helps keep pH levels steady and regulates the stress hormones (Jensen 2000a). This of course is the reason behind more and more teachers providing drinking water in their classrooms throughout the day.

Cognitive Behavioral Training

Cueing systems and reminders

Simple cueing devices whether they be tactile, fragrant, verbal or visual, support individuals who don't have well-developed self-regulatory skills. Without reminder systems in place it is easy for them to forget and lose their way. These gentle external triggers help keep students on track and arouse their wavering internal capacities. Verbal cueing may include anything from a friendly whisper of encouragement to openly calling time-out and making an assertive statement as, *You will need to put your pen down now and listen, so you'll know what to do*. Nonverbal cueing reduces obvious teacher intervention, but still encourages the student to give their best effort. Bill Rogers (1997), when discussing simple cueing systems, uses the acronym P.U.S. (Privately Understood Signals). Begin by making time to talk with the student, and agree on reminder signals, or secret signals, to achieve what you want. Build in times to meet and review progress. The bonus is that this private language is likely to strengthen your relationship as well.

Visual reminders

These of course are reminders that can be readily seen by the learner; anything that visually attracts their attention and is capable of persuading them to remain engaged with the task at hand.

- Coach students to look at your face when you speak as it helps them to listen, remember and follow instructions. Develop eye contact messages together. What a powerful silent language! Work on it and rehearse the meaning behind a wink or different types of looks.

- A colored fingernail, a drawing or a stamp on the hand, colored wrist bands, colored tape around pens or several pictures of the student's choice located at strategic points around the classroom can each serve as triggers to stay on task.

- Devise a simple chart that represents individual items that need to be completed during the lesson in order to have the task completed. Color, stamp or put a sticker on the chart as each of the sub-tasks are completed.

- A 'voice-o-meter' on the classroom wall will set the noise expectation during the lesson and provide a visual prompt.

- Simply moving closer to a student and lingering nearby can be a reminder to keep their head down and stay with the task.

- As you walk past a student's desk place a pen and a pencil together on their desk. This predetermined signal indicates 'You're doing really well with the task.'

- Place a blue counter on their desk as they are working to recognize their progress. Three of these over the day might achieve the coveted classroom award.

- Stopwatches, kitchen timers, five- and ten-minute timers, three-minute egg timers and the clock are helpful. Timers help students grasp that sustained periods of concentration are limited. It adds an edge to perseverance.

Auditory reminders

While it is practical in the busy classroom for teachers to call out instructions, it is obvious that as students become accustomed to the voice they tend to tune out and respond less. Surprise students by whispering an instruction, or

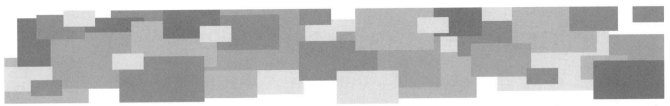

invent a key word that once said, students know nothing else will happen until all is quiet. As often as you can, do without words. Try imparting instructions through mime.

Try playing music when at times when concentration is required, or play an intermittent beep tape on the tape recorder as a reminder to students whether they are paying attention to the task. It is a widely accepted idea promoted by a bevy of well-respected ADHD researchers. When students hear the beep, they think, *What am I doing at the moment? Am I focused? Am I doing what I need to be doing?* If not, it is a cue to help bring them back to task.

Tactile reminders

Interact physically with the child; a touch on the arm can be just enough to sustain the perseverance of an inattentive student.

Set up signals to trigger the student's persistence. Your hand on their shoulder might mean *You'll need to think about getting on with the task now.* Placing a soft foam ball in their hand delivers the same message.

Fragrant reminders

Once or twice a day, at times when quiet, focused, on-task attitudes are required, burn a fragrant oil burner as a reminder for students to persevere. This seems to work best when used for the same lesson each day. Rosemary and lime oils are commonly recommended to enhance concentration, while cedar wood and frankincense are used as calming agents.

Blackline masters

- What would it take?
- Negative self-talk
- Secret self-talk translations
- How well did you pay attention?
- A promise to yourself
- Mini-milestones and celebrations
- My support network
- My support team: Job descriptions
- Red-hot ticket menu
- Board game: Getting off to a better start
- Voice-o-meter

What would it take?

Question: What is it that needs to change?

_____

_____

_____

_____

_____

_____

List one or two little things it would take to make a positive change.

_____

_____

_____

_____

_____

_____

What do you say to yourself?

Do you say: 'I can't', 'I'm useless', 'I'm dumb', 'It doesn't matter.'

_____

_____

_____

Negative
self-talk

What do you say about others?

Do you say: 'He always does that','They're weak!'

_____

_____

_____

_____

What you say about events?

Do you say: 'That won't happen', 'I never can ...'

_____

_____

_____

_____

_____

Secret self-talk translations

Check the boxes you hear your inner critic say. Add others that you sometimes think.

What my inner critic says

* This is boring.
* This is weak.
* Boring! Done this before.
* This will take too long.
* This is stupid.
* Why do we have to do this?
* I don't like this.
* ...
* _____
* _____
* _____
* _____
* _____
* _____

What I am really thinking

* It might be hard.
* I don't know what the teacher means.
* I don't want to look at this.
* How can I organize this?
* I don't understand it.
* I don't know this.
* This is really new. I'm not sure about it.

Rephrasing to positive self-talk

* I'll look at this bit first.
* I can ask someone.
* It was tricky before. I can try again.
* I can plan this by ...
* I'll get Dad to read some to me.
* I'll do what I can, then I'll get help.
* To start with I'll listen. One step at a time
* _____
* _____
* _____

How well did you pay attention?

Did you use your attending skills?

Attending skills include good eye contact (meeting the teacher's eyes and nodding your head as you listen), sitting with your body directed towards the teacher, your feet on the floor and your hands still, and listening so you can remember what has been said. There is a special look people have when they are paying attention!

Name _____

Date tried _____/_____/_____

| Not at all | A bit | Enough | Good | Perfectly |

Date tried _____/_____/_____

| Not at all | A bit | Enough | Good | Perfectly |

Date trie _____/_____/_____

| Not at all | A bit | Enough | Good | Perfectly |

Date tried _____/_____/_____

| Not at all | A bit | Enough | Good | Perfectly |

Date tried _____/_____/_____

| Not at all | A bit | Enough | Good | Perfectly |

Date tried _____/_____/_____

| Not at all | A bit | Enough | Good | Perfectly |

Date tried _____/_____/_____

| Not at all | A bit | Enough | Good | Perfectly |

Date tried _____/_____/_____

| Not at all | A bit | Enough | Good | Perfectly |

A promise to yourself

'What will success be for me this year?'

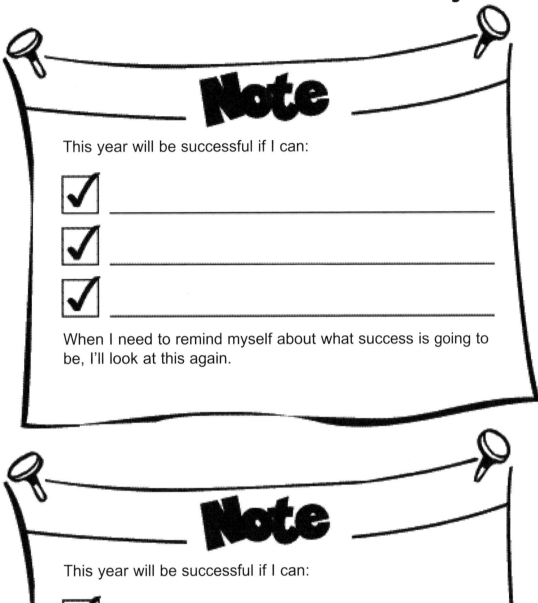

Note

This year will be successful if I can:

- ☑ _____
- ☑ _____
- ☑ _____

When I need to remind myself about what success is going to be, I'll look at this again.

Note

This year will be successful if I can:

- ☑ _____
- ☑ _____
- ☑ _____

When I need to remind myself about what success is going to be, I'll look at this again.

Mini-milestones and celebrations

Break the year into pieces. If you can put one assignment together, maintain a behavior or complete homework tasks over one week, try doing the same next week. Small steps add up to a successful week or term. Work out a celebration to mark the end of each milestone.

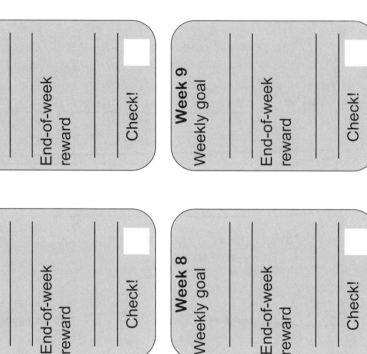

Week 1
Weekly goal
_____
_____

End-of-week reward
_____

Check! ☐

Week 2
Weekly goal
_____
_____

End-of-week reward
_____

Check! ☐

Week 3
Weekly goal
_____
_____

End-of-week reward
_____

Check! ☐

Week 4
Weekly goal
_____
_____

End-of-week reward
_____

Check! ☐

Week 5
Weekly goal
_____
_____

End-of-week reward
_____

Check! ☐

Week 6
Weekly goal
_____
_____

End-of-week reward
_____

Check! ☐

Week 7
Weekly goal
_____
_____

End-of-week reward
_____

Check! ☐

Week 8
Weekly goal
_____
_____

End-of-week reward
_____

Check! ☐

Week 9
Weekly goal
_____
_____

End-of-week reward
_____

Check! ☐

Week 10
Weekly goal
_____
_____

End-of-week reward
_____

Check! ☐

My support network

Arranging a support network is a smart move. Have you thought about it? Having people around you to talk to, to share problems with, to laugh with, to give you advice and to celebrate with is a success-building strategy.

Select a few people who might become part of your support network.

Name _____

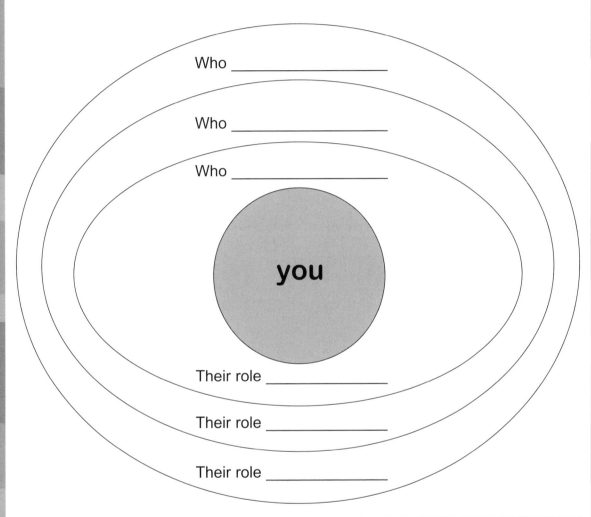

Who _____

Who _____

Who _____

you

Their role _____

Their role _____

Their role _____

Agencies
* Children's Help Line
* Family Planning
* Youth Advocacy Center
* Teen Challenge
* Youth Hotline
* Lifeline
* Church
* Crisis Care

Professionals
* doctor
* psychologist
* youth leader
* minister or priest

Friends
* boyfriend
* girlfriend
* best friend
* friend's parents

Family
* Mother
* grandmother
* brother
* aunt or uncle
* Dad
* grandfather
* sister
* cousin

School
* school counselor
* sports coach
* a teacher you trust

Others
* dance teacher
* karate teacher
* music teacher
* neighbor

My support team: Job descriptions

To be successful this year I'm choosing a support team. They are:

Myself

Job description
- [ ]
- [ ]
- [ ]
- [ ]
- [ ]
- [ ]
- [ ]

Name _____

Job description
- [ ]
- [ ]
- [ ]
- [ ]
- [ ]
- [ ]
- [ ]

Name _____

Job description
- [ ]
- [ ]
- [ ]
- [ ]
- [ ]
- [ ]
- [ ]

Name _____

Job description
- [ ]
- [ ]
- [ ]
- [ ]
- [ ]
- [ ]
- [ ]

Name _____

Job description
- [ ]
- [ ]
- [ ]
- [ ]
- [ ]
- [ ]
- [ ]

Name _____

Job description
- [ ]
- [ ]
- [ ]
- [ ]
- [ ]
- [ ]
- [ ]

Red-hot ticket menu

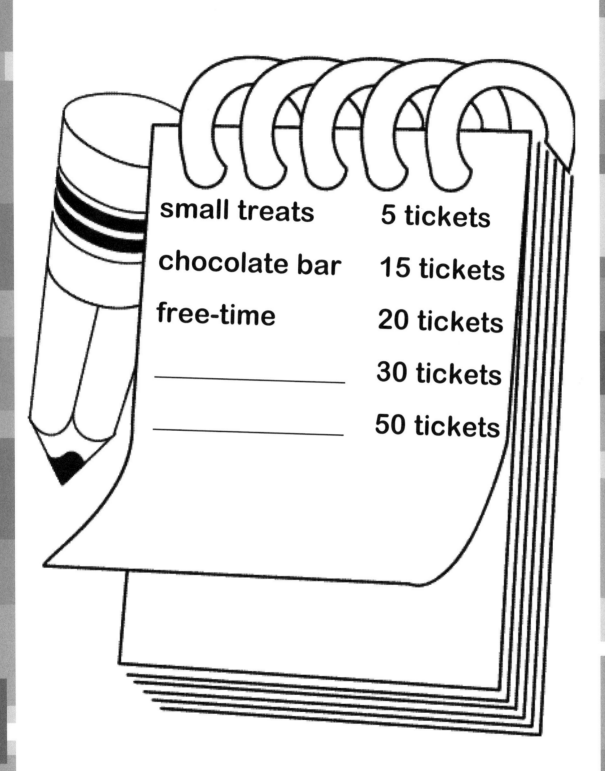

small treats	5 tickets
chocolate bar	15 tickets
free-time	20 tickets
_____	30 tickets
_____	50 tickets

Board game: Getting off to a better start

Voice-o-meter

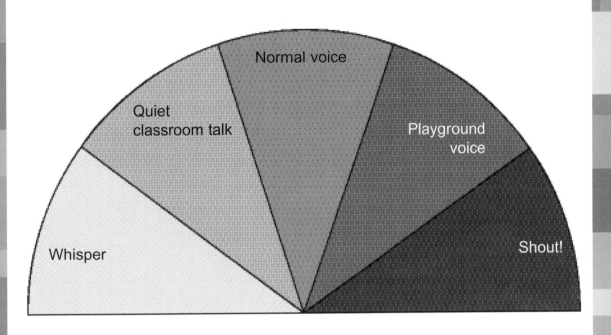

Cut out pointer and attach to Voice-o-meter with a split pin.

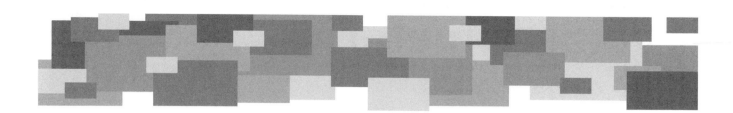

The last word

All children are inexperienced and learning. They are in rehearsal. So, of course it is natural to see difficulties emerge in the course of their development. However, those with more pronounced differences usually present exaggerated behaviors which affect flexibility, persistence, organization, motivation, concentration and cooperative capacities. Their delayed coping mechanisms result in fluctuating performances, and this generates problems in the domains of school, learning, friendships and relationships within families themselves. Even on good days, life can suddenly become surprisingly challenging for these children and those around them.

Yet, the world would be a poorer place without the exchanges and contributions made by these individuals. These are the children educators never forget. Hard work, laughs, tears, wins, losses and testing times emblazon them in our memories. A few years later, when we hear about them, we immediately reflect on the role we played in guiding their journey. Did I make a difference? Was my influence positive, insipid or damaging? Did I embrace their differences, tolerate them or turn a blind eye? Did I discount my contribution by succumbing to, *Yes, but that won't work because ... ?* Was I, individually or as part of a team, instrumental in helping put them on the success pathway?

The unquestionable wisdom of hindsight tells us it doesn't cost anything to make all the difference in the world to a child. Making a difference by navigating our way through the obvious, and not so obvious, pitfalls is our greatest legacy to students. Reflection intensifies the realization that it is too easy to define an individual by their apparent shortcomings. Our most impressive contribution is to uplift their positive elements, no matter what, as these are the qualities that will overcome their naturalistic difficulties in the future. This requires us to focus on individuals being whole, healthy human beings. They may have problems, but as with all children, the best way to help is to provide nurturing, energizing and optimistic interventions. The promotion of self-esteem, confidence, skill-building and relationship-building permits individuals to change. Reinforcing deficit, disobedience, disorder and syndrome does not.

One simple fact remains. There are no quick fixes for many of our children. To be of benefit we must adjust our expectations and circumvent the classic pitfall of expecting too much, too rapidly, without any tangible structuring. Remain mindful of the genuine gap between what we want from these children and what they are able to give. Their success is linked to our attitude. Nothing breeds success like success itself, but it is all too easy, too common, to see children fall into failure-cycles which breed disappointment, withdrawal, demoralization and downright refusal.

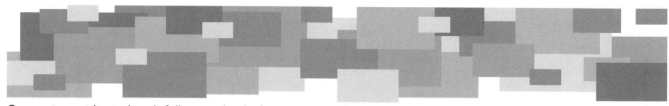

Our part must be to break failure-cycles before young, unknowing victims fall prey to too much failure. They may lack the awareness to identify failure-cycles and how to escape, but we do not.

Clever, proactive management couched in sustainable cognitive-behavioral techniques is our best ally and offers children the best chance to walk the success pathway. CBT strategies, promoted in a win-win spirit, engage young individuals to learn more about their attributes, build vision, set goals and live the exhilaration of experiencing success.

So many of our children have bright futures, particularly if their difficulty is managed early and well. This book shouts to parents and educators, 'Yes, you can do it!'. The ignition of constructive change starts with you, and becomes all the more effective when understandings, approaches and resources are teamed. It is your combined day-to-day management that shapes what children learn, how they learn, how they relate to others and how they see themselves. You make the difference. Trust your instincts and participate in redesigning the future of a child or student right now. Start with small steps that target one behavior or one change. Then, behold the amazing ripple effect!

At the first glimmer of light of dawn, a young man walked at the edge of the seashore. There had been a storm the night before, and he knew this would be a good morning to find seashells. With pants rolled up above his ankles, he walked along looking down for what treasures he might find. Then the young man looked up and could barely make out a figure of a very old man ahead of him.

The young man watched as the old man bent down to pick up an object from the sand, and toss it into the surf. As he got closer, and the light of morning began to turn the sand pink, he noticed that the old man was picking up starfish that had been tossed up on the beach by the storm.

There were thousands of them, but one by one the old man had picked them up and tossed them back into the surf. Nearing the old man, the young man introduced himself, and said, 'Excuse me, but there are thousands of starfish stranded here on the beach. You can't possibly make a difference!'.
The old man smiled and looked at him, then picked up another starfish. He tossed it back into the sea. 'I certainly made a difference to that one, didn't I, son?'

(Author unknown)

Appendix 1
Common clinical diagnoses and their implications

Specific Learning Difficulties (SLD)

Specific Learning Difficulties is a broad term used to describe a group of disorders which affect language and learning. This group of disorders is thought to affect between 3 per cent and 10 per cent of the population (Rivalland 2000). Such a diagnosis is sought when a noticeable discrepancy becomes apparent between an individual's intelligence and their acquisition of reading, writing and spelling and/or math skills despite support by sound teaching practice (Snowling 2000). Most commonly, the term incorporates conditions described as Dyslexia (specific reading disorder), Dyscalculia (specific calculation disorder), Dyspraxia (specific speech disorder), and Dysgraphia (specific writing disorder), and boys are about three times more likely to attract identification than girls. Students with Specific Learning Difficulty frequently have trouble following instructions, attending and remembering. They are likely to appear poorly coordinated and consistently present poor handwriting. Not surprisingly, their more general organizational levels are usually regarded as inadequate. They are commonly described as lazy, lacking in ability, poorly motivated, disorganized and slow learners. Sometimes the frustration and humiliation they have endured to acquire basic reading, spelling, writing or arithmetical skills badly compromises the development of their social skills, friendships, compliance, self-confidence and optimism. Family tensions, poor teacher understanding and lack of intelligent learning support certainly help to compound matters.

Dyslexia

Dyslexia, a difficulty with reading, spelling, writing and sometimes mathematics, affects between 3 per cent and 7 per cent of the population (Chinn 1991). Most agree it is an inherited condition and is identified in boys four times more frequently than girls. Current research indicates that identification may be problematic in girls and this may help to account for this diagnostic gender imbalance (Miles, Haslum & Wheeler 1998). While Dyslexia, as a single diagnosis, accounts for memory difficulties, it also coexists with other learning disorders, such as ADHD and ADD (Knivsberg, Reichelt & Nodnland 1999). There are, of course, typical behavioral patterns associated with Dyslexia.

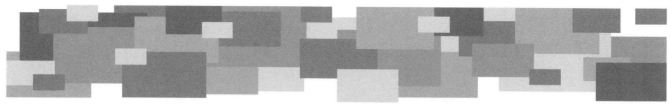

Before starting school, children later diagnosed as Dyslexic are often reported to have experienced a history of ear infections, with or without glue ear. They are likely to have demonstrated consistent minor difficulties in pronouncing longer words and locating the right word when speaking, and are likely to have started talking later than most.

As the student begins school, teachers and parents notice difficulties in their ability to acquire basic reading, writing and spelling skills. They appear not to be keeping up and are seen as underachieving. They may be able to spell a word verbally, but not write it down; the link between sounds and letters (phonology) does not develop as it does for others. Their reading lacks fluency and speed. They consistently trip over small words, read words that are not there, keep forgetting the same simple word from one page to the next and regularly lose their place, having to rely on their finger to keep track. They sound out syllables as they read, but forget them before they are able to blend the entire word. Their short term auditory memory lets them down. Naturally, these students are encouraged to try harder, and many do, but they tire quickly and can only read for short bursts. Well-intentioned help from parents often amplifies the child's frustrations.

These students are the children who can learn for their spelling test and gain full marks; however, when tested on the same spelling words two or three weeks later they achieve little accuracy. One of the classic observations is the misspelling of the same words over and over, year in, year out. Examples include *whent* for went, *thay* for they, *dun* for done, and *seaid* or *sed* for said. A further indicator is poorly developed written language. Students with Dyslexia are slow to learn to write, may experience letter reversal difficulties, mix upper- and lower-case letters and, even though they work more slowly than other students, produce untidy and inaccurate work. Commonly, their written language has words missing or may contain words not intended to be there.

Their memory difficulties may not be isolated to reading, spelling and writing; mathematics can also present difficulties. Number reversals (e.g. 25 becoming 52), copying inaccuracies and misreading of written information skew mathematical outcomes. Significant difficulty in learning and retaining simple formulas, remembering the sequential steps involved in basic math operations and recalling number sequences and patterns (especially the multiplication tables) undermine mathematical confidence and progress.

The complex interplay of overt and subtle memory and communication difficulties also affects organization and concentration, and promotes a stream of seemingly careless errors. Some have social problems as part of their learning difficulty. Their social judgment is impaired and as a result they do not socialize easily, feeling isolated, 'picked on' or 'put down'.

Learning difficulties often convince children that they are 'dumb'. Loss of confidence, in combination with their primary difficulty, results in secondary social, emotional, motivational and persistence difficulties. As school life is taxing, students may avoid learning tasks, time waste, forget, lose books, tune-out, become resistant to accepting help and resort to covering up their difficulties by becoming disruptive.

Attention Deficit Disorder (ADD)

Thompson and Sears define Attention Deficit Disorder as 'a collection of traits that reflect the child's inborn, neurologically based temperament ... [including] selective attention, distractibility, impulsivity, and sometimes

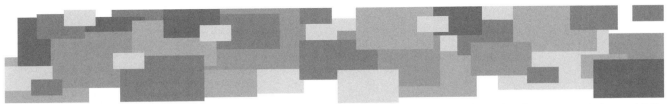

hyperactivity. Depending on how they are perceived and shaped, the combination of traits can work to a child's advantage or disadvantage' (2000, p. 3). Attention Deficit Disorder without hyperactivity appears more difficult to determine than Attention Deficit Disorder with hyperactivity. As individuals with ADD are not physically overly restless, their behavior does not usually attract attention. The serious, silent inattentive component can be easily overlooked. Also, girls identified with ADD seem to be diagnosed later than boys and in significantly fewer numbers. Debate continues as to whether boys have an increased propensity to be identified with this disorder, or whether traditional community attitudes overlook this difficulty in girls because generally they appear more compliant and responsive.

Problems are viewed through behaviors related to poor planning, poor conversion of thoughts to written work and reduced work output. In classic circumstances, children with ADD seem in a world of their own. They drift off, daydream and are noticed gazing or staring. Their quiet, constant inattentiveness impacts heavily on starting and finishing tasks not to their liking: getting organized in the morning, successfully retrieving an item from another room, remembering instructions, eating snacks and helping out around the house. When they are asked to help, and do comply, they are likely to mishear and tackle the task incorrectly. They have an inclination to become overly absorbed by computer games, television, magazines or books for long periods to the exclusion of other more urgent activities. Friendship difficulties can be a feature as their lack of attending inhibits keeping up with the pace of interaction. The luckier ones build friendships with quieter children who over time appreciate their individual style.

At school their inattentiveness cunningly undermines completion of written work. Sometimes they start well enough, but lose the thread. At other times starting schoolwork can be difficult: they are not sure where to start, appearing unsettled, uncertain of instructions, unsure which resources are needed and where they might be. Typically, their desks, lockers, schoolbags and bedrooms are in disarray, reflecting, to a large extent, their internal disorganization. These children and young adolescents can also carry the burden of associated learning difficulties. Interestingly, there is likely to be a person somewhere in the family who has similar characteristics, as Attention Deficit Disorder without hyperactivity is viewed as an inherited condition.

Attention Deficit Hyperactivity Disorder (ADHD)

These are the children we notice first. On the go as if driven by a motor, they have far more energy than most, are described as 'wound up' and find it impossible to keep still. They have to move, have to talk and have to touch. Their impulsivity is immediately recognized as they touch things they were asked not to touch. They cannot seem to help it. These individuals are described as 'over the top' - loud, excitable and explosive - struggling to find the brakes when playing jokes, play fighting or just having fun. Their excitability can verge on dangerous and jumps to new heights when they are overtired, overexcited or in the midst of a new situation (Reimers & Brunger 1999).

At school, students with ADHD work quickly and erratically, often making the same 'silly' mistakes they made yesterday and the day before. They are forever sidetracked, genuinely finding it hard to pay attention and stay with one thought or activity for long. Commonly, they call out in class, even when asked to wait their turn. Teachers find them wandering the classroom fiddling with the belongings of others and engaging half a dozen students on different topics in the space of a minute or two. When checked, they are almost always sorry, but a few minutes later they are doing it again. The combination of inattentiveness, impatience, impulsiveness and excitability has dire consequences for learning. Even though the student may be in the classroom full time, in reality they are only available to listen and gather information on a very part-time basis.

Learning problems, immaturity, poor memory, compulsiveness and mood difficulties also feature in the ADHD profile (Green & Chee 1997). Typically, wide fluctuations in attention and cooperation are noticed, depending on the nature of a task or the context in which the task is given. Many display chronic problems in sustaining attention for most study-related tasks; yet are able to concentrate very well on interests which highly motivate them.

Peers tend to avoid these children because of their oversensitive, overactive, impulsive and unpredictable behaviors. They are viewed as poor sports or team players as they cannot wait their turn. They have to win; and when they lose, their temper explodes just as quickly at school as it does at home. Once they lose their temper, overreaction and tantrums are unavoidable, even when the child becomes an adolescent.

ADHD and ADD are considered neurobiological conditions involving dysfunction in a variety of brain networks linked to the operation of executive functioning (Barkley 1990). The executive system is responsible for regulating thinking (without emotion); planning; and starting, maintaining and completing behaviors. ADHD and ADD are now viewed as disorders of performance, not specifically a lack of knowledge or skills. As a neurobiological condition, it is usual that an adult somewhere in the family also has this condition; often, despite their difficulties, the adult will have made their way successfully in the world. Recognition of this can be wonderfully affirming to students, helping to buoy their spirits and steer them in safer, more thoughtful directions.

Asperger Syndrome (AS)

In a student with Asperger Syndrome, the unusual physical and language mannerisms are often noticed first. Poor or fleeting eye contact is accompanied by a monotone voice which is consistently louder than convention dictates. Odd speech patterns and the hint of an unusual accent draw attention to the condition. Often dubbed 'little professors', these individuals hold pedantic, one-sided conversations. Their intent is locked on to the topic of their preoccupation, whether the listener is interested or otherwise. During the conversation they are likely to be standing either too far away or too close, as gauging social-physical proximity is challenging.

Currently diagnosed in 1 in 250 people, individuals with Asperger Syndrome develop an intense passion for particular interest areas, sometimes cultivating quirky, highly refined splinter skills (Aston 2002). A hallmark is the development of remarkable information about dates, trains, electrical circuits, computers, weapons, street directories, stickers, timetables and obsessions concerning specific computer games, hobbies (for example *Warhammer*) or television programs.

Their parents talk about their remarkable over-sensitivities and inflexibilities to texture, taste and smell. These cause difficulties in wearing new clothes, having their face washed or hair brushed. Some mothers report that their child, as a baby, demanded to be breast fed by being held in a specific way, and even now cannot bear it if their toast is not spread and cut exactly to their requirements. Outright refusal to try new foods is common.

The need to have things in order and have routine also features highly. Particular lights on the power board may need to be switched on before going to sleep, magazines may need to be stacked on particular tables in a particular order, and toys may need to be grouped according to size, shape, cost, theme or color. In the more controlled home situation, parents tend to compensate for their child's inflexibility fairly successfully.

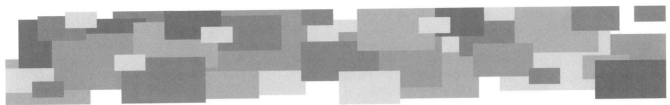

In day-to-day school life, such children are noticed as clumsier than most. Their stiff-legged walk, with arm movements that don't quite fit, draws attention. When they become excited or agitated, habits such as running on the spot, twirling, twirling hands and flapping are typical. Teachers almost always comment on their poor sporting ability (both poor motor control and emotional difficulties when losing in competitive situations), untidy handwriting, insistence on writing only in upper case, immature drawings and untidy book work.

A hallmark of students with Asperger Syndrome is that they read accurately, but with reduced comprehension. This is reflected in their social comprehension, as they are the children who will take things literally. A classic example emerges as the teacher says, 'Come on class, hurry up! Pick up your feet!'. The student with Asperger Syndrome may physically pick up their feet as they walk. Taking things very literally means these students may not understand ordinary jokes, irony or metaphors, yet often develop a bias towards offbeat humor similar to Monty Python or Mr. Bean.

At school, these students become unsettled, even upset, if something unexpected occurs. Naturally the social fluidity of school presents great challenges (Myles & Simpson 1998). Starting kindergarten, commencing a new year at school, a new student joining the class group, and beginning a new term can be fraught with difficulties and require proactive preparations (Klein & Moses 1999). Needless to say, most of these children do not enjoy surprises.

Inflexibility and egocentricity impact on friendships, as they find it difficult to read social situations and understand the facial expressions or gestures of others. This results in them often making inappropriate comments. As much as they want to get it right, these children can swing from being emotionless when strong emotion is called for, to becoming overly anxious and emotional when faced with small issues (Myles & Southwick 1999). Consequently, it is common to find these individuals more comfortable mixing with much older or younger social groups and enjoying this safer, more predictable contact (Attwood 2001).

Individuals identified with Asperger Syndrome usually become more aware of their social difficulty as young adolescence, which brings both benefits and difficulties. A recent study found a high incidence of depressive symptoms in Asperger youths, and identified a strong relationship between feeling different, being socially isolated and depression (Hedley & Young 2003). Over time, with constructive family support, a responsive school environment, formal social-skills training and exposure to safe, accepting social groups, most students with this condition learn to intellectualize what is required to fit in and feel more connected.

Language Disorder (LD)

As the name implies, this cluster of difficulties relates to the internal organization of language, the use of speech and written language capacities (Clark & Ireland 2003). As these students enter school and more formal learning begins, teachers notice difficulties concerning their response to language. They appear to listen, but often misinterpret, tackling a task inappropriately or wrongly even though the instructions were explicit. They often 'get the wrong end of the stick', only half completing tasks and putting them off as they are unsure about what really needs to be done.

Cognitive Behavioral Training

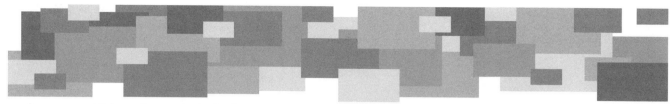

As young children, these students do not seem to enjoy listening to stories. Converting what is heard to what they need to do is consistently challenging, as they tend to forget, get confused and have a greater natural disposition to be disorganized. They are likely to prefer solitary activities; perhaps using a familiar computer game, drawing, painting, making things or immersing themselves in constructing something with *Legos*.

It is common to see students with Language Disorder struggling to hear against general background noise. They are both sensitive to and easily distracted by noise. They require optimal conditions to deliver what is expected in the classroom (Klein & Moses 1999). These students seem to tire quickly and tune out from listening earlier than their peers. Subsequently, teachers suggest parents have their hearing checked, but once tested their hearing usually proves to be normal.

As difficulties are encountered at school, parents begin to share their child's early history. Children with Language Disorder are late learning to talk and often need speech therapy. As young children they have early articulation difficulties and are challenged by producing rhyming words, remembering sounds and blending sounds. It is difficult for them to pick up correct grammar and tell a story in sequence. They find it challenging to count, recite common nursery rhymes, days in the week, months in the year and the alphabet. Phonological difficulties impact on both reading and spelling progress. In classic circumstances they can find it difficult to read words by sight, so their reading remains stilted and lacks fluency for a considerable time, even with significant intervention.

Sequencing of language difficulties cause them to mix words out of order, such as, 'I always hate that doing.' They also tend to have difficulties with word-finding; that is, the capacity to access and retrieve desired words at speed on demand. These students draw on word substitutes as 'that thing,' 'stuff,' 'you know,' 'like what we had' and resort to gesturing. They consistently forget names, words and routines that are familiar and depend on others to recall them. Persistent sequencing and word finding difficulties leave these children as reluctant speakers. They are reluctant to speak to unfamiliar people, rarely volunteer to speak in class and hesitate or refuse to talk on the telephone at home.

Parents and students alike explain how they often get muddled up and confused. They say yesterday for tomorrow, 'open the light' and 'switch the hot water off'. Their difficulty in saying what they mean causes great internal frustration (Bernstein & Tiegerman-Farber 1997). Parents frequently mention angry 'in the heat of the moment' outbursts. Their difficulty in sequencing thoughts, retrieving words and expressing their point of view can lead to emotionally charged circumstances. Alternatively, the child gives up, saying, 'It doesn't matter.'

Auditory Processing Difficulties (APD)

Auditory processing is understood as the 'brainwork' of hearing. It concerns a specific set of skills which enable individuals to act on what they hear. Audiologist and researcher Frank Musiek refers to auditory processing as how well the ear speaks to the brain, and how well the brain understands what the ear is saying (Chermak & Musiek 1997). Each of us is reliant on adequate auditory processing skills to communicate, remember, prioritize attention to a task, persist, filter background noise from voices and learn new information. This disorder has on occasions been described as auditory dyslexia, auditory comprehension deficit and word deafness.

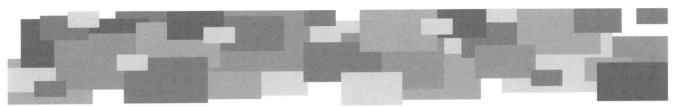

Auditory Processing Difficulties are frequently linked to maturational delays and range from mild to severe. The incidence of APD is gauged at 3 to 5 per cent of the population (Chermak & Musiek 1997). While APD can be diagnosed as a single, stand-alone difficulty, it also coexists with Language Disorder, ADD, ADHD, Dyslexia and Specific Learning Difficulties with regularity (Wilson 2003). Interestingly, it is not uncommon for teachers and parents to anticipate a child may have ADHD or ADD and be surprised when an audiologist diagnoses severe APD. This is because there are many similarities in the behaviors and listening of children with these conditions.

Children diagnosed with APD usually exhibit a cluster of traits or characteristics (Ferre 1997). When at kindergarten, they may enjoy music but have trouble learning the words and consistently have difficulty staying seated for story time. Naturally, the classroom is dominated by spoken language and the acoustic conditions are often poor. Therefore APD can be more apparent in the learning situation than in the home, and signs become stronger as the child progresses through school. Teachers find themselves instinctively touching these students and gesturing to gain and keep their attention as they seem 'tuned out' and respond indiscriminately to instructions or questions.

Such children may prefer to play alone and avoid social groups. Much of play is about negotiating the rules of games, and this is something which the child with APD finds challenging.

As school progresses and instructions become more frequent and complex, teachers increasingly rely on the auditory modality to communicate with students. Students with APD tend to misunderstand what is said and respond by saying, 'What was that?', 'I don't get it', 'I didn't hear', 'It's too noisy' or 'Huh?'. They have difficulty receiving or remembering verbal clues. As this becomes more apparent, hearing tests are called for and usually yield normal results, although a history of early ear infections may be recognized.

Parents and teachers describe these children as 'day-dreamers', or as having 'selective hearing', or being 'in a world of their own'. Their difficulty in catching essential information in the classroom, and even within the busy family situation, intensifies in noisy situations, as their capacity to filter distracting background noise from critical instruction is impaired. As a result students in the classroom can become anxious and stressed when required to listen (Tan 1999). Despite looking like they are listening, and wanting to listen, they have trouble interpreting what they hear. Depending on personality traits, associated learning issues and their history of success verses failure, the student may ask for the information to be repeated, or rely on others to re-explain and show them what to do. On the other hand, they may look as though they are not interested or have a short attention span. They may appear distracted, disorganized or dependent, or they may take on the role of class clown or the joker.

Without identification by a qualified audiologist, intervention and proactive management, prolonged Auditory Processing Difficulties have an impact on speech and broad-based literacy development. The erosion of learning skills is inevitable despite an individual's good intentions and sound intellectual abilities. Their enduring struggle to pay attention, to discriminate, associate, integrate and organize what is heard takes its toll on verbal communication, friendships, confidence and schoolwork. Unchecked, auditory processing problems can be at the root of slowing of school performance, increasing off-task responses, poor motivation, forgetfulness and growing disruptive behaviors in the classroom. Students often find support in simple management or compensatory strategies such as receiving short, focused directions and sitting close by when instructions are being given, and benefit when teachers provide additional visual clues (assignments or directions on the board or in a notebook) and arrange a peer tutor as a back up system.

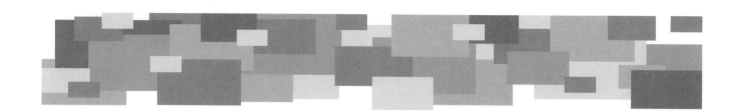

References

Aesop. Aesop's fables, trs Vernon Jones. Ware, Hertfordshire: Wordsworth Editions, 1994.

Amen, D. G. (2002a). Seven ways to optimize your brain and your life. Retrieved 17 July 2003 from <http://www.brainplace.com>.

Amen, D. G. (2002b). Healing ADD: The breakthrough program that allows you to see and heal the 6 types of ADD. New York: Berkley Books.

Armstrong, K. (2003). The circles. Melbourne: Hardie Grant Books.

Armstrong, T. (1997). The myth of the ADD child. USA: Pearson Education.

Armstrong, T. (1999). ADD/ADHD alternatives in the classroom. Retrieved 13 July 2003 from <http://www.ascd.org/readingroom/books/Armstrong>.

Aston, M. (2002). The other half of Asperger Syndrome, 2nd edn. USA: Autism, Asperqer Pub CD.

Attwood, T. (2001). Asperger Syndrome: A guide for parents and professionals. London: Jessica Kingsley Publications.

Barkley, R. (1990). Attention Deficit Hyperactivity Disorder: A handbook for diagnoses and treatment. USA: Guilford Press.

Barkley, R. (2001). A theory of ADHD: Inhibitions, self-control and time. Paper presented at the ADHD in the Third Millennium conference for the Children's Hospital Education Research Institute at Westmead, NSW.

Beamish, W., Bryer, F. & Wilson, L. (2000). Positive behavioral support: An example of practice in the early years. Special Education Perspectives, 9(1), 14-29.

Bernstein, D. K. & Tiegerman-Farber, E. (1997). Language and communication disorders in children. Boston: Allyn & Bacon.

Bisland, A. (2001). Mentoring: An educational alternative for gifted students. Gifted Child Today, 24(4), Autumn, 22-64.

Bloom, B. S. (ed.) (1956). Taxonomy of educational objectives: The classification of educational goals. Handbook 1: Cognitive domain. New York: Longman.

Booth, T., Ainscow, M., Black-Hawkins, K., Vaughan, M. & Shaw, L. (2000). Index for inclusion: Developing learning and participation in schools. Bristol: Centre for Studies on Inclusive Education.

Brock, A. & Shute, R. (2001). Group coping skills program for parents of children with Dyslexia and other learning disabilities. Australian Journal of Learning Disabilities, 6(4), December, 15-25.

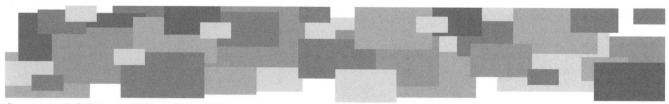

Cameron, J. & Pierce, W. D. (1994). Reinforcement, reward, and intrinsic motivation: A meta-analysis. Review of Educational Research, 64, 363-423.

Cameron, J. & Pierce, W. D. (1998). The debate about rewards and intrinsic motivation. In A. W. Woolfolk, Readings in educational psychology, 2nd edn. Ohio: Allyn and Bacon.

Chapman, J. (2003). Teachers told to make subjects more fun. Advertiser, 1 October, 3.

Chermak, G. & Musiek, F. (1997). Central auditory processing disorders: New perspectives. San Diego: Singular Publishing Group, Inc.

Chinn, S. J. (1991). Factors to consider when designing a test protocol in mathematics for dyslexics. In M. Snowling & M. Thomson (eds), Dyslexia: Integrating theory and practice. London: Whurr Publishers.

Chinn, S. J. (1999). What to do when you can't learn the times tables. London: Ideas Taking Shape Inc.

Church, K., Gottschalk, C. & Leedy, J. (2003). Enhance social and friendship skills. Intervention in School and Clinic, 38(5), May, 307-310.

Clark, L. & Ireland, C. (2003). Talk, listen and learn. Sydney: HarperCollins Publishers.

Clinch, R. (2000). Secret kids' business. Moorabbin, Victoria: Hawker Brownlow Education.

Coenen, M. E. (2002). Using gifted students as peer tutors. Gifted Child Today, 25(1), Winter, 48-55.

Cohen, J. (1986). Theoretical considerations of peer tutoring. Psychology in the Schools, 23, 175-186.

Corrie, L. & Leitao, N. (1999). The development of well-being: Young children's knowledge of their support networks and social competence. Australian Journal of Early Childhood, 24(3), 25.

Custer, S., McKean, K., Meyers, C., Murphy, D., Olesen, S. & Parker, S. (1990). SMARTS: Studying, memorizing, active listening, reviewing, test taking and survival skills. A study skills resource guide. USA: Sopris West.

De Bono, E. (1987). Six thinking hats. USA: Little Brown and Co.

Dempster, M. & Raff, D. (1992). Class discussions: A powerful classroom strategy. Moorabbin, Victoria: Hawker Brownlow Education.

Department of Education and Children's Services (2002). Negotiated education plan [Electronic version]. Retrieved 15 January 2004 from <http://www.decs.sa.gov.au>. South Australia: DECS.

Ellis, A. (1985). Expanding the ABCs of rational emotive therapy. In M. Mahoney & A. Freeman (eds), Cognition and Psychotherapy. New York: Plenum, 313-323.

Fabes, R. A., Fultz, J., Eisenburg, N., May-Plumber, T. & Christopher, F. S. (1989). Effects of rewards on children's prosocial motivation: A socialization study. Developmental Psychology, 25, 509-515.

Ferre, J. M. (1997). What are CAP and CAPD, and why test for them?. San Antonio: Communication Skill Builders, a division of The Psychological Corporation.

Flavell, J. H. (1970). Metacognitive aspects of problem solving. In L. B. Resnick (ed.), The nature of intelligence. Hillsdale, New Jersey: Erlbaum.

Foot, H. & Howe, C. (1998). The psychoeducational basis of peer-assisted learning. In K. Topping & S. Ehly (eds), Peer-assisted learning. Mahwah, New Jersey: Erlbaum, 27-43.

Friend, M. & Cook, L. (1996). Interactions: Collaboration skills for school professionals, 2nd edn. New York: Longman Publishers.

Gardner, H. (1993). Multiple intelligences: The theory in practice. New York: Basic Books.

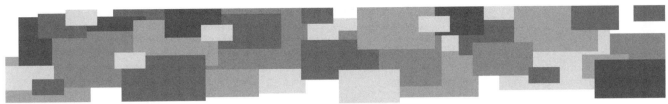

Garth, M. (1994). Inner garden. Australia: HarperCollins Publishers.

Gerber, P. J., Ginsberg, R. & Reiff, H. B. (1992). Identifying alterable patterns in employment success for highly successful adults with learning disabilities. Journal of Learning Disabilities, 25, 475-487.

Giorcelli, L. (2000). Wrap around. ACTIVE Newsletter, Hyperactive Children's Association of Victoria, June.

Glasser, W. (1999). Choice therapy: A new psychology of personal freedom. London: Perennial Press.

Glasser, W. (2000). Reality therapy in action. London: HarperCollins Publishers.

Goodfellow, N. (2003). Guiding lights on the roads out of school. Advertiser, 23 July, 25.

Gottesman, R. L. (1979). Follow up on learning disabled children. Learning Disability Quarterly, 2, 60-69.

Graham, S., Harris, K. R. & Reid, R. (1992). Developing self-regulated learners. Focus on Exceptional Children, 24(6), 1-16.

Green, C. & Chee, K. (1997). Understanding ADHD. Moorebank: Doubleday Books.

Hallowell, E. (1997). Worry: Controlling it and using it wisely. New York: Pantheon.

Hannell, G. (2002). Identifying children with special needs: Check lists for professionals. South Australia: Palmer Educational Publications.

Harris, S. (1999). Remember our first love. Educational Leadership, 57, May, 76-77

Hedley, D. & Young, R. (2003). Social comparison and depression in thirty-six children and adults with a diagnosis of Asperger Syndrome. Autiser, Autumn, 3-4.

Heggen, B. (2003a). Breakfast puts spring in their day. Advertiser, 14 September, 39.

Heggen, B. (2003b). Schools 'out of date'. Sunday Mail, 19 October, 7.

Hendren, R. L. (1999). Disruptive behavior disorders in children and adolescents. Washington, D.C.: American Psychiatric Press Inc.

Hoffman, F. J., Sheldon, K. L., Minskoff, E. H., Sautter, S. W., Steidle, E. F., Baker, D. P., Bailey, M. B. & Echols, L. D. (1987). Needs of learning disabled adults. Journal of Learning Disabilities, 20, 43-52.

International Baccalaureate Organization (2002). Candidates with special assessment needs, 2nd edn. Switzerland: IBO.

Jenks, P. (2003). Navigating time travel. Perspectives, International Dyslexia Association, 29(1), Winter, 7-11.

Jensen, E. (2000a). Brain compatible strategies. Thousand Oaks, CA: Corwin Press.

Jensen, E. (2000b). Different brains, different learners. Thousand Oaks, CA: Corwin Press.

Johnson, D. J. & Blalock, J. W. (eds) (1987). Adults with learning disabilities: Clinical studies. New York: Grune & Stratton.

Joseph, J. (2002). Brainy parents – brainy kids. Australia: Focus Education Australia Pty Ltd.

Kanfer, F. H. & Goldstein, A. P. (1991). Helping people change: A textbook of methods, 4th edn. New York: Pergamon Press.

Kanfer, F. H. & Schefft, B. K. (1988). Guiding the process of therapeutic change. Champaign, Illinois: Research Press.

Kavale, K. A. (1988). The long term consequences of learning disabilities. In M. C. Wang, M. C. Reynolds & H. J. Walberg (eds), Handbook of special education: Research and practice. Tarrytown, New York: Pergamon, 303-344.

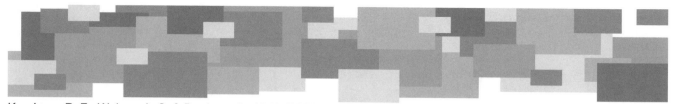

Kernberg, P. F., Weiner, A. S. & Bardenestin, K. K. (2000). Personality disorders in children and adolescents. New York: Basic Books.

Klein, H. B. & Moses, N. (1999). Intervention planning for children with communication disorders. Needham Heights, Massachusetts: Allyn & Bacon.

Knivsberg, A., Reichelt, K. & Nodnland, M. (1999). Coexistence between Dyslexia and ADHD. British Journal of Special Education, 26(1), March, 42-47.

Kohn, A. (1996). Beyond discipline: From compliance to community. Alexandria, Virginia: Association for Supervision and Curriculum Development.

Lasley, T. J. & Matczynski, T. J. (1997). Strategies for teaching in a diverse society: Instructional models. Belmont, California: Wadsworth Publishing Company.

Lepper, M. R., Keavney, M. & Drake, M. (1996). Intrinsic motivation and extrinsic rewards: A commentary on Cameron and Pierce's meta-analysis. Review of Educational Research, 66, 5-32.

Maag, J. W. (2001). Rewarded by punishment: Reflections on the disuse of positive reinforcement in schools. Council for Exceptional Children, 67(2), 173-186.

Maag, J. & Katsiyannis, A. (1999). Teacher preparation in E/BD: A national survey. Behavioral Disorders, 24, 189-196.

Marron, J. A. (2002). Way to go: Positive reinforcement programs for your child with Attention Deficit/Hyperactivity Disorder (ADD/ADHD). Exceptional Parent Magazine, July, 68-70.

McGrath, H. (2000). Behavior management middle primary. Glebe, NSW: Blake Education.

Miles, S. (2002). Inclusive education: An assessment of the impact of Salamanca. Social Spectrum, 4: 16-18.

Miles, T. R., Haslum, M. N. & Wheeler, T. J. (1998). Gender ratio in Dyslexia. Annals of Dyslexia, 48, 27-55.

Minton, P. (2002). Using information and communication technology (ICT) to help Dyslexics, and others, learn spelling. Australian Journal of Learning Disabilities, 7(3), 26-31.

Myles, B. S. & Simpson, R. L. (1998). Asperger Syndrome: A guide for educators and parents. Austin, Texas: Pro-ed.

Myles, B. S. & Southwick, J. (1999). Asperger Syndrome and difficult moments: Practical solutions for tantrums, rage and meltdowns. Shawnee Mission, Kansas: Autism Asperger Publishing Co.

Newton, D. (2003). Teaching study skills and learning strategies to therapists, teachers and tutors: How to give hope to disorganized students. Perspectives, International Dyslexia Association, 29(1), Winter, 27-31.

Noddings, N. (1998). Teaching themes of care: Readings in educational psychology, 2nd edn. Ohio: Allyn and Bacon.

O'Malley, J. M., Chamot, A. U., Stewner-Manzanares, G., Kupper, L. & Russo, R. P. (1985). Learning strategies used by beginning and intermediate students. Language Learning, 35(1), 21-46.

Parker, J. (1999). Effective teaching and learning strategies for all students. Moorabbin, Victoria: Hawker Brownlow Education.

Parkinson (2003). Television program, Australian Broadcasting Corporation, Sydney.

Petersen, L. (2002). Social savvy: Help your child fit in with others. Camberwell, Victoria: ACER Press.

Petersen, L. & Adderley, A. (2002a). Stop, think, do social skills training: Early years of schooling ages 4–8. Camberwell, Victoria: ACER Press.

Petersen, L. & Adderley, A. (2002b). Stop, think, do social skills training: Primary years of schooling ages 8–12. Camberwell, Victoria: ACER Press.

Petersen, L. & Le Messurier, M. (2000). Friendship neighbourhood: STOP and THINK workbook. Adelaide: Foundation Studios.

Pfiffner, L. J., Rosen, L. & O'Leary, S. (1985). The efficacy of an all positive approach to classroom management. Journal of Applied Behavior Analysis, 18, 257-261.

Pohl, M. (1998). Teaching thinking skills in the primary years. Moorabbin, Victoria: Hawker Brownlow Education.

Pohl, M. (1999). Learning to think: Thinking to learn. Moorabbin, Victoria: Hawker Brownlow Education.

Prior, M. (2003, October 20). Bullying: Are our schools doing enough? Age, 11.

Rankin, J. & Reid, R. (1995). The SM rap - or here's the rap on self-monitoring. Intervention in School and Clinic, 30, 181-188.

Raskind, M., Goldberg, R., Higgins, E. & Herman, K. (1999). Patterns of change and predictors of success in individuals with learning disabilities: Results from a twenty-year longitudinal study. Learning Disabilities Research and Practice, 14(1), 35-49.

Raskind, M., Goldberg, R., Higgins, E. & Herman, K. (2002). Teaching 'life success' to students with LD: Lessons learned from a twenty year study. Intervention in School and Clinic, 37(4), March, 201-208.

Reid, R. (1996). Self-monitoring for students with learning disabilities: The present, the prospects, the pitfalls. Journal of Learning Disabilities, 29, 317-331.

Reid, R. & Harris, K. R. (1993). Self-monitoring of attention versus self-monitoring of performance: Effects on attention and academic performance. Exceptional Children, 60, 29-40.

Reiff, H., Gerber, P. & Ginsberg, R. (1997). Exceeding expectations: Successful adults with learning disabilities. Austin, Texas: Pro-Ed Inc.

Reimers, C. & Brunger, B. (1999). ADHD in the young child: Driven to redirection. Plantation, Florida: Specialty Press.

Rivalland, J. (2000). Definitions & identification: Who are the children with learning difficulties? Australian Journal of Learning Disabilities, 5(2), 12-16.

Rogers, B. (1995). Behavior management: A whole school approach. Gosford, NSW: Ashton Scholastic.

Rogers, B. (1997). Cracking the hard class. Gosford, NSW: Scholastic Australia Pty Ltd.

Ryan, T. (1990). Thinker's keys for kids. Woodridge, Qld: Logan West School Support Centre.

Sears, B. (1999). The Zone. New York: HarperCollins.

Senior Secondary Assessment Board of South Australia (2002). Handbook: Alternative Assessments for Students with Disabilities. Wayville, SA: SSABSA.

Shochet, I. M., Osgarby, S. M., Holland, D. & Whitefield, K. (1997). Resourceful adolescent program: Group leader's manual. Brisbane, Qld: School of Applied Psychology, Griffith University.

Shore, K. (1998). Special kids problem solver. USA: John Twiley.

Sinclair, B. & Ellis, G. (1992). Survey: Learner training in EFL course books. English Language Teaching Journal, 46(2), 209-225.

Smith, B. (2004). Success … in spite of early learning problems. Self-published. Hobart: Print Centre. ISBN 1-875489-22-3.

Snowling, M. (2000). Dyslexia. Oxford, UK: Blackwell Publishers.

Spalding, B. (2002). The contribution of a 'quiet place' to early intervention strategies for children with emotional and behavioral difficulties in mainstream schools. British Journal of Special Education, 27(3), 129-134.

SSABSA – see Senior Secondary Assessment Board of South Australia

Swindoll, C. R. (1982). Strengthening your grip: How to live confidently in an aimless world. Nashville, Tennessee: Thomas Nelson/W Publishing Group.

Tan, L. (1999). Auditory processing at school. Camberwell, Victoria: Listening Works. (Phone Lesley Tan: (03) 9809 1327. Email: admin@listeningworks.com.au)

Taylor-Neumann, N. (2002). Proactive teaching 2: Rules, discipline, self-esteem & relationships. Australia: ADHD Seminars. (Phone: (08) 8339 4119. Email: tayneu@ozemail.com.au)

Thomas, A. & Pashley, B. (1982). Effects of classroom training on Learning Difficulty students' task persistence and attributions. Learning Disability Quarterly, 5(2), 133-144.

Thompson, L. & Sears, W. (2000). The ADHD book: New understanding, new approaches to parenting your child. New York: Little, Brown and Company.

Tomlinson, C. A. (1999). The differentiated classroom: Responding to the need of all learners. Alexandria, Virginia: Association for Supervision and Curriculum Development.

Van der Kley, M. (1991). Classroom management. Christchurch, New Zealand: Purse Willis and Aiken Ltd.

Van der Kley, M. (1997). Disruptive children. Christchurch, New Zealand: Purse Willis and Aiken Ltd.

Weiner, B. (1998). History of motivational research in education: Readings in educational psychology, 2nd edn. Ohio: Allyn and Bacon.

Westwood, P. (1999). Common sense methods for children with special needs, 3rd edn. London: Routledge.

Wiersma, U. J. (1992). The effects of extrinsic rewards in intrinsic motivation: A meta analysis. Journal of Occupational and Organizational Psychology, 65, 101-114.

Williams, F. E. (1991) Classroom ideas for encouraging thinking and feeling. Moorabbin, Vic: Hawker Brownlow Education.

Williams, J. (2003). Study and organizational skills: Practical suggestions and sensible plans. Perspectives, International Dyslexia Association, 29(1), Winter, 4-6.

Wilson, W. (2003). Confused about APD? ACQuiring Knowledge in Speech, Language and Hearing, 5(3), 123-126.

Wubbles, T., Levy, J. & Brekeinams, M. (1997). Paying attention to relationships. Educational Intervention, 6(2), April, 82-86.

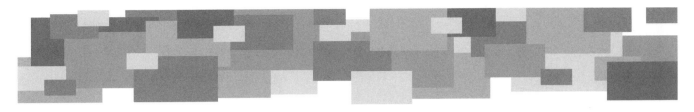

Further reading and useful websites

ADD and ADHD

Books & articles

Barkley, R. A. (2000). Taking charge of ADHD: The authoritative guide for parents, revised edn. New York: Guilford.

Department of Education, Training and Employment (1999). Attention difficulties, poor impulse control, overactivity or ADHD: Teaching and managing children and school students. Adelaide, South Australia: DETE.

Flick, G. (1998). The ADD/ADHD behavior change resource kit. USA: John Wiley.

Kewley, G. (2001). ADHD: Recognition, reality and resolution. Camberwell, Victoria: ACER Press.

Reid, R. & Maag, J. W. (1998). Functional assessment: A method for developing classroom based accommodations and interventions for children with ADHD. Reading and Writing Quarterly, 14, 9-42.

Rief, S. F. (1993). How to reach and teach ADD/ADHD children: Practical techniques, strategies, and interventions for helping children with attention problems and hyperactivity. USA: John Wiley.

Spencer, S. & Rohena, E. (2003). Students with attention deficit disorders: An overview. Intervention in School and Clinic, 38(5), 259-266.

Wallace, I. (1997). You and your ADD child. Australia: HarperCollins.

Zentall, S., Moon, S., Hall, A. & Grskovic, J. (2001). Learning and motivational characteristics of boys with AD/HD and/or giftedness. The Council for Exceptional Children, 67(4), 499-519.

Websites

ADD: <http://www.familyvillage.wisc.edu/lib_adhd.htm>.

ADHD - A teenager's guide: <http://www.add.org/content/teens/tguide.htm>.

ADHD in girls: <http://www.helpforadd.com/girls.htm>.

Children and adults with AD/HD: <http://www.chadd.org>.

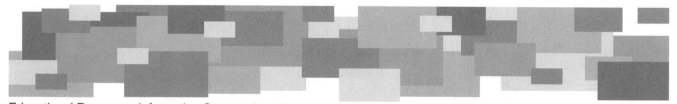

Educational Resources Information Center: <http://www.ericec.org/digests/e569.html>. Includes information on gifted education and ADD. Offers instructional strategies which can be used at home and in the classroom.

Information on ADD & ADHD: <http://www.helpforadd.com/info.htm>.

A kid's guide to ADHD: <http://www.add.org/content/family/guide.htm>. Written for children aged between seven and twelve years.

What you need to know about ADD: <http://www.add.about.com>. An extensive site containing information, support and intervention ideas for ADHD students.

Asperger Syndrome

Books & articles

Adreon, S. & Stella, J. (2001). Transition to middle and high school: Increasing the success of students with Asperger Syndrome. Intervention in School and Clinic, 36(5), 266-271.

Faherty, C. (2002). What does it mean to me? A workbook for explaining self-awareness and life lessons to the child or youth with high-functioning autism or Asperger's. Arlington, Texas: Future Horizons.

Haddon, M. (2003). The curious incident of the dog in the night-time. Oxford: Random House Children's Books.

McKean, T. A. (2001). Soon will come the light: A view from inside the Autism puzzle. Arlington, Texas: Future Horizons Inc.

Vermeulen, P. (2000). I am special: Introducing children and young people to their autistic spectrum disorder. Jessica Kingsley: London.

Williams, K. (2001). Understanding the student with Asperger Syndrome: Guidelines for teachers. Intervention in School and Clinic, 36(5), 287-292.

Websites

Asperger Syndrome Support Network: <http://www.vicnet.net.au/~asperger>.

Online Asperger Syndrome information and support: <http://www.udel.edu/bkirby/asperger>.

Tony Attwood: <http://www.tonyattwood.com.au>. Authoritative Asperger website.

University students with Autism and Asperger Syndrome: <http://www.users.dircon.co.uk/~cns>. An informative site dedicated to offering practical advice on Asperger Syndrome.

Auditory Processing Disorder

Books & articles

Bellis, T. J. & Jarnes-Bellis, T. (2003). Assessment and management of central processing disorders in the educational setting: From science to practice. New York: Delmar Learning.

Tan, L. (1998). Auditory processing at home. Camberwell, Victoria: Listening Works. (Email admin@listeningworks.com.au)

Tan, L. (1998). Behavior, communication and auditory processing. Camberwell, Victoria: Listening Works. (Email admin@listeningworks.com.au)

Tan, L. (2001). Auditory processing in the under sixes. Camberwell, Victoria: Listening Works. (Email admin@listeningworks.com.au)

Websites

American Speech-Language-Hearing Association: <http://www.asha.org>.

Maelstrom: <http://www.capd-pro@maelstrom.stjohns.edu>. An Internet resource for professionals contributed by St. Johns University in New York.

National Coalition on Auditory Processing Disorders, Inc.: <http://www.ncapd.org>. For parents.

Cognitive behavioral training

Books & articles

Braswell, L. & Bloomquist, M. L. (1991). Cognitive behavioral therapy with ADHD children. New York: Guilford.

Ellis, G. (1999). Developing metacognitive awareness: The missing dimension. Retrieved 16 June 2003 from <http://www.britishcouncilpt.org/journal/j1004ge.htm>.

Greenberger, D. & Padesky, C. (1995). Mind over mood: A cognitive therapy treatment manual for clients. New York: Guilford.

Kite, A. (2000). A guide to better thinking. London: NFER-Nelson.

Matthews, J. (2001). Digging deep: A practical program to encourage young people to name, own and deal with their emotions. Camberwell, Victoria: ACER Press.

Spence, S. H. & Donovan, C. (1998). Cognitive behavior therapy for children and families. New York: Cambridge University Press.

Wragg, J. (1991). Is what I'm doing helping me? Camberwell, Victoria: ACER Press.

Developing emotional resilience

Books & articles

Canfield, J. (1998). Improving students' self-esteem: Readings in educational psychology, 2nd edn. Ohio: Allyn and Bacon.

Janas, M. (2002). Twenty ways to build resiliency. Intervention in School and Clinic, 38(2), November, 117-121.

Leung, P. (2001). Passing the baton: Teachers and parents working together to identify and manage depression in children. Classroom, (2), 10-12.

Webb, J. (2001). Teaching tips for enhancing students' self-esteem and fostering individuality. Classroom, (2), 16-17.

Friendship-building and relationships

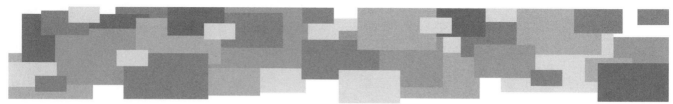

Books & articles

Bernard, M. (2002). Increasing your child's tease tolerance. Social Spectrum, 3, 2-3.

Bulkeley, R. & Cramer, D. (1994). Social skills training with young adolescents: Group and individual approaches in a school setting. Journal of Adolescence, 17, 521-531.

Francey, S. & McGrath, H. (1992). Friendly kids, friendly classrooms. Melbourne: Longman Cheshire.

Frankel, F. & Myatt, R. (2003). Children's friendship training. New York: Brunner-Routledge.

Howes, C. (2000). Social-emotional classroom climate in child care, child-teacher relationships and children's second grade peer relations. Social Development, 9(2), 191-204.

Lavoie, R. (2002). The teacher's role in developing social skills. Let's Talk About Dyspraxia, (22), October, 15-17.

Lawhorn, T. (1997). Encouraging friendships among children. Childhood Education, 73(4), 228-233.

Rigby, K. (2001). Stop the bullying. A handbook for schools. Camberwell, Victoria: ACER Press.

Homework

Books & articles

Clark, F. & Clark, C. (1989). Hassle-free homework. New York: Doubleday.

Hennessy, N. (2003). Homework hints for parents. Perspectives, International Dyslexia Association, 29(1), Winter, 33-35.

Johnson, L. (1992). My posse don't do homework. New York: St. Martin's Press.

Power, T. (2002). Homework success for children with ADHD. Guilford Press: New York.

Inclusive education

Books & articles

Holzschuher, C. (1998). How to manage your inclusive classroom. Moorabbin, Victoria: Hawker Brownlow Education.

Jenkinson, J. (2001). Special education: A matter of choice. Camberwell, Victoria: ACER Press.

Lang, G. & Berberich, C. (1995). All children are special: Creating an inclusive classroom. Armadale, Victoria: Eleanor Curtain Publishing.

MacNaughton, G. & Williams, G. (2000). Techniques for teaching young children: Choices in theory and practice. Melbourne: Addison Wesley Longman Pty Ltd.

Penrose, V., Thomas, G. & Greed, C. (2001). Designing inclusive schools: How can children be involved? Support for Learning, 16(2), 87-91.

Sleishman, P. (2000). The use of negotiation in the management of adolescent behavior. Special Education Perspectives, 9(1), 30-43.

Learned helplessness

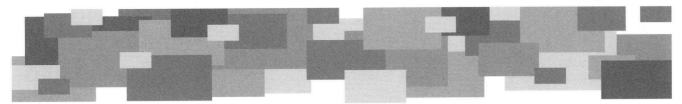

Books & articles

Boggiano, A. K., Shields, A., Barrett, M., Kellam, T., Thomspon, E., Simons, J. & Katz, O. (1992). Helplessness deficits in students: The role of motivational orientation. Motivation and Emotion, 16, 271-296.

Learning styles

Books & articles

Anderson, L. & Krathwohl, D. (eds) (2001). A taxonomy for learning, teaching and assessing. Moorabbin, Vic: Hawker Brownlow Education.

Butler, K. (1995). Learning styles: Personal exploration and practical application. Moorabbin, Vic: Hawker Brownlow Education.

Schwartz, L. (1988). Creative capers: Using Williams' taxonomy. Moorabbin, Vic: Hawker Brownlow Education.

Vialle, W. & Perry, J. (2002). Teaching through the eight intelligences. Moorabbin, Vic: Hawker Brownlow Education.

Websites

Oz-TeacherNet <http://rite.ed.qut.edu.au/oz-teachernet/index.php?module=ContentExpress&func=display&ceid=29>.

Managing behavior

Books & articles

Barrett, P., Turner, C., Rombouts, S. & Duffy, A. (2000). Reciprocal skills training in the treatment of externalising behavior disorders in childhood: A preliminary investigation. Behavior Change, 1(4), 221-234.

Maag, J. W. (2000). Managing resistance. Intervention in Schools and Clinics, 35, 131-140.

Martin, G. & Pear, J. (1996). Behavior modification: What is it and how to do it, 5th edn. Upper Saddle, New Jersey: Prentice Hall.

Porter, L. (2000). Student behavior: Theory and practice for teachers, 2nd edn. Melbourne, Victoria: Allen & Unwin.

Rogers, B. (1994). Behavior recovery: A programme for behaviorally disordered students in mainstream schools. Camberwell, Victoria: ACER Press.

Rogers, B. (1998). You know the fair rule and much more: Strategies for making the hard job of discipline and behavior management in schools easier. Camberwell, Victoria: ACER Press.

Websites

Stop think do: <http://www.stopthinkdo.com>.

Mentoring

Books & articles

Clark, E. (1995). Mentoring: A case example and guidelines for its effective use. Youth Studies, 14(2), 37-42.

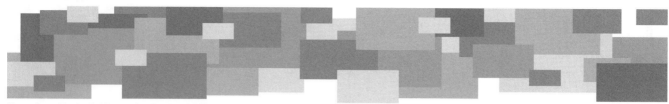

Davalos, R. A. & Haensly, P. A. (1997). After the dust has settled: Youth reflect on their high school mentored research experience. Roeper Review, 19, 204-207.

Dondero, G. M. (1997). Mentors: Beacons of hope. Adolescence, 32, 881-886.

Hawke, R. (2000). The keeper. Melbourne, Victoria: Lothian Books.

Rogers, B. (1992). Peer support: Peers supporting peers. National Foundation for Educational Research, 1(7), 29.

Websites

Article Insider: <http://selfhelp.articleinsider.com/43342_effective_mentoring.html>.

Mentoring UK: <http://www.mentoring-uk.org.uk>.

Organization and planning

Books & articles

Brent, M., Gough, F. & Robinson, S. (2001). One in eleven: Practical strategies for teaching students with a language learning disability. Camberwell, Victoria: ACER Press.

Coil, C. (1992). Motivating underachievers: 172 strategies for success. Moorabbin, Victoria: Hawker Brownlow Education.

Dodge, J. (1994). Study skills handbook: More than 75 strategies for better learning. New York: Scholastic.

Edwards, P. (1996). Seven keys to successful study, 2nd edn. Camberwell, Victoria: ACER Press.

Parks, S. & Black, H. (1992). Organizing thinking, Book 1. Moorabbin, Victoria: Hawker Brownlow Education.

Raffini, J. P. (1994). Winners without losers: Structures and strategies for increasing student motivation to learn. Boston: Allyn and Bacon.

Parenting

Books & articles

Hall, J. (2001). Fight-free families. Sydney, NSW: Finch Publishing.

Irwin, C. (1999). Parenting girls. Brisbane, Qld: Pandanus Press.

Matthews, A. (1990). Being happy: A handbook to greater confidence and security. Singapore: Media Masters Pty Ltd.

McCann, R. (2000). On their own. Boys growing up under fathered. Sydney, NSW: Finch Publishing.

Mellor, K. & Mellor, E. (2001). Easy parenting. Sydney, NSW: Finch Publishing.

Mellor, K. & Mellor, E. (2001). The happy family. Sydney, NSW: Finch Publishing.

Pallotta-Chiarolli, M. (1998). Girls talk: Young women speak their minds and hearts. Sydney, NSW: Finch Publishing.

Websites

Michael Carr-Gregg's home page: <http://www.geocities.com/ozzypsych/MichaelCarr-Gregg.html>.

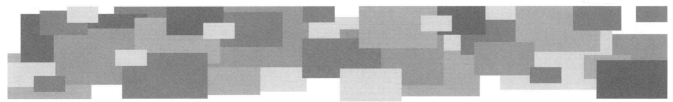

Parenting SA – Helping parents be their best: <http://www.parenting.sa.gov.au>.

Australian Institute of Family Studies Information for Parents: <http:www.aifs.org.au/sf/parenting>.

Adelaide's child: <http://www.adelaideschild.com.au>.

Brisbane's child: <http://www.brisbaneschild.com.au>.

Canberra's child: <http://www.canberraschild.com.au>.

Melbourne's child: <http://www.melbourneschild.com.au>.

Sydney's child: <http://www.sydneyschild.com.au>.

Parentlink: <http://www.parentlink.act.gov.au>. A government initiative to promote attitudes and behaviors that nurture and support children and strengthen families.

Relaxation

Books & articles
Garth, M. (1991). Starbright: Meditations for young children. New York: HarperCollins.

Garth, M. (1994). Moonbeam: A book of meditations for children. New York: HarperCollins.

Rickard, J. (1994). Relaxation for children. Camberwell, Victoria: ACER Press.

Thomas, P. (2002). The magic of relaxation: Tai chi and visualization exercises for young children. Castle Hill, NSW: Pademelon.

Specific Learning Difficulties & Dyslexia

Books & articles
Cogan, J. & Flecker, M. (2004). Dyslexia in secondary school: A practical handbook for teachers, parents and students. London: Whurr Publishers.

Cook-Sather, A. (2003). Listening to students about learning differences. Teaching Exceptional Children, 35(4), March/April, 37-42.

Gorman, C. (2003, July 28). The new science of Dyslexia. Time Magazine.

Jordan, D. (1996). Overcoming Dyslexia in children and adults. Austin, Texas: Pro-Ed.

Prior, M. (1996). Understanding Specific Learning Difficulties. New York. Psychology Press.

Sheehan, A. & Sheehan, C. (2000). Lost in a sea of ink: How I survived the storm. Journal of Adult and Adolescent Literacy, 44(1), September, 20-33.

Snowling, M. & Hulme, C. (eds) (1997). Dyslexia: Biology cognition and intervention. London: Whurr Publishers.

Websites
British Dyslexia Association: <http://www.bda-dyslexia.org.uk>. Offers information for schools, teachers, parents and students.

A Dyslexic child in the classroom: <http://www.dyslexia.com/library/classroom.htm>. A guide for teachers and parents.

DYXI: <http://www.dyxi.co.uk>. A site for Dyslexics, written by Dyslexics and promoted as a contact for Dyslexics, their parents and educators.

I am Dyslexic.com: <http://www.iamdyslexic.com>. Sensible understandings and accommodating strategies written by teenagers with Dyslexia.

International Dyslexic Association: <http://www.interdys.org>.

Specific Educational Learning Difficulties Association: <http://www.speld-sa.org.au>.

Using computers

Books & articles

Alliance for Technology Access (2000). Computer and web resources for people with disabilities: A guide to exploring today's assistive technologies, 3rd edn. Alameda, California: Hunter House, Inc.

Cook, A. & Hussey, S. (2001). Assistive technologies: Principles and practice, 2nd edn. St. Louis, Missouri: Mosby.

Dobbs, C. (2002). Using the computer as a resource for early intervention activities. Australian Journal of Learning Disabilities, 7(3), September, 35-37.

Websites

AlphaSmart: <http://www.alphasmart.com>. Information about the AlphaSmart word processor.

QuickPAD: <http://www.quickpad.com.au>. Information about the QuickPAD word processor.

Regency Rehabilitation: <http://www.regencyrehab.cca.org.au>. Information on a range of assistive technologies.

ScanSoft: <http://www.scansoft.com/speechify>. Information on RealSpeak, Speechify and Dragon NaturallySpeaking products.

Voice Perfect: <http//:www.voiceperfect.com>. Information on RealSpeak, Speechify and Dragon NaturallySpeaking products.

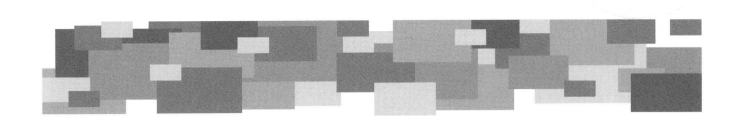

CORWIN PRESS

The Corwin Press logo—a raven striding across an open book—represents the union of courage and learning. Corwin Press is committed to improving education for all learners by publishing books and other professional development resources for those serving the field of PreK–12 education. By providing practical, hands-on materials, Corwin Press continues to carry out the promise of its motto: **"Helping Educators Do Their Work Better."**